MW01681580

The Big Voice in the Sky

Stadium Drama for Youth Football Before and During the COVID Pandemic

Gregory E. Johnson

Copyright © 2025 by Gregory E. Johnson

All rights reserved. No portion of this book may be reproduced in any form without written permission from the publisher or author, except as permitted by U.S. copyright law.

ISBN: 979-8-9929964-0-1 (E)

ISBN: 979-8-9929964-1-8 (P)

ISBN: 979-8-9929964-2-5 (H)

ISBN: 979-8-9929964-7-0 (A)

The Big Voice in the Sky is a fictional account inspired by the experiences of a pair of amateur stadium sports announcers compressed to the opening home gameday of two consecutive youth tackle football seasons: 2019 and the 2020 COVID-19 pandemic year. All characters and organizations portrayed in this novel are fictional composites based on the author's imagination. Any similarity between the portrayal of organizations and individuals to actual people or organizations is unintended and purely coincidental.

Book cover by illustrative artist Liz C. The cover shows members of a youth football team in a huddle with helmets raised overhead in celebration. Behind them, the stadium stands rise to the press box, where two figures, the broadcast team, observe the activities on the football field.

To my brother, Don.
He is the epitome of a self-made man, enabled by support from Shirley, his devoted partner in life.

Acknowledgements

Thanks to my family for their support during this endeavor, those who read the draft and offered feedback as well as those who pretended to read the draft and told me what a great job I did. I appreciate their tolerance in letting me appropriate elements of their personas for some characters in this book.

A cadre of Beta readers helped sort through issues with the early drafts. Thanks especially to the first Beta reader, Brian Walther, for his detailed critique of the initial draft—he had a target rich environment. Thanks also to Donald Johnson, George "Denny" Wright, Jeffery Johnson and his son Lane, Katrina Highfill, and Leona Johnson for their valued feedback.

Thanks to authors Don Sapaugh, James Padgett, and Pam Kaster for insights on how to navigate the book publishing business.

For my first novel, I experimented with different elements of grammar and rhetoric where appropriate. Why? For the fun of it. One of my favorite non-fiction books, *The Elements of Eloquence* by Mark Forsyth, was inspirational in this regard.

I also used this opportunity to pay homage to two of my favorite authors: William Shakespeare and Ernest Hemingway.

Most fictional player names were inspired by fictional characters from favorite science fiction TV series from the author's past. The surnames represented the proportional ethnicity observed for hometown youth football teams. The nicknames are real. The players and parents picked their preferred nicknames.

Youth tackle football game videos were consulted for this novel. Examples of videos, such as some youth Senior Super Bowl performances, are available on YouTube (search DaParson Films) courtesy of Dr. Mark Redd.

Multiple references regarding tackle football, especially those sources that mentioned the potential effects on youth tackle football participants, were consulted for this book. *League of Denial* by Mark Fainaru-Wada and Steve Fainaru chronicles the history of revelations regarding the relationship between head impacts and chronic brain disease and the associated health aftermath for tackle football, primarily for the professional athletes but also extending to the Pop Warner level.

Head Games by Christopher Nowinski provides a data-supported discussion of tackle football, head trauma and potential adverse health effects with focus on youth football participation.

The Center for Disease Control (CDC) website has a presentation titled "*What Parents Need to Know About Brain Safety and Youth Football.*"

The *New York Times* posted a pertinent online interactive report based on research conducted at Boston University that recounts four families whose young sons committed suicide. Each son exhibited chronic traumatic encephalopathy (CTE). A summary is available on Instagram/NYTimes/They Started Playing Football as Young as 6. They Died in Their Teens and Twenties with C.T.E. (full report available by subscription).

The Aspen Project, a nonprofit organization, monitors youth athletic participation on an annual basis. The online report, *Project Play: State of Play 2022*, from their website (https://projectplay.org/state-of-play-2022/introducti on) was consulted for this book to obtain the level of participation in youth sports during the time period covered by the novel.

Finally, thanks to all parents, volunteers and paid employees who contribute to a safe, positive gameday experience for the boys and girls who participate in the youth football program.

As an updated note, the book was re-edited one year after its initial release. The re-edited version corrected oversights from the original editing. In order to enhance accessibility, additional descriptors with context were included for the book cover and closing photograph of the two brothers in the press box. While scene and point-of-view changes in the book have visual cues, the audiobook required additional wordage to provide the listener with verbal cues for clarity.

Contents

Opening Day 2019: First Season

Chapter One

Unto the Breach

I don't intend to harm a child—or anyone else for that matter. Obey the ten miles per hour speed limit. Swing my vision between the SUVs and pickup trucks around me as I steer my F-150 through the parking lot to the central aisle that runs toward the main gate. Parking is congested, but several vacant spots dot the lot near the entrance. Come to a complete stop at the intersection of the parking lot lane and the central aisle. Switch on the left turn indicator. Look left, right, left. Take foot off brake and—

A flash in front of my truck.

Brake!

What the f—! My heart pounds at twice its normal rate. The adrenalin rush wakes me up more than the thermos of caffeine I consumed on the hour drive here. During the time it takes to shift my right foot from the brake to the accelerator, a blue jersey no taller than my engine hood darted across the front of my truck.

A few seconds later, a pair of twenty-something adults emerge from behind the SUV parked to my immediate right—the man glues a cell phone to his ear as they stroll past the front of my truck without a glance to either side. They'll never realize how we almost turned a pleasant family outing into a tragedy. I know.

I'm tempted to honk at them, but I no longer use my truck's horn. This is Texas. They might be armed, take the honk as a personal insult, and retaliate in a disproportionate manner. My truck windshield is not bulletproof.

For the drive to Deer Park, the pickup truck navigation system provides directions for the most efficient highway route, the best way to avoid traffic congestion from perpetual road construction or from the inevitable automobile wreck. Turn off the main north-south artery through town at the Catholic church, drive past the elder care facility, past a Baptist church, and the east side of the structure comes into view. My truck operates in cruise control most of the way to provide an uneventful Saturday morning drive. At this point, the guidance directions cease, and the driver selects the safest route to the target destination. I thought I had done so.

Screw this. I'm getting away from the entrance. Turn on the truck's right turn signal. Look left, right, left. Remove foot from brake and let the idling truck creep into the intersection. Swing right and right again to retreat deeper into the parking lot. I park about seventy yards from the main entrance. Since I need to burn more calories anyway, at least the longer hike provides some health benefit.

What a way to start the day. I almost run over a child. Okay. Reset. I'm tempted to just return home, but that's not an option. I made a promise.

No time to dawdle; the rising sun has cleared more than a foot above the east horizon. Text brother and mute phone. Sling the binoculars' strap around my neck, behind the collar on my maroon polo shirt so the strap doesn't chafe the skin. Slide the reading glasses into my pocket—always wear a shirt with a pocket. Tug down my gray baseball cap with the burgundy "DP" on the front and grab my notebook. Twist around in the driver's seat, hook my left shoe under the open door and tug myself outside the truck.

The cell phone vibrates in my pocket to warn me my brother replied to the text. I read the message, glance to the west where a man, dressed in a bulging red T-shirt, blue shorts and a maroon "DP" baseball cap, waves at me. Dodge the moving SUVs and stationary parking logs to get to my younger brother.

"Good morning, Earl. How are you on this magnificent September morning?" reaches me from several yards away through the din of the parking lot.

"Can't complain," I say as I step alongside him.

Dan, a leather pouch under his left arm, extends his right hand to swallow mine and squeezes the fingers of my right hand to a purple shade for several seconds. His casual dress and broad grin belie his stressful weekday job, revealed only by his eye's prominent webwork of skin creases and furrows between the eyebrows that formed from decades of bridging the world between port shipping line managers and union longshoremen.

"I hope you are ready for an all-day celebration of children and football," he says.

"I'll help out for as long as you need me. If I weren't here, I'd just waste the entire Saturday. You know...sleep in late, lie on a plush sofa most of the day, watch split-screen college football games on high-def TV, guzzle Shiner Bock while Sandy lies on her rug next to me."

Dan moves his 6-foot-4-inch frame with a purpose—always as though he's in a perpetual footrace to outrun time itself—so I quick-time my pace to keep up with him. The sidewalk leads us around the outskirts of the stadium. Our ten-yard-long silhouettes ripple through the fence posts as we traverse the sidewalk parallel to the eight feet tall black metal picket fence that guards the stadium perimeter. From the heart of the community, perhaps a dozen concrete pillars, each too wide for a pair of adults to wrap their arms around, rise from the pavement to lift the concrete steps that comprise the ninety-yard-long eastern bank of seats for the ten thousand capacity venue. Abshier Stadium, a concrete testament to football, lords over the surrounding neighborhood.

"I appreciate your help. When the Darts organization director asked me to announce all the home games this season, I felt I had to accept."

"That's flattering: the director for the entire Darts organization so highly regarded the job we did last season during the Freshman home games that he wants us to work all the games this year."

The monotone male voice from the stadium speakers indicates the Pee-Wee game progress. "Yeah, I told him there is no way we can get here early enough for the Pee-Wee game, but we could handle the other four games."

We hear the stadium entrance before we see it. The toddlers come equipped with their own audible warning system—screaming and hollering and crying—so adults know when they need to dodge or to run the other way....A smudged cartoon mouse smiles at me from the pavement. Oblivious feet kick around the cap lost by some toddler....Some garbled name-yell draws my attention to the mom who grasps an imaginary leash in a vain attempt to restrain the preschooler in front of her....One dad, a mobile human jungle gym with shoulders for his little girl to crawl over, reflects a stoic face as she giggles while she tugs off his Astro cap and puts it on his head backwards...."'Scuse me. 'Scuse me." Another dad wobble-walks sideways, both hands strain from the straps of his blue canopy tarp bag, as he passes through the gate. He bumps the bag a few times against others in his general path....Every fourth adult talks or texts, face down, during their zombie-walk through the congested entrance. Awareness by nearby pedestrians avoids pinball collisions.

The police officer stationed at the main gate grins as he watches the spectacle. He has mastered the art of looking bored and attentive at the same time: slouching against his patrol car, sipping a steaming cup of coffee, darting his eyes between every person who enters or exits the main gate.

A "Deer Park Darts" banner, weather-resistant vinyl with a clustered trio of darts with Royal blue feathers trimmed in gold, dangles from the length of a six-foot-long folding table inside the gate to our left as we enter. A male voice shouts to us from that direction. "Dan! Dan Jordan! Good morning!"

We turn to greet a man in his late thirties who dresses with the comfortable formality associated with his light blue button-down long-sleeve shirt, dark slacks, and white tennis shoes. Dan shifts his leather case to under his left arm to meet the man's outstretched right hand.

"Glad to see you," he says. "The parents loved your Freshman stadium calls last year. I got tons of compliments about the way you add to the game experience, the way you keep fans informed of action on the field, the way you call out the player names, the way you generate excitement in the stands. I'm sure all the parents who attend these games will appreciate your efforts this season."

No pressure. I'd be satisfied if we avoid several hundred irate parents from storming the press box, dragging us outside and hanging us from their canopy poles.

"I promise, we won't let you down," Dan replies. He nods toward me. "My brother, Earl. He'll help me out again in the booth this season." He swings his head to tell me, "This is Gabriel Anderson, the Darts organization manager."

"Please call me 'Gabe.' Glad to meet you."

I shake Gabe's hand and toss a "howdy" to him.

"He has a son, one grade higher than my Matthew, who plays on the Darts Junior squad," Dan tells me.

A woman's voice calls Gabe from behind him.

"The Pee-Wee game must be winding down now. We need to head up to the press box soon. Catch you later," Dan says.

"Later. I'm here all day if you need anything," Gabe says as he spins toward his summoner.

"I need to stop at the concession stand before we climb up the stairs." Dan queues up with parents and kids in front of the concession stand. Let's see...colas, snow cones, candy, donuts, popcorn, chili Frito pie. Nothing I should eat. No aroma from the barbeque pits. Too bad. I make exceptions to my forever diet for barbeque.

I spin around to see the crowd segregate into different groups past the entrance. Some adults and children scramble in and out of the toilet area to the immediate north. Several kids tote black helmets, shoulder pads and yellow jerseys to the visitor player dressing room located further north under the stands. The ramps leading up into the stadium seats occupy space on both sides of the concession stand. "Okay, ready to roll," Dan says, a plastic bag in his right hand.

The ramped tunnel funnels us upward three feet onto the base of the stands, several feet above field level. Oops—dodge the fresh cherry-colored stain from the snow cone pile near the ramp to the stands. The instant transition from shade to sunlight blinds me for a moment when I emerge from the tunnel, a reminder to wear sunglasses next time. As I reel around and look up, Dan bounds every other step upward toward the top of the stands. More power to him. I climb one step at a time.

I ascend through the lower tiers of rows where adults, families, and friends of the players on the field scatter to get an unobstructed view of field action. Then I pass through the central sections of the stands, where most canopies are erected. Different families cluster under the tarps to provide shade from the soon-to-be oppressive sun. Skilled families adjust the rear legs of their canopy to a reduced pole height so the overhead tarp exhibits no slant. Other spectators scatter throughout the upper rows of the east side of the stadium. Can't linger in one spot, or I'll block their vision to the field of play.

Dan leans against the galvanized chain-link fence at the top of the stadium to catch his breath. After I reach him, I hunch over and huff-and-puff with him while I scan the field. Though over fifty years have passed since my playing days, the memories that resurface whenever I see youth tackle football still surprise me. I forget what I ate for breakfast yesterday, but I recall some plays as though I'm still on the football field. My coach's favorite offensive play targets me from my tailback position: the quarterback receives the snap from under center, whirls around and jabs the football into my gut, so hard he knocks the breath out of me after my first forward step; the diminutive fullback leads the path to the offensive guard; the pair assaults the defensive linemen right across the line of scrimmage; I clutch the football with both arms and dive into the least obstructed side of our guard, seldom an open hole; the defenders drag me to the turf and smother me under a pile of pads and helmets. I'll never forget that play—the "meat grinder."

"Fifty-two steps," I tell him.

"You counted every step?"

"You bet I did. Fifty-two steps from the ramp to the top row. And the pain in my knees tells me stadium steps are taller than the stairway steps at home."

"We need to get in better shape."

"No kidding. I'll drop twenty pounds if you drop thirty," I promise.

"Hah. That sounds easy," Dan says. "Too bad there's no elevator on this side. The remodeled press box on the west side includes an elevator. We get the original press box, good enough for our needs." Dan nods toward the reflected glare from the far side press box. "Besides, the rising sun blinds the west press box during the morning games."

We scrunch our legs to squeeze sideways the fifty yards between the top row of metal seats and the press box wall to reach the entry. I wish we had a breeze flowing through the stands. Even though the stadium opens at the north and south ends, not much wind flows through the stadium this morning. The press box door scrapes against the floor as it opens to another eight steps up into the main observation room.

***

"Ahh...this feels good." Dan extends his arms wide, shoulder high, in front of the air conditioner vent above the hallway entrance.

"Save some for me," I say as I look over the press box area. The observation room counter spans enough length for two average size men to lie head-to-toe. The viewing window extends the length of the counter. Between the recessed fluorescent lights in the drop-down ceiling and the wall of windows, natural and artificial light floods the press box. Several rolling chairs form a pile against the back wall composed of mottled white paint on drywall opposite the brown vinyl countertop. Square tiles run down the press box floor past two separate booths and a second observation room. Thank God—there's a toilet at the end of the hallway.

We exchange waves through a plexiglass window into the adjacent booth to the twenty-something year old man calling the Pee-Wee game. We each roll a chair with five wheels under metal spokes that support gray plastic seats with a burgundy cushion to the counter. My chair rolls back to the wall before I sit down.

"Remember, this floor has a noticeable slope."

"Yeah, I forgot. Either feet on floor or elbows on counter to keep the chair from rolling to the back wall." I roll the chair back to the counter, plop down, set feet on the floor and spin to the window to bring the field into view.

Dan sets his pouch and plastic bag on the counter and tells me, "I bought some bottles of water and sports drinks to last the day. No lunch unless you want something from the concession stand."

"I'll be okay. I suspected we wouldn't eat lunch today, so I stopped at Whataburger on the way here and wolfed down a burger for breakfast." A few candy bags spill from the plastic sack. "You still toss down the cherry sours?"

"I pop a few during the football practices. Parents notice my fondness for cherry sours and some of them offer small bags to me. What can I do?" he says. "You're welcome to some if you want."

"I better not," I say as I pat my too-apparent gut. Flavored balls of sugar are never on my diet.

Dan pulls the 11 inches wide by 17 inches long spiral sheet logbook from his pouch and hands it to me. "Thanks again for keeping the game log sheets. It helps me keep up with action on the field while I call the game. And when parents quiz me about something that happened during the game."

"No problem," I reply as I put on my glasses. My eyes are weird. I see typical size font fine from five feet away, but I need reading glasses to discern or write within arm's reach. I title four pages, four sections per page, to cover home and visitor teams' first half and second half. Each sheet includes column headings (ball yard line, down and distance, yards gained, general notes) and rows for each play. The football announcing mission requires entry of plays into a written spreadsheet, a less-than-exciting part of the task and thus well suited for an engineer.

The spreadsheets in hand, I scan the field. A woman armed with a pen and clipboard stands beside a mustard-yellow canopy along the visitor sideline. Women coaches on the football field are rare. I bet she keeps track of the players to ensure they each meet the minimum number of plays per league requirement. Three other yellow-shirted coaches, all men, stand along the sideline and focus on the action on the field. One coach from each Pee-Wee team huddles on the field with their corresponding defensive and offensive squads. The on-field coach strikes me as a good idea to assist these six- or seven-year-olds line up and maintain order for each play. When I played over fifty years ago, my league had an on-field coach for every age group.

"It's rare we have much time to talk. How's the family doing?" I ask as the Pee-Wee game winds down.

Dan looks up from the roster notes. "Cheryl, Matthew and I are all doing all right. I still work fifty to sixty hours a week and have some obvious health issues." He thumps his ample belly. "Cheryl had a rough stretch after her hip replacement, but she's recovered now and active as ever with family and friends. And Matthew, for a kid who spends too much time staying up late playing video games, is doing well in fourth grade. Cheryl tutors him and makes sure he finishes his homework before he settles in for the evening to play video games."

"Children have so many entertainment options now compared to when we were growing up. I don't see how kids stay focused on anything. It seems to me Matthew adjusted pretty well since he moved in with you and Cheryl."

"Oh, yes. His parents,"—Dan shakes his head—"so many drug issues, legal problems. We couldn't let our grandson go into foster care. I still recall," Dan says with a smile, "that four-year-old boy, not even waist high to me, his tiny, trembling fingers clutching my hand, looking up to me with an open mouth, gap toothed, staring wide-eyed as we board the flight from Seattle to Houston. His first airplane ride to someplace he'd never been. A year of daycare, then kindergarten, and now elementary school. So far, so good."

I shift my gaze to Dan. "Speaking of Matthew, how's his dad doing?"

Dan hunches over in his seat and stares into my eyes. "Sean is doing great. He's clean now and doesn't want to return to Victorville or anyplace like it. That last stint in a maximum-security prison...it...he..."—Dan drops his face to the floor for a few seconds and jerks his eyes to mine—"epiphany! That's the word I'm looking for. He had an epiphany. He realized he had wasted more than half his life on drugs and jail and lost time with his sons. Sean wanted his life to go in a different direction starting his first day from of prison."

"Good, good," I say as I nod my head.

"I got him a job at the port container yard. Sean doesn't mind the hard work—and he's sure motivated. I talk to his supervisors a few times a week. They tell me Sean has a great attitude and work ethic. He always shows up on time, works extra hours whenever needed. One told me that Sean, for a smaller guy, is capable of physical labor that larger men struggle with."

"I'm glad he's getting a second chance, especially employed in a union job. If he sticks with it, then the job should provide a decent income for life. How's your other son, Bryan, doing?"

"Bryan"—Dan tilts back in his chair and smiles—"doesn't communicate much with us. When we talk, it's always a positive conversation. He's a captain now, stationed at Fort Bliss."

"Is this his second military post?"

"His third. He started at Fort Jackson for boot camp, then to Fort Benning for officer school and Ranger training, and now at Fort Bliss for he-won't-tell-me-what training. Bryan does well at every position, every base he's assigned to. He told me he loves the army and plans to make military service his life."

"He's found his calling. Let's hope both sons are cruising to successful, happy lives now."

Text messages draw Dan's attention to his cell phone while I wrap up labeling the gameday log sheets. I stand to stretch my legs and watch the outside activity, so, of course, my chair rolls to the back wall. The stadium football field aligns in a north-south orientation with concrete stands that rise on the east and west sides to meet a chain-link fence that runs along the top of the stands. Each stadium row consists of a continuous metal bench with the assigned seat and row designations painted along each pew, far preferable to the pair of rusty metal bleachers and row of lawn chairs that lined the field where I played youth football.

I guestimate three hundred spectators scattered throughout the stands near the end of this first Pee Wee game. Multiple colored square and rectangular shaped canopies dot the stands. A quick count shows nine blue, four maroon, two gray, two brown, two black, and one burnt-orange canopy. One misguided soul has erected a canopy with a Dallas Cowboys logo. I'll keep track of the various canopies to see how the color palette changes during the day as families erect and dismantle their tents. No special reason. Just curious.

The press box door scrapes open to announce an entry. I glance at the twenty-something-year-old man sporting a black baseball cap and yellow tee shirt who emerges into the observation room. "Good morning, gentlemen," he says. "I hope you are doing well this immaculate morning."

Someone's in a good mood. Black Cap exhibits a more rapid breathing rate, but nowhere close to the extreme panting Dan or I exhibited when we entered the press box. Maybe he's been sitting on a higher row in the stands for a while.

"We're fine," Dan says. "Looking forward to announcing today's games."

"I'm here for the Freshman game. I get to see my boy play football with his friends on a cloudless September morning. Life can't get much better than that."

The Pee Wee players on the field execute plays in a competent manner. I recall the Pee Wee games were a circus when I watched this age group decades ago.

"I brought the LaPorte team rosters."

"I'll take them," Dan says as he rises to accept the paper with the lists of names from Black Cap. He pins his chair between his rump and the counter. "Any hard-to-pronounce names?" he asks while he scans the visitor team rosters.

"No, the names are pretty straight-forward," Black Cap replies as he hunches over Dan's shoulder. "Be sure to get my boy's name right. He's here." He taps a spot on the top page.

"I'm surprised to see youth tackle football going so strong," I say to nobody in particular while I scan the activity on the field. "The publicity surrounding tackle football and head trauma doesn't seem to discourage parents from enrolling their kids. Some people don't want anyone's kids to play the sport anymore. I saw on the news a state legislator proposed a bill to ban tackle football for children under thirteen years old."

"Hey!" Black Cap spins and takes two long strides at me. I turn toward the yell. He thrusts his right forefinger outward from in front of his chest multiple times at my face. I lean backward, my eyes wide and mouth agape, and turn my face toward the left. "My father played football. I played football. By God, my son is playing football. Nobody is taking our football from us!" Black Cap's ears are so red they might explode off the sides of his head at any moment.

The stadium speakers fall silent as the current game announcer, open-mouthed with unblinking eyes, focuses on the drama in the observation room instead of the action on the field. Dan folds the roster sheets in half as he glides within arm's reach of Black Cap's left shoulder. Dan's indifferent chair creeps toward the back wall. Black Cap whirls around, shoves the chair against the other chairs to unleash a metallic "clang" that reverberates throughout the observation room. He stomps out of the press box and scrapes the door shut in a none-to-gentle manner.

"Jesus. Who was that?" I ask. Talk about a Jekyll and Hyde moment.

"A parent dropping off the rosters for the visiting LaPorte squads."

"Man, I didn't mean to stir up anything. I thought I was making a harmless comment," I say as I use my handkerchief to wipe stray spittle from my face and wish Black Cap had discovered mouthwash. I hope he doesn't lead the mob that storms the press box. "He behaved like I challenged his Second Amendment rights."

"Forget it. He misunderstood what you meant," Dan says. "Even when the Astros make a World Series push, in Texas, football is king."

"Well, I'm all for parents deciding what is best for their own children. But if I had a boy, to be honest, I'd try to steer him away from tackle football. The potential consequences of sustained head trauma worry me."

"An expert opinion from the man who played a grand total of one year of youth tackle football." Dan retrieves his chair and sits down at the counter.

"Okay, so I'm not the professional youth footballer you are. You played, what, three years?"

"Four. Four unspectacular years slugging it out as an interior lineman in the trenches on both sides of the ball. No glorious moments. I stuck it out until I graduated from the program."

"Okay, fine. But I bet neither one of us ever thought about getting injured, for sure not injuries we might carry into our old age."

"You mean, like our current age," Dan says.

"Hah. I know, I know. So far, we're only normal nuts, not crazy nuts. I don't want to end up like Dad with onset Alzheimer's."

"And Dad never played football. He's ninety years old. It comes with getting older, a lot older."

"There's been plenty in the news about professional football players and brain damage and mental issues and suicides. I wouldn't want to set up a kid with that in his future. I came across an interactive online video put out by *The New York Times* that shows kids with extensive tackle football history, some as young as eighteen years old, can suffer the same effects."

"*The New York Times*. Then I'm sure it was fair and balanced."

"Okay, but don't disregard everything from the newspaper because you hate their politics. The portion of the video I find hard to forget is the final tribute two mothers create for their deceased sons—each one tattoos a loving, hand-written sentiment from their pre-teen boy onto their forearm. Each mother carries her lost child's declaration of love for the rest of her life, so all the world bears witness."

"That is tragic," Dan agrees, "but it's got to be rare. Millions and millions of kids have played tackle football for decades, and there's no epidemic of suicides from footballers, not counting the pros."

"Hmm. I can't argue with you on that point." Hard to determine how common impact-induced brain disease is—or how to put its frequency in relationship to other life risks—when no corresponding medical information exists for the ex-footballers who fail to exhibit serious mental problems or for the general population, for that matter. But I hate to make choices in ignorance. I hope I'm not contributing to long-term health issues for these kids. For now, I'm here for my brother.

"Cheryl and I have a personal perspective. No one has a crystal ball into the future. Life is full of risks, and a sport that challenges Matthew mentally and physically will make him tougher, better able to take on whatever comes his way later in life. We can tell he's not going to play professional football or college football, and maybe not even high school ball. We want him to get involved in a team sport, get some exercise, get away from the computer screen. We signed Matthew up for baseball, basketball and football. Football is the only sport he wanted to play a second time. As long as he wants to play, we'll support his choice."

Dan turns his gaze to the field. "The Pee-Wee game is wrapping up." The players and coaches from each team walk along opposite sides of the midfield stripe in reverse directions and touch hands in the traditional display of sportsmanship.

The three officials cross the field to rest before the start of the next game.

"Any idea how much the officials get paid?" I ask.

"They get paid as much as we do."

"They're not paid anything?"

"Correct. They volunteer their Saturdays to officiate all five youth football games."

"Game officials may work under a blazing sun or in heavy rain. You must be committed to what you're doing to be out there in this Gulf Coast heat and humidity," I comment.

"The officials are like teachers on the field. You sometimes see an official talk to a kid after a penalty to tell him what he did wrong to draw the yellow flag."

"Kudos to them. I couldn't be out there all day."

A shout comes from the announcer's booth. "Is that Dan?"

"Yes."

"Do you want to auction off the game ball?"

"I can."

"Please."

Dan scurries into the announcer's booth after the Pee-Wee game announcer steps out. "I'm Jonas, by the way. Gabe texted me that you are announcing the rest of the games."

"Glad to meet you. This is my brother, Earl." I nod to Jonas as he hurries through the observation room.

"Good luck, guys. I have to run to meet my wife and kids." The scraping door declares his rapid departure from the press box.

"Help me watch for bidders," Dan yells from the booth.

"You got it," I holler back.

Dan plops down in the chair in front of the stadium microphone and depresses the mic button that sends his voice through the stadium speakers. **"Good morning, football fans. It's time to auction the game football. LaPorte fans, anyone can bid on this lifetime memory. Now, who will start us at $50? Only $50 for a lifetime memory. Thank you, sir, from the north forty-five. Now, who will give me $100?"**

We both scour the stands for anyone who waves their arms at the press box.

"At the north twenty, thank you, sir. I need $150 now."

The original bidder again waves both arms overhead from several rows below the right side of the press box.

"Got you. At the north forty-five again. Thank you, sir. Looking for $200 now. This game ball is a lifetime memory. Put it on your mantle. Put it in your trophy case. Still looking for two hundred. I have one myself. You will never regret owning a game ball, a memory that lasts a lifetime. Going once...You may never get another chance to get a game ball...Going

twice...Last call...Sold! Thank you, sir. Please collect the football at the Darts organization table beneath the stands."

"One hundred fifty dollars to get a game football with an emotional attachment. Strikes me like a pretty good deal."

"I want the winning bids to be higher," Dan says, "not only to help with league expenses, but especially when we get to the designated Fireballs donation day. On that Saturday, all winning game ball bids go to the Deer Park Fireballs. I recall the league donated over a thousand dollars last year to support mentally impaired kids and adults who compete in a bunch of different sports."

"Good cause. Back in a minute," as I exit the booth.

The adjacent booth, same size as the announcer's booth, stands empty. The far observation room, half the size of the main observation area, contains a camera mounted on a tripod. The camera focuses onto the field. A high school age male reclines as much as his stubborn chair allows while he stares into his cell phone.

"Good morning," I say from the open doorway.

"Good morning, sir," says the camera operator as he jumps with enough force to hurl the wheeled chair clanking against the side wall.

"The older gentleman, the retired professor who recorded the games last year, he isn't here today."

"No, sir. He's preparing for the church mission trip to Africa, so I handle the camera today. I'm Jonathan."

"Nice to meet you. I'm Earl. A church missionary trip sounds impressive. I didn't remember he went overseas on church missions. Do you know what they're doing?"

"No, sir. But I am sure Dr. LePrince will be happy to fill you in when their church group gets back."

"That's okay. Just curious." Pointing to the camera, "So you have to be here to record each game today?"

"Yes, sir. I set up the camera in the morning and dismantle it at the end of the day. I'll adjust it to focus on the part of the field that's active during the football game and switch it off during idle times between games. Not difficult. The worst thing is the job consumes my entire Saturday."

"I guess that's why Dr. LePrince pays you the big bucks."

"Hah. Yes, sir."

"All right, then, we'll see you later." I wish I had video from my youth tackle football days, although I'd cringe at half the things I did—or didn't do—on the field.

"Yes, sir. Have a good day."

I'm not used to someone being so polite to me. He focuses his attention back to his cell phone while I head into the bathroom and feel a little guilty for the "Eddie Haskell" vibe sensed from Video Teen. That's a reference nobody born this century recognizes.

Once back in the announcer's booth, I stand in the middle and extend both arms outward from my sides. My fingertips touch each wall. "I've seen airplane bathrooms bigger than this booth. There's enough room for two chairs if we bump sides. I'll stand during the game and bend over to record the plays in the log sheet. I get a better view through my binoculars of game action when I stand, anyway."

"However you want to handle the spotter role suits me fine. I appreciate your help." Dan has team rosters, binder with league information, and personal notes scattered around the mic. And cherry sours to his far right.

I arrange the game log sheets on the counter to Dan's left. Pen at the ready on top of the sheets. Reading glasses next to the pen. Observe the play on the field with my binoculars. Stoop over and put on reading glasses. Use the pen to record the results of the active play and start the row for the next play. Set down pen. Remove glasses. Stand erect. Use binoculars. Repeat. That's the plan. It's analogous to the classic dipping or drinking bird toy that, once activated, bobs up-and-down "by magic" toward an open glass of water.

"We worked well together when we only dealt with the individual Freshman home games last season," I tell him. "I bet doing all four games for each of the six home Saturdays during the regular season won't be too tough."

I hope those words don't come back to haunt me.

Chapter Two

Be Not Too Tame

The Darts' players—in white helmets, blue jerseys with gold trim at each sleeve and white numbers bordered by gold trim—hop up and down as though they stand barefoot on hot concrete during a Texas summer. An inflated plastic tunnel, resembling a helmet with painted feathered darts on the side, dominates the southwest corner of the end zone. The mob of eight-year-old kids on the far side of the field cluster behind the puffed-up helmet. One boy grasps a pole that flies a teal-blue flag, three darts feature Royal blue feathers trimmed in gold, and leads the charge of screaming players through the helmet tunnel to their far sideline blue canopy.

In contrast, the opposition Bumble Bees' players on the near side each sport a black helmet, mustard-yellow jersey with black numbers, black padded pants, and white cleated shoes. An intertwined yellow 'BB' marks each black helmet.

"If I remember correctly," Dan comments, "the Bumble Bees were once called the Killer Bees until a few years ago. Some parents complained about the name sounding too violent, so they changed their name to the Bumble Bees."

"I like the color scheme of their uniforms. The black and yellow mimics bumble bee colors in nature. I don't recall seeing any other team with colors coordinated with a mascot."

Dan organizes his home team rosters and notes for the upcoming game while I inspect the field below.

This field is a galaxy far, far away from the field on which I played over 50 years ago. All football fields have identical dimensions: just over 50 yards wide and 100 yards long with 10-yard-deep end zones at each end of the field. Not all football fields are the same. The western half of this field gradually emerges from the retreating shadow of the east stands, shimmering in the morning sunlight, to highlight the turf—artificial turf. Artificial turf for youth tackle football.

My God, I played youth tackle football on a grassy junior high football field with splotches of overgrown grass so high in parts of the field that blades of grass reach up like ankle grabbing twelfth defenders. Sandburs are prevalent throughout my field, and the burs make the grass-burns that accompany tackles more painful. I pluck burs from my white socks, which act like bur magnets, after every game.

No burs on this field. The artificial turf comprises alternating dark green sections, the color of rind on a ripe lime, and light green sections, the color of pulp within the lime, that span across the width of the field every five yards. I expect this turf to keep its form throughout the season. When I played, we chewed up the central area of the grass field so much that it deteriorated into more dirt than grass by the end of the season.

I like order. I appreciate the geometric precision of the white stripes that slice across the field to separate each alternating green section. Mini-stripes along the white sideline boundaries denote one-yard increments. Crisp, sharp lines without fading along the edges intersect at perfect right angles. The yardage mark numbers every ten yards are clear enough to be seen from anywhere in the stands, including the press box, without binoculars. When I played, faded white dirt ruts cut across the field every five yards. Portable rubber inverted V-shaped markers, similar in thickness to heavy mudflaps on 18-wheelers, were positioned like teepees along the sidelines every ten yards for sideline markers.

I'm no architect, but the engineer in me appreciates the design and construction efforts applied to the idealized football arena realized by this stadium. I shake my head—all this with youth football. Hah, I swear, even the overhead birds refuse to soil the pristine green turf of Abshier Stadium.

If I played youth football on a field like this, then it would have been the most impressive sports venue in which I ever competed.

After a few deep breaths, Dan presses the microphone switch, and the big voice in the sky emanates from the stadium speakers: **"Are you ready for some footbaaall!? We have an exciting lineup of Freshman, Sophomore, Junior and Senior games today. Welcome to Deer Park's Abshier Stadium on this ideal, chamber-of-commerce morning to see the Freshman Deer Park Darts versus the LaPorte Bumble Bees coming up next."**

"Do we do the anthem?" I ask.

"No. The Pee-Wee game announcer should have done it before the first game ."

"Just wondering. I don't see an American flag on the pole outside the north end zone."

"The old flagpole isn't used anymore. Cheryl and I go to a lot of high school games with friends to watch their kids play. Those games use the fancy, high-tech scoreboard to show a rippling flag with the anthem lyrics. Also, the church across the south stadium parking lot always flies the American flag on one pole at the same height as the Texas state flag on the adjacent pole. That marker serves as a reference point for facing the flag."

"Bang!" echoes from outside the press box as tarp poles strike a metal seat. A family starts to erect a blue tarp, eight feet long and six feet wide, in front of the press box announcer's booth. Their canopy obstructs the press box view to the field along the near sideline and to the visitor player's tent area.

"Please do not erect tents in front of the press box. It blocks our view to the field," the big voice in the sky informs them. **"Thank you for your consideration."**

Two young adult males look at each other and say I-don't-know-what—I'm not a lip reader—back and forth for a minute. They fold the poles, wad up the tarp and move thirty yards east of us, about half-way down the stands.

"They didn't need to move all the way across the stadium," Dan says. "They could have erected their tarp several rows lower, and we'd have been fine."

"Well, we have a clear view of the entire field now."

Three officials stride to the center of the field for the coin toss ceremony. The zebra's shirts display alternate black and white vertical stripes, while their black shorts feature a single vertical white stripe down each outer leg. The lead official wears a white cap, while the other two officials wear black caps.

"I need to read the sportsmanship announcement and rosters. Keep an eye on what's happening on the field?"

"You got it."

Dan's alter-ego, the Big Voice, begins the recital: **"Our youth sports organization is committed to teaching sportsmanship to our youth through playing football. Regardless of the final score, all the players prove their willingness to work and sacrifice with the goal of achieving athletic excellence while enjoying the game of football. We encourage you to cheer and applaud for them. Please act in accordance with our goal by exhibiting sportsmanlike conduct. Do not use profanity or direct insults toward teams, fans or game officials.**

"We encourage you to honor the performances of the cheerleaders and drill teams. They also practice every week and travel to away games to support their teams.

"The gameday officials also officiate high school football games. Years of studying, training, and annual testing go into their ability to officiate. These volunteers help teach young players the rules of the game and ensure a fair contest. These games are not possible without them. Please demonstrate the same respect for them you would have for any dedicated person in a position of responsibility."

Show respect for a dedicated person in a responsible position—many would consider that a naive notion. I'm glad some old-fashioned values still linger. Can traditional values survive in such a cynical age? Perhaps the trick is determining what values are worth keeping.

"No alcoholic beverages or tobacco products are allowed on school property per state law.

"Thank you for your help to make this a positive gameday experience."

Three players from each team straddle the midfield stripe on their respective sidelines. For this age group, the shoulder pads stretch beyond their torsos to exaggerate their apparent chest sizes. Some jersey numbers scrunch together so much on these young frames the numbers are hard to make out.

After the lead official points his right hand toward each sideline, two opposing trios stride side-by-side along the 50-yard line until they meet at midfield. The deliberate approach provides the clearest view of the player's jersey numbers. The jersey numbers crinkle together, but I take my best guess and jot their numbers in the margins of the game log sheet.

"Welcome again to today's Freshman game between the Deer Park Darts versus the LaPorte Bumble Bees. Here is your Freshman Darts roster.

Number 1. Kenny 'Shake-N-Bake' Argo, *Line*-man!

Number 2. Matt 'M&M' Martinez, *Line*-man!

Number 3. Wesley 'Grenade' Addams, *Line*-man!

Number 5. Dylan 'Hawkeye' Hunter, *Line*-man!

Number 6. Samuel 'Big T' Austin, *Line*-man!"

The lead official directs each team captain to shake the hands of their counterparts. The official shows the ceremonial coin to each captain. At least I presume he handles a coin. From the press box, the coin flip resembles a pantomime act they perform for the fans. Even through my binoculars, I can't make out a coin. A visiting captain must have called "heads" or "tails." The official tosses the coin head-high and lets it fall to the turf. All six captains hunch over—their helmets collide—to see the coin before the lead official picks it up and shows each of them the coin's upward-facing side.

"Number 7. Doug 'Juggernaut' Phillips, Running back.
Number 9. Dave 'Prime Time' Nunez, Quarterback.
Number 11. Simon 'Showboat' Trevor, Wide receiver.
Number 13. Vic 'Mad Dog' Dampouse, *Line*-man!
Number 19. Leo 'Wampus' McCoy, *Line*-man!
Number 21. Jay 'The Jet' Kirk, *Line*-man!"

The lead official aligns the team captains face-to-face: Bees face north from the south 49-yard line and Darts face south from the north 49-yard line. After the official taps the shoulder of the nearest Dart player, he extends both arms in front of his chest and crosses them once parallel to the ground. He moves beside the nearest Bee captain, extends both arms in front of him and draws his arms back to his chest. The player positions indicate the Bees attack the Darts from south to north or left to right from the press box vantage point.

"Number 30. Isaac 'Flash' Ramos, Running back.
Number 34. Enos 'Hot Wheels' Sinclair, Running back.
Number 51. Andrew 'Tank' Munos, Running back.
Number 56. Jamie 'Thunder' Sommers, *Line*-man!
Number 64. Dean 'Hot Sauce' Prince, *Line*-man!
Number 76. Ryan 'Rhino' Wells, *Line*-man!"

Each set of team captains trots back to their respective sidelines.

"Number 79. Dave 'Dynamite' Lester, Running back.
Number 87. Otto 'Bear' Goldman, Wide receiver.
Number 90. Will 'Gorilla' Robbins, *Line*-man!
Number 98. Ed 'Destroyer' Striker, *Line*-man!
Number 99. Chris 'Crusher' Kochanski, *Line*-man!"

"Ready?"

"Shoot."

"Darts win the toss and defer. Captains are 10, 34, 56."

"Okay."

"Bee captains are 1, 17, 27."

Dan jots the numbers on scratch paper and scans the team rosters.

From the voice in the sky: **"Darts won the toss and deferred their choice to the second half. Bees receive the opening kickoff. The Dart team captains today are Dave 'Prime Time' Nunez, Enos 'Hot Wheels' Sinclair and Jamie 'Thunder' Sommers. The Bee captains are Jabari 'Man with the Plan' Mills, Bobby 'Fireball' Draper and Cal 'Gonzo' Drummer."**

"I like your '*line*-man' emphasis."

"Yeah, the linemen don't get much recognition during the game, so I give them a little extra love during the roster roll call. Since most players play both an offensive and defensive position, I only mention the offense—Oh...some music." He scrolls through music selections on his phone, and "Welcome to the Jungle," a traditional classic rocker played before many professional sporting events, streams from the stadium speakers.

I look down at the Dart roster next to Dan. In a way, the variety of names, especially the surnames, provides an interesting "sort-of look" into the ethnic makeup of the community, the degree of diversity present in the local neighborhood like the view through a windshield swept by worn wipers during the rain—not perfect, but adequate to see what's happening around you.

A squad of eleven players from each team trots onto the field for the kickoff. For most games, the kicker mounts the football tip-down-on-tee at the middle of their 40-yard line. In this case, the Darts' kicker places the tee at the far hashmark intersection with the 40-yard line, almost one-third inward from the far sideline. Two sets of hash marks, each about two feet long, traverse the length of the field lengthwise like railroad crossties without the rails to assist football placement during the game. In theory, the off-center kickoff position reduces the amount of field the kicking squad needs to cover.

"Jersey 6 kicking off."

"Samuel 'Big T' Austin is kicking off for the Darts."

The lead official points to the kicker, and Dan stops the music. Big T carries the wave of attackers with him to the 40-yard line. The young kicker drives the football along the ground—not sure if it's on purpose. The football bounces past the first line of Bee blockers. One player, Catch Me If You Can, knocks the ball down at the Bee 43-yard line, covers it, and hugs it from a fetal position as a mother might hug her precious baby.

"Number 49 covered the ball."

"Jim 'Catch Me If You Can' Holden covers the football for the Bees. First and ten from the Bees' 43-yard line."

While I record "43B" in the ball location cell of the game log sheet and write "receive KO" in the comments for the first line, the Bee offensive and Dart defensive squads filter through the special teams players that jog off the field. The black-helmeted Bees with mustard-yellow jerseys, black helmets and black pants provide a glaring contrast against the white-helmeted Darts with blue and gold jerseys and white pants who array against them.

As a kid, I never appreciated the planning and organization skills required to configure the offensive and defensive formations for youth football.

The Bumble Bees adopt a basic I-formation that teaches the eight-year-old players game fundamentals, run blocking, play execution—not much emphasis on a passing game expected at this age. The Bees establish their attack formation: six linemen crouch in the classic football three-point-of-contact position to the ground, both legs and one hand, to maximize leverage against the defensive linemen arrayed opposite them; the quarterback hunches behind the center to receive the hiked football; one running back, the fullback, crouches three yards behind the quarterback; the second running back, the tailback—the same position I played on offense for my Senior squad over fifty years ago—stands six yards behind the quarterback; two Bee wide receivers split several yards apart from each end of the offensive line to threaten downfield.

The offensive players, frozen before the snap, display more discipline than I exhibit as an eight-year-old. I'm not a football player at this age, but I play little league baseball. We practice on an open field that borders a bramble patch. As one of the outfielders, I often line up in a group with several other boys and wait for my turn to catch a fly ball from our coach. We spend more time scouring the bramble patch for wild blackberries than watching for fly balls. The baseballs are covered with dark blue and black stains by the end of practice. So much for our self-discipline.

The Darts counter their opponents: five defensive linemen crouch in a three-point stance—helmet-versus-helmet—along the line of scrimmage; three linebackers space several yards behind the defensive line so they can reinforce at the point of attack; two defensive players, the cornerbacks, split wide to defend against the wide receivers; one player sets up fifteen yards behind the defensive line to act as a deep safety—the defensive position I played during my olden days of youth football.

The far sideline official organizes the three members of the chain gang. One pole aligns with the football at the Bee 43-yard line while the other pole stretches the attached chain ten yards across midfield to the 47-yard line. The third pole, topped by the down indication box, shares the Bee 43-yard mark with "1" displayed by the placard that crowns the pole. Two teens and a dad handle the yardage poles. I bet the parents either bribed or threatened their teens to handle the chains.

During on-field activity, Dan sets the rosters to the left of the stadium mic and circles the quarterback and running back names. I start the game log sheet second row with "43" in the ball location cell and "1/10" in the down/distance cell. I will complete the rest of the row after the play. We train our binoculars, or 'noculars, toward the field.

The quarterback, Man with the Plan, receives the snap, whirls to his right and jabs the ball into the tailback's stomach.

The running back, Fireball, hurtles headfirst at the right offensive guard. He bounces backwards off his own lineman. Retreats five yards. Sprints ten yards toward his right, the near sideline.

Two Dart players, Crusher and Mad Dog, cut him off.

Fireball spins around. Retreats five more yards. Reverses course to the far sideline for 30 yards.

More Darts, Dynamite and Destroyer, threaten him.

Fireball reverses direction. Retreats 20 yards back toward the near sideline.

Fireball, penned in by Dart players, faces the line of scrimmage. Darts to the right of him. Darts to the left of him. He clutches the football in both arms and charges at the Darts in front of him along the original line of scrimmage.

A mass of blue jerseys engulfs Fireball.

Snorts and giggles fill the announcer's booth. "He ran from sideline to sideline for a two-yard gain. A lot of energy expended, but he found a way to move forward in the end," I say.

"*Dynamic* run by halfback, Number 17, Bobby 'Fireball' Draper for two yards. Brings up second down and eight to go from the 45-yard line."

Independent, simultaneous group activities begin for the upcoming play. The Bee offensive players huddle ten yards behind the football to coordinate the plan of attack. After several seconds, the huddle disintegrates. Two wide-outs sprint to their assigned positions while the rest of the unit trots to the line of scrimmage.

Dart defensive players loiter near their assigned areas to await the Bee frontal assault. They resume their ready positions as the Bees assemble along the line of scrimmage.

As the players ready for the upcoming play, one chain gang pole holder changes the down indicator to "2" and positions the pole at the far 45-yard sideline.

Meanwhile, I record "HB dive" in the comments and "2" in the yards gained cell. I start the next row with "45" in the ball location cell and "2/8" in the down/distance cell.

The Big Voice makes the second down call: **"Quarterback keeper up the middle. Chris 'Crusher' Kochanski takes him down! Gain of three yards on the play. That makes it third down and five yards to go for a first down."**

The pattern or rhythm of play continues with a huddle by the offensive players, realignment by the offense against the defense, and down indicator pole relocation by the chain gang. In the booth, the active line is completed, and the next line is started in the game logbook.

'Noculars are raised. Football is hiked. Play is run.

"Quarterback keeper to the left end. Small gain by 'Man with the Plan' Mills. Gang tackled by the right side of the Darts line. That means a big fourth down play is coming up. Fourth and three. Okay, Darts fans. Let our defense hear you! Make some noise!"

The active row ends, the future row starts.

'Noculars are raised. Football is hiked. Play is run.

"Handoff to the deep back around the left side. Hit behind the line! Great tackle! Dave 'Prime Time' Nunez and Jay 'The Jet' Kirk. Loss of two yards on the play. The ball goes over on downs to the Darts."

The change in football possession reverses the pattern of play. Now, the Darts go on the attack.

The Darts prepare their assault in a split backfield formation: six linemen across the line of scrimmage, quarterback Prime Time, running backs Juggernaut and Flash split apart several yards behind the quarterback, and two wide receivers split ten yards apart from each end of the offensive line.

The Bees oppose with five defensive linemen, three linebackers behind the defensive line, two cornerbacks, and one deep safety.

Both teams substitute several players who have more specialized defensive or offensive skills—or to get their required number of plays per league mandate.

"I didn't see any sign of speed for the Bumble Bees. Have you heard anything about their team?" I ask.

"Not much. They lost their opening home game, and we also lost our opening road game."

The first two Dart plays, one where Flash dives into the line and Prime Time sweeps around the end, gain eight yards. Third down and two yards needed for a first down.

A second before Hawkeye hikes the football to Prime Time, a yellow jersey jumps across the line of scrimmage on the left side of the offense. No penalty flag thrown.

Prime Time wheels right. He jabs the football into halfback Flash's gut.

Flash squeezes between M&M and Destroyer.

"Handoff to the tailback into the right side."

Flash charges over the yellow jersey in front of him. The Bee grabs a leg and hangs on while Flash drag-steps forward twice.

The middle and left outside Bee linebackers envelop Flash.

"Tough run by 'Flash' Ramos for five yards. And that is enough for a Darts...First Dooown!"

The conflict continues in a grind-it-out manner. The quarterback or running back with the football determines the flow of play. Offensive linemen propel themselves at the opposing defensive linemen at each snap of the football. The defensive linemen try to break free from the offensive linemen and drag the ball carrier to the turf. Contrasting color uniforms seldom appear in the opposing team's backfield—unless they jump early. The linebackers, unencumbered by offensive linemen, are most effective in reaching the ball carriers. I suspect both teams position their quickest, more aggressive defensive players at linebacker.

Neither team passes. The wide receivers and opposing cornerbacks stand and watch the play's progression unless the football hurdles right at them.

Neither team punts. When teams cannot make a first down to retain possession, they turn the ball over on downs.

The press box door scrapes open near the end of the first half, and a pair of footsteps climbs several steps to announce entry into the press box viewing area. Two women, one perhaps in her late twenties and one in her late thirties, each wearing yellow jerseys tucked into their jeans, wave to us as they stoop over at the waist and breathe heavily. One jersey displays a black "10" on it, while the other shows "65." I don't wonder which team they support.

After she catches her breath, Yellow 65 pokes her head into the announcer's booth. "Good morning. We're here for the Bumble Bees ladies drill team."

"You're in the right spot."

"Can we find out how much time remains before halftime?"

"Well, I can check," Dan replies. **"Officials, how much time is left until halftime?"**

I focus my binoculars on the white-capped lead official. He looks to a device tethered to his left wrist, raises his right hand and holds up four fingers...five fingers...four fingers...five fingers.

"Four and five."

"Forty-five seconds before halftime."

Right thumb up from the lead official.

"Okay, ladies. Forty-five seconds to go."

"Thank you."

The Bees execute the last running play. The lead official waves his arms over his head and retrieves the football. Halftime. The score: Darts 0, Bees 0. Both teams jog off the field to regroup, the Darts to the home team locker room under the southwest corner of the stands and the Bees to the visitor locker room under the northeast corner of the stands. The officials stride to the northeast area under the stands to take their break.

"We have a nail-biter at halftime," the Big Voice declares. **"Still anyone's game. Please stay in your seats for the halftime performance by the ladies spirit squad from LaPorte."**

***

"I have to get here earlier before the next halftime, so I have time to catch my breath," Yellow 10 says.

"Believe me, we sympathize. I guess your jersey numbers match your boy's jersey numbers?" I ask.

"Sort of," Yellow 10 says. "My son graduated from the Bees' youth football program last year, but my daughter is in her second year on the spirit squad. I still wear my boy's old jersey. I mean, not his actual jersey but the same jersey that I wore when he played, to show support for my daughter and the Bee teams."

"I have one son on the Sophomore team and one son on the Senior squad. Thankfully, I got the number '65' for both their uniforms. Otherwise, I'd be changing jerseys between games to avoid one of them feeling slighted," Yellow 65 tells us. "It's my daughter's first year on the spirit squad." She nods toward the field. "Okay, how do I start the music?"

Dan lifts a cord that dangles from the booth window counter to the electronic equipment on a shelf at the back wall of the booth. "This cord ties my phone to the receiver for the speaker system. You can connect your phone, start the music, and it plays through the stadium speakers. Depress this button on the mic and you can speak while the music plays."

"Understood. It seems straightforward. Thank you."

We squeeze out of the announcer's booth for the two women to enter. Dan rolls a second chair into the booth so they can sit side-by-side. Yellow 65 drops in front of the mic and connects her phone to the receiver cord.

On the field, thirty girls form five clusters spread outward from the near side midfield stripe. Each girl wears a mustard-yellow pleated skirt and sleeveless top with black trim at the bottom of the skirt, across the waist, and along the

V-neckline. Black "Bees" letters are written across the front of each top. Every girl carries a pair of shiny tinsel pom-poms, one black and one yellow.

"Do the visitor pom-pom teams still get the first two halftimes and the home team squad the last two halftimes?"

"Yeah, that's my understanding. Still a combined eight through twelve-year-old squad," Dan says. "The Pee-Wee team has their own six- or seven-year-olds for cheerleaders who hop around and wave pom-poms for their game."

"Since we only called the early Freshman game last season, I never got to see the home team's performance. I'm curious to see how the home and visitor shows compare."

"Me too. The girl's performances add a lot to the panorama, the spectacle of Saturday at the stadium."

Yellow 65 speaks through the stadium speakers: **"Good morning. We are happy to be here on this beautiful morning. Please give a hand to your 2019 Honeybees spirit squad."**

The music starts, an updated remix of the pop rock classic "Let 'Em In," to send the five clusters of girls to form parallel, single-file lines and march, pom-poms held against their hips, toward the middle of the field.

They step in place until everyone reaches their designated spot. The music stops, and the girls spin around in unison to face the east press box. They exhibit varying sizes, apparent even without binoculars, from mid-thigh height to some likely as tall as chest high to me.

"Allow me to introduce our young ladies."

Yellow 65 announces each girl's name over the stadium speakers. The girl raises her arms overhead when she hears her name and shakes her pom-poms before returning to the hands-on-hip position. Every girl displays a broad smile during the introductions, as though the ready position includes an exaggerated smile.

At the end of the roll call, Yellow 65 continues, **"These are your 2019 Honeybees! Ladies, here is your music."**

No time to watch the routine—I need to compile the first half statistics. After a little math, I pass the summary to Dan.

"Here are the first half stats. As you might expect, the numbers are both even and unremarkable when neither team sniffs the other side's end zone."

Dan looks up from his cell phone. "Thanks, man. Not a major barnburner. Somebody, a tired player or a weak backup who requires his minimum number of plays, needs to make a mistake for us to score."

"So, the game is not a barnburner, but the game is a nail-biter."

"Okay, I'll work harder on my sports cliches."

Time to watch the pom-pom squad. I didn't expect to recognize their music for this routine since, after all, the song was from this century. A dynamic female vocalist declares all days are great days, we are all beautiful regardless of the naysayers, beautiful in every way.

The young ladies form into two parallel columns along each 45-yard line and face the east press box as the song starts. The girls, fifteen to a line, start from a standing hands-on-hip position. Taller, and I presume the older and more experienced girls, are in the front of each line.

To my engineer's eye, both lines replicate the same pattern: Arms to front. Arms extend sideways. Left arm rotates skyward. Right arm joins skyward. Left arm returns sideways. Right arm sideways—the rapid movement of the yellow and black pom-poms glistens against the sunlight at each arm movement—and elbow bends follow for each arm to bring pom-poms to their chests and back to full forward extension. Simultaneous elbow bends and back to full sideways extension. Swing both arms forward. Return to the ready position.

From the ready position, the foremost girl drops to one knee while she flings arms sideways. After she drops to the ground, the girl behind her matches the drop-motion. The other girls also drop to their knees in a front-to-back sequence. Once the girls are all on one knee, the rear girl rises—oh, my knees ache from watching them kneel and rise—and hurls her arms skyward. The team members in front of her repeat the motion in a back-to-front sequence.

Another song starts, and the thirty girls form into a single line that faces the press box with the taller girls anchored near the center of the line. For this song, a female singer encourages the audience to holler at the DJ to crank up the volume. Another unrecognizable song.

The girls drop their pom-poms behind them, clasp each other's shoulders and begin their leg kick routine: Alternate single left leg and right leg kicks in front of them. Then twist off center to angle their leg kicks toward one side and then the other. The girls near the center of the line maintain their constant smiles, but no smiles for the shorter girls toward the ends of the line, only clenched teeth and furrowed brows. All the girl's chests heave after the set as they strain to catch their breath.

The final set creates a formation where some girls recline and conduct leg kicks from the turf while others stand and emphasize arm action. Six taller girls recline to form an inner arc or "smile" ten yards wide and fifteen yards deep. The other twenty-four girls stand in a broader arc below them to form a pattern that reminds me of a smile within a smile.

Then, a surprise.

A country music song streams from the stadium speakers during the final routine, in contrast to the earlier modern pop tunes I was unfamiliar with. The country song lyrics describe a father, a working man who cares for his wife, boy and girl, who makes sacrifices to perform his duty, who mans the front lines, willing to pay the ultimate price for freedom and liberty, who is called, per the title of the song, an "American Soldier."

As the music fades, the girls align themselves into five parallel lines and march off the field, hands on hips, to the near sideline to conclude their routine.

"Nice job, ladies," Dan says to the two women as they leave the announcer's booth. "Your team impresses with how well they coordinate the choreographed motions, something that requires quite a bit of practice, I bet."

"Thank you. The girls work just as hard as the boys during the weekly practices."

"A country song incorporated into a drill team routine," I say. "I haven't heard that before with the different teams I've seen rotate through our stadium."

"We changed our original music," Yellow 10 says. "One of our girls—her father is being redeployed to Afghanistan, and we want to show our support for their family."

"Ooh. Well done," I tell them.

"What branch of the military does the father serve in?" Dan asks. "I have a son serving now as an army officer."

"Mm, I know he's also in the army," Yellow 10 says. "I think he's a sergeant, but I can't say regarding his service details." Yellow 10 looks at Yellow 65, who shakes her head.

"No problem. I'm curious if he crossed paths with my boy."

"We'll be back for the next halftime," Yellow 65 says as the two women exit from the press box.

After the press box door scrapes close, Dan looks at me and nods. "Nice tribute. Bryan wants to go where the action is, but Cheryl and I pray he never gets transferred to Afghanistan...Oh, dead air."

Dan scrambles back into the announcer's booth and drops into the chair in front of the mic. I remove the extra chair and place the game log sheets toward the left side of the counter while Dan sets the roster sheets to left of the mic.

"Please give another hand to the Lady Bees spirit squad for their outstanding halftime performance."

***

The three officials wait at midfield as both special teams jog onto the field. The Bee kicker places the tee where the 40-yard line intersects the nearside hash marks. All eleven Bees align across their 35-yard line with five players between the hash marks and the near sideline. Meanwhile, the Darts position their return squad in a 5-4-2 pattern with five players along the 50-yard line, four along the 45-yard line, and two at the 40-yard line.

Before the kickoff, the Big Voice relays: **"Some unofficial halftime statistics for you. The visiting Bees used four possessions to make two first downs, ran 17 plays and gained 61 yards. The home team Darts used their three possessions to make five first downs, ran 18 plays and gained 78 yards. Both teams still trying to get on the board.**

"The Darts receive the ball to open the second half. Cal 'Gonzo' Drummer kicking off for the Bees."

Dan triggers "U Can't Touch This," a song in which the lead singer declares he has talent that can never be surpassed, through the stadium speakers until the lead official points to the Bee kicker. Gonzo leads the wave of yellow attackers and drives the football on the ground to his left. It bounces through the first line of Darts. Most of the black-helmeted Bees blow through the first line of white-helmeted Darts despite the effort to impede Bee progress. A Dart player, Rhino, covers the ball at the 40-yard line before three Bees pounce on top of him.

"Ryan 'Rhino' Wells covers the football for the Darts. First and ten from the 40-yard line."

Pre-snap activities commence. While the far side official aligns the chain gang on the field, the offense and defense set their formations as in the first half. In the press box, I update the game log sheet.

"The Darts quarterback is Dave 'Prime Time' Nunez. Center is Dylan 'Hawkeye' Hunter."

Prime Time receives the snap. He whirls to his left and slides the football into the hunched-over halfback's stomach.

Head down, the Juggernaut squeezes the ball in both arms. He hurtles between the center Hawkeye and left guard Wampus.

Two defensive linemen collapse on either side of the fullback's legs while the middle linebacker throws his yellow jersey into the fullback's helmet and pads.

"Handoff up the middle to fullback Doug 'Juggernaut' Phillips. *Determined* run into the teeth of the Bees' defense for a two-yard gain. Second down and eight to go for the first down."

Two more running plays, Tank up the middle behind Rhino and Prime Time around the left end Gorilla, gain six yards.

On fourth and two yards to go, a black helmet breaches the offensive line: pre-snap collision at the line of scrimmage. The far side official drops his yellow penalty flag and waves his arms over his head as he runs to the football. He places both hands on his hips for a moment and points toward the Bee side. He retreats to the far sideline while the lead official faces the east stands, puts both hands on his hips, points to the Bee side, and advances the football five yards up the field.

"Illegal procedure. Offsides on the Bees. That penalty advances the ball to midfield, and that's enough for another Darts...First Dooown!"

'Noculars are raised. Football is hiked. Play is run.

"Quarterback keeper to the left side. 'Prime Time' Nunez for four yards to the Bees 46-yard line. Second and six coming up for the Darts."

The active row ends, the future row starts.

'Noculars are raised. Football is hiked. Play is run.

"Pitch to the tailback around the left side. He gets around the corner! Pushed out of bounds. Fine gain of seven yards by 'The Flash' Ramos."

"Yellow flag down."

"Penalty on the play."

The far side official runs to the lead official while clasping his left wrist and then pointing to the Darts side.

"Holding. It's against us."

The lead official stands at the original line of scrimmage and faces the east stands. He raises his left hand in front of his face, grabs the wrist with his right hand and then points to the Dart side. The side official tosses the football to the lead official, who then paces ten yards back into Dart territory. He holds up two fingers to the chain gang on the sideline to show the next play remains second down.

"Holding against the Darts. That brings up second and sixteen to go from the Darts' 44-yard line."

"Too bad. That was the best offensive play we've had all game," I say.

"We can still get something going, but the negative yardage plays sure make it harder."

The teams continue to battle between the 30-yard lines. One or two players run on and off the field every play as both coaches make frequent player substitutions. Regardless of alternating players, the action along the line of scrimmage continues as black-helmeted Bees and white-helmeted Darts hurl themselves against each other. Any attempted passes fall incomplete.

Without an operating game clock, I can only guess how much time remains in the game. The two Sophomore squads warm up beyond each end zone, the Bees to the north end nearest the visitor locker room and the Darts to the south end nearest the home team locker room—a clue to indicate the Freshman game advances late into the fourth quarter.

Both teams display similar preparation routines: they conduct basic stretches and sprints to get loose followed by the offensive squad executing basic running plays while the defensive squad sets up in front of a coach directing the back-and-forth motion of the players in front of him. Some kids respond right away to the coach's directions, while others are sluggish—I know the feeling. I could use more caffeine myself. Even though I'm more interested in the player warm-ups than the game in front of me, I keep track of field activities and game logbook entries.

The pivotal moment happens late in the fourth quarter.

The Dart quarterback, Prime Time, receives the snap from center Hawkeye. Prime Time spins right. He extends the football outward. No running back there to receive the handoff. Both tailbacks run wide to the quarterback's left.

Busted play.

The eight-year-old quarterback maintains composure under pressure. Prime Time draws the ball back and repositions it under his right arm. He sprints right behind the offensive line.

"Quarterback keeper to the right side."

Prime Time slants through a gap between M&M and Destroyer.

Prime Time shrugs off the arm tackle attempt from a Bee linebacker.

"He breaks a tackle!"

Prime Time—cuts to the outside.

He's down the sideline! At the 30...to the 20...to the 10...Touch-dooown! Dave 'Prime Time' Nunez with the score!"

"How many yards?"

"Thirty-eight."

"Thirty-eight yards on the play. The Darts lead six to nothing. Extra point attempt coming up."

I close out the active logbook row with "+6" circled for emphasis, with the TD note in the comments cell, and start the next row before the extra point try.

"That came out of nowhere," I say.

"I hope one touchdown is enough. Lucky plays don't come in bunches."

With the football three yards away from the goal line, the Darts set up in an I-formation. The Bees position six players in a three-point stance along the line of scrimmage to defend against the Dart assault. Three linebackers stand along the goal line to reinforce the defensive line at the point of attack. Two cornerbacks match up against the two wide receivers.

The Big Voice describes the play: **"Handoff to the fullback. Tank—straight into the teeth of the defense. Stuffed at the line of scrimmage. The extra point is no good. The score remains Darts 6, Bees 0. The Darts kickoff is coming up."**

"Recap?"

"Shoot."

Dan jots the numbers on scratch paper as I relay plays, yardage and outcome.

"Scoring drive recap. Fifty-four yards on five plays, capped off by a touchdown run of 38 yards."

Dan turns to his phone, scrolls down a music list and selects "Enter Sandman." A solid rocker with lyrical images of nightmares and monsters in the room bursts from the stadium speakers as both teams set up for the kickoff.

The music stops before the Dart kicker, Big T, sends the bouncing football to the 36-yard line, where a yellow jersey, Catch Me If You Can, picks it up. The Bee receiver darts toward the far sideline to evade the onrushing wave of blue jerseys. His chosen path fails. Juggernaut, Prime Time and Big T swarm over ball carrier.

For their final possession of the game, the Bees use a different offensive formation—one that includes three wide receivers and one running back. The Darts counter with three cornerbacks to match each wide receiver and two deep backs to prevent a long gainer from the offense. The pass-oriented formation generates three incomplete passes. Game time expires with a final score of Darts 6, Bees 0.

Each coach and their players walk single-file along opposite sides of the 50-yard line in the post-game sportsmanship ceremony as players and coaches touch the hands of their counterparts as they pass by one another. After they reach the end of the procession, the Darts curl around and sprint to the far sideline while the Bees spin and jog back to the near sideline. Applause from the stands greets all the players.

"Game ball."

I focus my attention on the stands to my left while Dan concentrates to his right.

"Folks, it's time to auction off the game ball. Bidding is open to anyone from either team. Now, who will start us off with a $50 bid for this lifetime memory? Only $50...Thanks you, sir, from the north 20-yard line. Who will give me $100?"

"Low at midfield."

"I have $100 from the forty. Thank you, sir. Looking for $150. Only one fifty for a lifetime memory. Put it on your fireplace mantle...on your bookshelf...in a trophy case. I see $150 at the north 20-yard line. Looking for $200 now...This could be your last chance to get a memory like this."

A bidder, halfway up the midfield stands, waves his hands over his head.

"Thank you from higher midfield. Now looking for $250. Only–"

The bidder at the north 20-yard line waves his right hand overhead.

"Got you! Thank you, sir, from the north twenty. We have $250 now. Looking for $300. You may never have this opportunity again. Put this football on your fireplace mantle. Put it in your trophy case. Put it on your bookshelf."

The bidder at midfield shakes his head and sits down as we continue to scour the stands. Dan begins the countdown.

"Going once...Going twice...Last call for this once in a lifetime opportunity...Sold! Thank you, sir. Please collect the game ball at the organization table located beneath the stands."

"Exciting game at the end," I say.

"Sure was. Calling a game is more fun when the game is on the line to the finish."

"It's sure hard to predict what's going to happen, especially for the younger kids."

"That's what makes the games interesting," Dan says. "Who can say what will happen next game?"

We've never called more than one game in a day. I hope we don't grate on people as the day progresses.

Chapter Three

More Perfect in the Use of Arms

Dan pops a cherry sour into his mouth. He wags his right forefinger toward the far sideline while he chews the soft red sourball, puckers his cheeks and swallows.

"The chain gang is the worst," he says. "As gameday announcer, I'm exempt from 'volunteer' assignments like trash pickup or Gatorade jug duty. But chain gang is the worst. Three people stand along the sidelines—in rain or shine, heat or cold—throughout the game. Two volunteers drag the first down chains: a rear rod person aligns to the original first down ball location and a forward rod person stretches the chain 10 yards downfield. Another volunteer, the box or placard operator, moves the down indicator pole to wherever the ball is spotted and flips the 12-inch-tall down indicator to the proper number. I did it once and finished the game showered in sweat. I took an actual shower and a nap afterwards ."

"Come on, man. It sounds like a free trip to a sauna."

"Riiight," Dan says. "If Sean were here today, then he might be out there dragging the chain gang poles down the sideline. He's working today, so he's free of the chain gang.

"In fact, Sean came by last night and picked up Matthew for their favorite pastime for father-son bonding: shopping for shoes."

"Shoes?"

"Yeah, Sean is an Air Jordan fanatic. At last count, he has eighteen pairs, still with their original boxes, piled in his bedroom closet. Hah, Sean even keeps a shoe cleaning kit in his car, just in case he smudges his shoes when he wears a pair in public. A few weeks ago, Sean bought Matthew a five-hundred-dollar pair of tennis shoes."

"Five hundred dollars for a pair of tennis shoes! I wear mine until water leaks through the sole or socks show through the canvas. Then I go to a discount shoe store to replace them."

"Sean wants to be a bigger part of Matthew's life now. I feel it's good for both to reconnect now that Sean is clean." Dan looks to the floor as he says, "We're extra careful to keep alcohol away from Sean—he's like a different person, a reverse hyper-aggressive personality, after he has a few drinks."

Dan doesn't elaborate, and I'm not comfortable asking for details.

"Anyway, since Sean has a stable income, he wants to do something nice for Matthew to help make up for lost time."

"If it works for them—great. Then this Sophomore team is Matthew's team?"

"Correct."

"How's the team doing this season?"

"This is one powerful team. It has all the key players from last year's playoff team and gained a couple of new players that are real game changers," Dan says. "They destroyed two teams in practice games and won big on the road last week for their season opener."

"Sounds good."

"It starts with our coach. He knows football and he knows kids. I remember, last year he arranged a pre-season practice game against a team in Texas City, a squad of all Black kids. Our boys were so intimidated. We lost by a score that approached thirty to nothing, and it would have been worse if their coach hadn't taken mercy on us."

"Hah. That's cute. One nice thing about a sport that requires you to travel outside your immediate community is kids get exposed to neighborhoods beyond their day-to-day experience," I say. "The world becomes more interconnected every year, and the sooner children interact with people who don't look like them, the easier time they'll have adapting to this diverse, integrated existence."

"It helped prepare them for the season. Practice games plus rigorous practices laid the foundation for the regular season games. The kids practice from 5:30 to 7:00 PM, four evenings a week during preseason, and three evenings a week once the season starts. Monday evening is for offense, Tuesday evening is for defense, and Thursday evening is for special teams. And every practice emphasizes tackling. Wednesday nights are reserved for church services, and Friday nights are reserved, of course, for high school football."

"You went to every practice? That's a major time investment."

"You make the time for your boy. Besides, Thursday evening practice is my assigned Gatorade day. All the organization teams practice at the same time on a junior high practice field, and I make sure each squad stays hydrated. I use the opportunity to browbeat the coaches for team rosters for Saturday's games.

"Also, that Freshman squad improved during the season, and they made the playoffs. And Matthew improved, too. He started out at linebacker. He did okay in practice but shied away from contact during the games. Once the opposing coaches saw this, they started running every play right at him. Our coach moved Matthew to defensive nose-tackle and told him to fall down and make a pile."

"The infamous pile-maker position."

"I told Matthew to make plays and not just fall to the ground. He didn't make many tackles, but he occupied blockers so his teammates could make the tackles."

"How's he doing this year?"

"Pretty good," says Dan. "He gets more time now as an offensive lineman than as a defensive lineman. And he gets time on the special teams unit."

"Remind me. What's his jersey number?"

"Thirty-two."

About two dozen screaming Darts charge through the inflated helmet tunnel to the far sideline tent as three figures clad in black and white stripes stride to the middle of the field.

"Almost time to start. Keep an eye on the coin toss while I read the roster?" Dan asks.

"Can do."

"I hope you are ready for some footbaaall! Darts football!" the Big Voice declares. **"Welcome to beautiful Abshier Stadium. You could not ask for more ideal weather. We expect a great game today between our Sophomore Deer Park Darts and the visiting LaPorte Bumble Bees."**

The white-capped official motions to each sideline. A trio of captains march in lockstep from each sideline to the center of the field. Their steady gait allows me to observe their jersey numbers, which I jot down in the margin of the game log sheet.

"Here is your 2019 Sophomore Darts roster.
Number 2. Dane 'Hammerhead' Jackson, *Line*-man!
Number 3. Sam 'Need for Speed' Carter, Running back.
Number 5. Michael 'Big G' Gideon, *Line*-man!
Number 6. John 'Godzilla' Demik, *Line*-man!
Number 9. Jules 'J-Dawg' Bass, Quarterback."

Through my binoculars, I watch the lead official start the ceremony by having each captain shake hands with the other team's captains.

"Number 10. Billy 'Blue Thunder' Riker, Running back.
Number 11. Luis 'Lights Out' Rodriguez, *Line*-man!

Number 14. Miles 'Beast Mode' Bannon, Running back.
Number 15. Will 'Kraken' Galen, Cornerback.
Number 18. Al 'Crackers' Carter, Wide Receiver."

The official shows each captain both faces of the ceremonial coin. Then he flips it a few feet above head level and lets it drop to the ground between the two sets of captains. I presume a visiting Bee captain calls "heads" or "tails." After the coin settles on the turf, a yellow jersey spins around and kicks at the artificial turf a few times. Calm down. It's only the coin flip.

"Number 20. Kyle 'Goose' Frye, Running back.
Number 24. Xavier 'X-Man' Gonzales, *Line*-man!
Number 28. Travis 'Terminator' Mays, *Line*-man!
Number 29. Brooks 'Bullet' Ford, *Line*-man!
Number 30. Bennett 'The Business' Cisco, *Line*-man!"

The lead official lines up the opposing captains face-to-face, with the Bees south of midfield facing north and Darts north of midfield facing south. He taps the nearest Dart captain on the shoulder, holds his arms parallel to the ground and crosses them in front of his body. The official steps alongside the nearest Bee captain, holds out both arms in front of his torso and draws his arms back to his chest.

"Number 32. Matthew 'Hit Man' Castillo, *Line*-man!
Number 39. Sam 'Slam' Torres, *Line*-man!
Number 40. Nathan 'Nate-Dog' West, *Line*-man!
Number 63. Tyrone 'T-Bone' Anasazi, *Line*-man!
Number 99. George 'Freight Train' Hamon, *Line*-man!"

"Ready?"

"Shoot."

"Team captains for the Darts are 9, 14 and 63. Team captains for the Bees are 7, 21 and 49. Darts won the toss and deferred."

Dan scrolls through the team rosters and the Big Voice relays: **"Team captains for the Darts are Jules 'J-Dawg' Bass, Miles 'Beast Mode' Bannon and Tyrone 'T-Bone' Anasazi. Team captains for the Bees are Riley 'The Dart' Tamm, Howard 'Titan' Washburn and Sherman 'Big Time' Book. The Darts won the toss and deferred their choice to the second half. Bees will receive the opening kickoff."**

I look down at the Bees' roster and grin. "A player nicknamed 'The Dart' plays against the Darts. A bit of a coincidence."

"Yeah," Dan comments. "I'm also intrigued by the different nicknames the players use. Many of the nicknames play off the kid's real name. Most are over-the-top dynamic to encourage aggressive play."

"We Will Rock You," a song of defiance from a band vowing to rock us, streams through the stadium speakers while teams line up for the kickoff.

The Dart kicker, flanked by five teammates on each side, mounts the football onto the tee at middle of their 40-yard line. Alongside the kicker, ten Darts lean forward at their 35-yard line to prepare for the downfield assault. The Bees set their return team with five players spaced along their side of the midfield stripe as their forward wall. They place four other players along their 40-yard line and two players at their 30-yard line.

"Will 'The Kraken' Galen kicking off for the Darts."

"Watch this kid kick. I see him at the Thursday practice session, the day they work on special teams. He is amazing."

The blue assault wave moves forward with The Kraken. He kicks the football in an arch, 30 yards high at its zenith, and it tumbles end-over-end to the Bees' 25-yard line. The Bee return man, Kamikaze, retreats a few steps, catches the football and launches up the field. Blue Thunder leads the Dart swarm that smothers Kamikaze.

"Number 19 on the runback."

"Tony 'Kamikaze' Verdaschi with the return. First and ten Bees from their 41-yard line."

"That *was* a nice kick. It covered 40 yards in the air. Nine-year-olds seldom produce high arching kicks with distance."

"I talk to his dad at the Thursday practice. Their family comes from Norway. He works in the petrochemical industry and is over here on a one-year assignment. His baby boy, before he could stand, crawled on the floor and pushed a soccer ball around with his head. He's been kicking a soccer ball since he learned to walk. The kid transitioned from a round soccer ball to the American football as though born to kick our oval-shaped cowhide."

As Dan speaks, I record "41B" for ball location and "receive KO" in the comments cell in the game log sheet. The next row starts with "41" for "ball location" and "1/10" for "down/distance."

"A kicker like that is unexpected for this age. And a nice weapon."

"For sure. During practice, he never misses an extra point kick," Dan says. "An automatic two-point conversion after a touchdown is a big edge in a close game. Our coach told him he'll try to find a situation where Kraken can attempt a field goal this season."

We raise our binoculars, or 'noculars, to watch the action on the field. The football is snapped to trigger the first down play.

Tank, the center, snaps the football to his quarterback, Big Time.

Big Time wheels right. He hurls outside his right tackle, Titan.

X-Man, the crouched blue jersey opposite the offensive tackle, dives into the quarterback's legs.

Big Time can't spring forward. He falls backward.

The outside linebacker, The Business, pounces on top of Big Time.

"Quarterback keeper into the right side of the line. Gain of two yards on the play."

"Who made the tackle?"

"Uh, Numbers 24 and 30."

"Tackle by Xavier 'X-Man' Gonzales and Bennett 'The Business' Cisco. Brings up second and eight."

In the game log sheet, I complete the active row and start the next row.

Dan's phone vibrates against the vinyl countertop. He reads the text message and comments, "Did I tell you Mom is here today?"

"Mom's here! She never goes anywhere she's never been before. I'm shocked she'd come out to the stadium."

"Yeah, Cheryl brought her. Mom has never seen her great grandson play, so Cheryl offered to bring her over today," he says. "They are somewhere low in the stands under our blue tarp."

A quick scan of the stands shows a dozen blue tarps. No way I can identify her tarp, and I sure can't abandon my post to find her. "I see Matthew isn't starting. He's on the bench under the far sideline tent," I say. "I hope he gets some playing time while Mom is here."

"He will, more so on the offensive line than the defensive line. But I hate his body language. I want him standing on the sidelines and encouraging his teammates on the field. I'll ride his butt some more about it."

"This is for Mom," Dan says. **"I want to give a special shout-out to Lee Jordan, eighty-five years young. She is here to see her great grandson play football for the first time. Welcome, Lee!"**

***

Several minutes earlier in the lower stands: "Here, Lee, grab my arm," Cheryl tells her. Lee's shoulder hugs the left wall, purse in her left hand, while Cheryl occupies the middle of the aisle to shield Lee from the indifferent children that run up and down the ramp. Lee moves with a light step as her flat slip-ons provide traction on the incline. "I set the tarp near the ramp, so it's not too far to walk."

"That's okay," Lee says. "I scoot along fine on flat ground. Climbing can be difficult." As soon as she emerges into sunlight, "Ooh, I wish I wore my sunglasses."

"It'll be alright. We'll be in the shade in a minute."

Four steps up, ten yards to the south they approach two couples under a canopy—a blue tarp with white trim along the edges. The squatters are in their late twenties, nondescript gray sweatshirts on the men and yellow tee shirts on the women. "Hello," Cheryl says as she nods to them. "You're under my tarp. You need to find somewhere else to sit now."

"No one else was here. And there are not any reserved seats for a youth football game," the man seated nearest them tells her. "This tent must have been erected for public use."

Cheryl stares him in the eyes. "Not quite how it works here. The individual parents, not some organization, decide if, when, or where to set up a tarp. I set this tent up earlier this morning. Me. Then I left to collect my guest. You need to move somewhere else now." The nearest squatter opens his mouth, but the tugs on his jeans convince him to keep quiet. The foursome moves southward along the row and climbs higher in the stands. "Thank you," Lee shouts at their backsides.

Cheryl trails Lee as they duck under the canopy. Once under the tarp, Lee scans the surrounding stands. "There are quite a few people here. I didn't expect so many."

"Yes, the crowd size has an ebb and flow to it. The crowds for the Freshman, Sophomore and Junior games overlap, so there can be over a thousand fans in the stadium sometimes. Plus, we're playing LaPorte today, and they're close enough to Deer Park to allow easy travel for the visiting fans." Cheryl turns to the field. "The Darts, in the blue jerseys, are on defense. The Bumble Bees wear the yellow jerseys. We are looking for number thirty-two on a blue jersey."

"What?" Lee asks as she cocks her right ear toward Cheryl's mouth.

"Number thirty-two," Cheryl repeats into the inadequate mechanical device in Lee's right ear.

Both women scan the field. No Number 32 visible. "He's not on the field right now. I expect we'll see him when the Darts go on offense."

Cheryl sends a text while Lee comments, "There's so much...passion. Someone yells and claps before and after every play. I see this kind of thing on TV, but it feels different when you're in the crowd."

"These"—Cheryl sweeps her left arm before them—"are all somebody's child, so the passion is always there." She turns to Lee and asks, "Have you ever been to a youth football game before?"

"What?"

"Have you ever seen a youth football game before?"

"No. Well...maybe one of Bryan's games a couple of decades ago," Lee says. "I'm more of a baseball girl. I played softball while growing up in Terre Haute. After I got married, AT&T transferred our family to Houston in the mid-1960s, so I've been rooting for the Astros since they changed from the Colt 45s."

The stadium speakers announce the game action. "That's Dan calling the game now."

"He sounds different. Most of the time, he's so serious. Here, he sounds like he's...having fun."

A specific announcement from the stadium speakers draws Lee's attention.

"I want to give a special shout-out to Lee Jordan, eighty-five years young. She is here to see her great grandson play football for the first time. Welcome, Lee!" the big voice in the sky says.

Lee smiles and scrunches her shoulders. "Oh...he didn't need to do that."

Cheryl smiles at Lee's reaction and points to the field. "There's been a change of possession. The Darts are on offense now." She cups her hands around her mouth and shouts, "Let's go, Darts!"

Lee joins in. "Go Darts!"

Cheryl doesn't need binoculars to see the jersey numbers at field level. "There. Number 32 on the left side of the Darts offensive line." Cheryl points while Lee squints her eyes to make out Matthew's jersey number. "He's crouched down now, but you'll see him when the offense huddles up."

The ladies clap and holler at every play. "Cheryl!" diverts Cheryl's attention from the field to the stairs. She waves at her grandson and hollers, "Hey, Kade!" A slender young man, a high school junior dressed in blue-jean shorts and a red tank-top, smiles and waves back. Cheryl and Lee butt-hop a few feet down the row to make room under the canopy. Cheryl asks, "Kade, you know Lee, don't you?"

"Of course. We've met many times."

"Thought so." To Lee, "Whenever Kade can make a game, he shows up to watch his younger brother play." Turning back to Kade, she says, "Matthew is starting on the offensive line."

Several minutes later, "scoot over" comes from behind the trio. A tanned, wiry fortyish man with short dark hair, faded blue jeans, and an oversized oil-stained sweatshirt hunches under the canopy and wedges between Cheryl and Kade.

"Dad," Kade says and smiles as the man clasps his shoulder as he sinks on the metal row.

"Sean," Cheryl says as she hugs her son. "Glad you could make it. I thought you were working today."

"I was at the port before dawn. Have to return in a couple hours. It worked out just right, enough time to catch Matthew's game." Sean tilts forward and looks at Lee. "Hello, Mrs. Jordan."

Lee leans forward and greets him in return. Sean then grabs Kade and gives him a bear hug.

"C'mon, Dad." Kade tries to wriggle out of Sean's grasp. "Matthew's out there now. Left side of the line."

Sean shifts in his seat to face the field of play. He cups his hands to his mouth and screams, "Matthew! Matthew!" Then he spews six rapid-fire thunderous handclaps—each as loud as the "whack!" Yordan Alverez generates when bat meets baseball on a monster 400+-foot home run—throughout the north side of the lower stands. Kade and Cheryl wince in reflexive reaction to each clap. "I want to make sure Matthew knows I'm here."

The couple sitting on the row in front of them twist around to face Sean and shoot him looks that say "what-do-you-think-you-are-doing?"

"You're not surfing today?" Sean asks Kade.

"Nah. I may go to Galveston or Surfside later this afternoon." Kade checks his cell phone to consult the Surfline app. "Still only one and a half foot high swells every four seconds. My longer board, you know, the blotchy gray fiberglass one, I'll take it if the waves pick up."

"I thought you liked mornings better."

"I do. The water isn't as choppy in the morning. What we need is a storm in the Gulf."

"Kade, don't you dare wish for a hurricane," Cheryl says.

"Not wishin'. Just sayin'."

Sean sends several more deafening handclaps across their section of the stands. The couple in front of them rises and moves twenty yards further south.

"Are you going out there by yourself?" Sean asks Kade.

"I'll be okay. There are always other surfers around."

"I saw on the news—a teenage girl was bitten by a shark a few weeks ago at Galveston Beach."

"I'm not worried about sharks. And I'm a decent swimmer, so I don't worry about drowning. It's the newbies and the jellyfish you need to watch for. I can avoid the amateurs, but the jellyfish are everywhere. Seems like I get stung every other year, but if that's the price I heed to pay to surf, then I'll live with it."

"Okay. Your call. Stay safe. I hope you're back home before dark."

"Well, I'm out of the water by sunset," Kade says. He turns from Sean to face the field. "Isn't that Matthew out there?"

Thunderous handclaps ensue.

The family—great grandmother, grandmother, father, and brother—applaud and cheer for Matthew over the next twenty minutes. Afterwards, Lee rotates her shoulders a few times and shakes her arms loose by her side. Cheryl notices her fidgeting and asks, "Lee, do you want to go back home now?"

"I think that would be best," Lee says as sweat drops build on her face.

Cheryl tells the boys: "You're welcome to camp out here. Strangers squatted under my tent earlier, so you can stand guard. I'll be back in about twenty minutes."

"Hah. Sure, we'll hold down the fort until you get back."

"Back in a bit," Cheryl says as she and Lee squeeze their legs past Kade and Sean, then double-foot each step down the stairs and shuffle down the ramp, Lee's arm on Cheryl. "Well, Lee, you're now the fourth generation of family to be involved with Matthew's youth tackle football experience."

Lee smiles at the comment.

***

Back to the press box: **"Handoff to the tailback...Fumble! The officials signal...Darts ball!"**

"I couldn't see who forced the fumble."

"Who made the recovery?"

"Not sure. The kids are patting Number 29 on his pads."

"Recovered by Brooks 'Bullet' Ford. First and ten Darts at the Bees' 40-yard line."

The squads swap roles as the defensive and offensive units form up. The Darts establish their tactical offensive formation: an 'I' formation that consists of six crouched down linemen, quarterback J-Dawg behind the center, fullback Beast Mode three yards behind the quarterback, tailback Blue Thunder three yards behind the fullback. Two wide receivers, Goose and Crackers, split fifteen yards to each side of the offensive line to provide a downfield threat.

The Bees counter the Darts with five defensive linemen on the opposite side of the line of scrimmage, three linebackers to reinforce against the point of attack, two cornerbacks to match against the wide receivers, and one deep safety to guard against long gains downfield.

As the teams set up for the upcoming play, the officials organize the chain gang to set their down and distance poles along the far sideline.

In the booth, I close out the Bee's possession and start a new line for the Dart's possession in the game log sheet.

Beast Mode gains seven yards on first down. The Bees hold Blue Thunder to no gain on second down. Third and three coming up.

"Quarterback keeper," the Big Voice relays for third down. **"He slices through the right side of the Bee's line. Tough run by Jules 'J-Dawg' Bass for five yards. And that is enough for a Darts...First Dooown!"**

The active row ends, the future row starts.

'Noculars are raised. Football is hiked. Play is run.

The quarterback, J-Dawg, receives the snap. He fakes a handoff to the fullback, Beast Mode. J-Dawg glides to his right.

The tailback, Blue Thunder, parallels J-Dawg's movement to the right.

All three Bee linebackers shift to confront the Dart's backfield movement.

"Quarterback keeper to the right..."

Goose, the Darts receiver on the right side who lined up five yards offset behind the outer lineman, sprints to his left between J-Dawg and Blue Thunder.

J-Dawg tosses the ball chest high in front of Goose.

Reverse!

Goose draws the football toward his stomach. He slices through the gap around left end toward the sideline.

"...tosses to the wide receiver...end-around."

The wide receiver on the left side, Crackers, blocks—hinders more than blocks—the cornerback opposite him against the sideline boundary.

Goose races down the sideline, the back of his blue jersey taunting the trailing yellow jerseys.

"Goose streaks down the sideline! At the 20...to the 10...the 5...touchdooown! 'Goose' Frye."

"How many yards?"

"Uh...28 yards."

"Twenty-eight yards on the touchdown run by Kyle 'Goose' Frye. Darts score first for a six to nothing lead. Extra point attempt coming up."

"Man, that kid is fast," as I add "TD reverse" and circle "+6" in the log sheet comments.

"He's most often the fastest player on the field."

"We need to feed him the ball more. He should start at halfback."

"Our head coach likes to spread the ball around," Dan says. "Besides, the starting halfback is an assistant coach's son."

"Aah."

The players line up for the extra point kick from the three-yard line. For each end zone, a goal post rises from a single ten-foot tall-pole that arches over the rear boundary of the end zone and morphs into a twenty-three-foot-wide horizontal bar with a twenty-foot-tall vertical pole on each end.

The Bees are not allowed to rush beyond the line of scrimmage for a declared kick. They hop up and down as though on miniature trampolines. They shout and wave their arms overhead in a chaotic, uncoordinated manner—like free-form signs of sky worship—to distract the kicker. The Dart offensive linemen squat in their customary three-point stance. The center snaps the football from the three-yard line to the ten-yard line, where J-Dawg kneels on one knee, catches the ball without trace of a bobble, and holds the football upright, tip against the ground. Kraken steps to the ball and drives it end-over-end through the middle of the upright poles at the back of the end zone. The lead official raises both arms skyward.

"The kick is good! Will 'Kraken' Galen. That makes the score Darts 8, Bees 0."

"Great start."

"I suspect we can name the score. We can't get ahead of ourselves, but it looks good early."

A clear line-of-sight exists from every spectator to the video electronic scoreboard—60 feet wide and 30 feet tall mounted 10 feet above the turf—erected at the south end of the stadium. "Man, sometimes the scoreboard remote controller works and sometimes it won't respond no matter how many times I press the score 'up' arrow." Dan punches the remote controller for the stadium scoreboard again, then again, and again. "Are the batteries getting weak?"

"If you point the remote at the electronics behind us instead of the scoreboard sixty yards away, then you might get a more consistent response."

"Oh...Of course," Dan says. The scoreboard shows "8" for the home team and "0" for the visitors.

Dan triggers a song with a Caribbean beat through the stadium speakers. A dynamic female vocalist urges listeners to let the music move them, make some noise, live life to the fullest. Since the music sounds like it's from this century, I have no idea of the singer's name.

"Who's that?"

"J-Lo. Cheryl and I caught her show in Las Vegas. Her energy, the live music—an amazing performance."

"A trip to Vegas is still on my bucket list. I don't gamble, but I like the live entertainment possibilities." One day.

The game continues with the Darts generating first downs after every two or three running plays. Dynamic scoring plays longer than twenty yards spur the game's pace. The Bees grind out running plays to chew up game clock, and each Bee possession ends with a change of possession after a fourth down failure.

Late in the second quarter, the press box scrapes open to interrupt the rhythm in the booth. The same two women who managed the Freshman halftime performance climb into the observation room, hunch over at the waist, and inhale and exhale like they're chasing breaths. They wave at us through the plexiglass window between the observation room and the announcer's booth.

"Officials, how much time is left before halftime?"

Through binoculars, I see the lead official look to the device tethered to his left wrist, hold up one finger—not his middle finger—...four fingers...thumb to forefinger. What does that mean?

"He's holding up one finger, four fingers, and making a zero sign."

"One minute forty seconds to go before halftime."

Right thumb up from the lead official.

"Thank you!" a lady shouts from the observation room.

The first half ends at home team 24, visitors 0.

***

We squeeze out of the announcer's booth to make room for the women. This time, Yellow 10 sits in front of the microphone. Yellow 65 rolls a chair from the back wall into the announcer's booth and sits beside her.

"Is Mom still here?" I ask.

"No," Dan mumbles as he chews, puckers and swallows another cherry sour. "Cheryl texted me she took Mom home a little before halftime."

As before, the girls begin as five clusters spread outward from the near side midfield stripe. Their mustard-yellow pleated skirts and sleeveless tops with black trim provide a sharp contrast against the field's green turf. Each girl marches onto the field while holding a pair of tinsel pom-poms, one black and one yellow, against her waist.

Yellow 10 begins through the stadium speakers: **"Good morning. We are glad to be at Abshier Stadium on this picture-perfect Saturday morning. Please give a hand to your 2019 Honeybees spirit squad."**

As the music starts, an updated remix of the rock classic "Let 'Em In," the five clusters of girls form parallel, single-file lines and march, pom-poms held against their hips, toward the middle of the field. They step in place until everyone reaches their designated spot. After the music stops, the girls spin around in unison to face the east press box.

"Allow me to introduce our young ladies." Yellow 10 announces each girl's name over the stadium speakers. As each girl hears her name, she raises her hands overhead, shakes her pom-poms, and returns to a hands-on-hip position.

Cheer squad introductions give me time to compile the half-time statistics. The Bees use five possessions to generate three first downs, run 16 plays and accumulate 60 yards. The Darts, with four possessions, generate seven first downs, run 21 plays, accumulate 142 yards and score three touchdowns.

"Is there a mercy rule?"

"Yes," Dan replies, "but I don't remember the exact score difference that triggers it—somewhere between a forty-to-forty-five-point lead in the second half. The league suspends the head coach for the next game if he goes over the allowable score difference. Not sure if the game is also forfeited. Also, if the score gets too lopsided, the game officials let the game clock run unless they call a time-out."

At the end of the roll call, Yellow 10 continues: **"Ladies, here is your music."**

"Here are the first half stats. As you might expect, the numbers are one-sided, to say the least."

"Thanks. Oh, remind me later. There are three kids with birthdays near this date, so I need to give them a 'Happy Birthday' shout out. I want to do it at the end of the third quarter."

The young ladies, with their ever-present smiles, again form two parallel columns along each 45-yard line that face the east press box. The same song from the prior halftime, with lyrics promoting a positive self-image, triggers the girl's coordinated pom-pom motions. I'm not qualified to judge the quality of the routine, but I find the sight of coordinated yellow and black pom-poms flashing in the sunlight mesmerizing.

Dan snaps me out of it. "I got a text from Gabe, the Darts organization manager. He said we missed a bidder for the game ball after the Freshman game."

"You're kidding. We both sweep our heads back-and-forth across the stands during the bidding."

"A tent might have blocked our view of the bidder. I need to come up with something different before this game's football bid."

The next song, the one that features a female singer who encourages everyone to shout at the club DJ to crank up the volume, triggers the girls to form a single line that faces the press box. They drop their pom-poms, clasp each other's shoulders, and begin their kick routine. Each girl on the team coordinates right and left leg kicks or rotations. As before, the girls near the center of the line maintain their constant smiles while the shorter girls toward the ends of the line clench their teeth and furrow their brows during their effort.

The final routine repeats the formation where six girls recline along an arc and conduct leg kicks from the turf while the others stand in a broader, encompassing arc and conduct arm pom-pom actions. A patriotic-themed country song, the tribute for a girl's father recalled for deployment to Afghanistan, again plays during this set. Afterwards, the girls form into five parallel lines and march off the field, hands on hips, to the near sideline at the end of their routine.

As the two ladies emerge from the announcer's booth, Dan stands and claps his hands. "Another fine job, ladies."

The ovation is contagious.

"Thank you," the ladies reply in unison as they both tilt their heads to avoid eye contact and nod to us on their way out of the press box.

Dan sinks into the chair in front of the mic while I roll one chair from the announcer's booth to the back wall. **"Let's give another round of applause to the Lady Honeybees spirit squad. Great job, ladies!"**

***

"I need to make a public service announcement for our trash pickup volunteers before the second half starts." Dan presses the mic button and the Big Voice says: **"As a reminder, the Darts organization is responsible for cleaning the stadium after the games today. Please help us out by throwing your trash**

in bins positioned throughout the stadium. Thanks in advance for your cooperation."

The three referees stride to the center of the midfield stripe.

"The officials are coming back onto the field, so we'll be kicking off soon. Some unofficial halftime statistics for you..."

Dan relays the stats while the two teams line up for the second half kickoff. He transmits "Eye of the Tiger" from the classic *Rocky* underdog movie through the stadium speakers. Meanwhile, the Bees and Darts repeat their kickoff alignment from the first half.

"The Darts will receive the kickoff to start the second half. Amos 'Tank' Burton kicking off for the Bees."

The lead official points to the kicker. Tank launches a line drive kick to his right—away from Goose. The wave of black-helmeted Bees overcomes resistance from the white helmeted Darts to pursue the bouncing football to a deep back. J-Dawg scoops up the football at the 39-yard line and sprints along the nearest sideline to escape the oncoming Bee onslaught. The Bees shove him out-of-bounds at the Dart 47-yard line.

"Jules 'J-Dawg' Bass returns the ball to the Dart 47-yard line. First and ten Darts."

The simultaneous pre-snap activity begins as the Dart offense opens in a different formation. Six offensive linemen anchor the front of a "full house" backfield as quarterback J-Dawg hunches behind the center. Fullback Beast Mode crouches three yards behind the quarterback. Running backs Goose and Blue Thunder split apart three yards behind the fullback. Wide receiver Need for Speed splits ten yards wide to the right of the offensive line.

The Bees oppose the Dart formation with six defensive linemen who adopt a three-point stance in preparation to bull-rush the player in front of them. Three reinforcing linebackers set five yards behind the defensive line. One cornerback sets wide to match the wide receiver. One deep safety sets up fifteen yards from the line of scrimmage.

'Noculars are raised. Football is hiked. Play is run.

"Quarterback keeper. 'J-Dawg' for 4 yards. That brings up second and six from the Bee's 49-yard line."

The active row ends, the future row starts.

'Noculars are raised. Football is hiked. Play is run.

"Handoff to Miles 'Beast Mode' Bannon. Gain of 4 yards on the play. Third and short coming up."

The active row ends, the future row starts.

'Noculars are raised. Football is hiked. Play is run.

"Handoff...Goose... sweep around the left end for a gain of 8 yards."

"Flag down."

"Penalty flag on the play."

The lead official raises his left arm, grabs his left wrist, and then points to the Dart side of the field.

"Holding against the Darts. That backs us ten yards. Third and thirteen to go from the Dart 44-yard line."

"That hurts."

The active row ends, the future row starts.

The Big Voice describes the third down pass play: **"Quarterback 'J-Dawg' drops back to pass...Incomplete! Pass intended for Sam 'Need for Speed' Carter. A big fourth down is coming up. Come on, Darts fans. Let out a cheer for our Darts offense!"**

For the fourth down play, J-Dawg hands the football to Beast Mode into the line for an eight-yard gain.

"Coach sure dialed up a conservative play that time," Dan says.

"I wish we ran that play on third down. Whatever."

"First and ten Bees from their 48-yard line."

On the field, the squads rotate their offensive and defensive players. The Bees prepare to assault the Darts with a split-backs formation, six offensive linemen in a three-point stance, a quarterback behind the center, two running backs set apart seven yards behind the quarterback, and two wide receivers.

To counter their offensive formation, the Darts resist with five crouched defensive linemen, three linebackers, two cornerbacks and a lone deep safety.

Meanwhile, the chain gang pole holders reverse their roles, with the former lead pole now set as the anchor pole at the line of scrimmage and the other pole stretched ten yards downfield.

In the booth, I complete the active line to close out the Dart's possession and start the next line in the Bee's section of the game log sheet to note where the Bee possession begins.

"A lot of different jersey numbers out there for the Darts."

"Coach is making sure his subs get their playing time in," Dan comments.

"Quarterback dive into the right side of the line. Riley 'The Dart' Tamm for 2 yards. That brings up second and eight from midfield."

'Noculars are raised. Football... is not snapped. Black and white helmets collide at the line of scrimmage.

A yellow flag rests on the ground at the far sideline. The side official runs to the football while waving his hands overhead. He leans over to speak to the lead official, who puts both hands on his hips and then points to the Dart side.

"Offsides, Darts. That gives the Bees a free five yards and brings up second and two to go from the Darts 44-yard line."

I update the log sheet to reflect the circumstances.

'Noculars are raised. Football is hiked. Play is run.

"Quarterback keeper around left end."

"Oh, no."

Only one Dart player, a cornerback, is within 15 yards of the sideline. Their wide receiver screens our cornerback from the Bee running back. Put Goose back in there, coach.

"He's free down the sideline! The 30...the 20...the 10...Touchdown Bees!

"How many yards?"

"Forty-four."

"Forty-four yards on the play. Riley 'The Dart' Tamm with the carry. Extra point try is coming up."

"The Coach will not be happy about that play," Dan says.

"I would sure hope not. At least it gives him the opportunity to show his kids they still need to improve."

"I'm confident The Coach will figure it out. At practice, he told me he studies the video from every game to see where his players need to be coached up. He'll keep them from getting complacent about their early success."

"Man, how does he find the time?"

"The Coach makes time. His son starts at quarterback, and he wants his boy—in fact, all the boys—to succeed."

The teams line up for the extra point attempt. The Bees have eight offensive linemen crouched in front of the quarterback and two running backs. To counter, the Darts use seven defensive linemen in three-point stances and four linebackers in support.

"Matthew is in the game. Number 32...over on the left side of the defensive line."

The Bee center, Titan, hikes the ball to his quarterback, Big Time.

At the same time, the deep tailback, The Dart, sprints right.

Big Time pitches the ball toward The Dart.

Dropped! The oblong football falls to the ground. The ball bounces backward; the back kicks the ball by accident; the ball skips right; it wobble rolls forward on the turf. The Dart scrambles onto the football.

A blue jersey launches on top of him. I shake Dan's left shoulder. "That's Matthew! That's Matthew!"

"*Bursting* through the line to break up the play, Number 32, Matthew 'Hit Man' Castillo!"

"That worked out well," Dan says. "Matthew got his name shouted through the stadium speakers. A stadium shout-out plus a win makes for a happy ride home."

"The extra point fails. The score is Darts 24, Bees 6."

On the field, the battle progresses much like the first half.

Off the field, halfway through the fourth quarter, the girls in the Bee's spirit squad cluster behind the Bee's tarp at the near sideline. A separate horde of girls, dressed in blue and white, twice as large as the Bee contingent, form a blotch at the north base of the near sideline. With an adult woman in the lead, the girls in blue stride toward the girls dressed in yellow. The adult carries a rectangular white box, almost two feet long, under her right arm.

All right, a spirit squad rumble is coming up.

I recognize Yellow 10 awaiting them at the front of the Bee's spirit squad. She holds something I can't see to her left side. Once the two groups stand a yard apart, each lead adult whips out a flower bouquet and hands it to their corresponding team leader. The Bee captain speaks to her counterpart—Yellow 10 stares at her captain and bobs her head every few seconds during the recital. Then the Dart captain replies to the Bee captain, and they exchange bouquets. The Bees, in unison, shout out a cheer and raise their pom-poms overhead. The Darts reciprocate with a cheer and pom-pom lift. All the girls clap as much as their pom-pom clenched hands allow. Afterwards, each girl in the Dart's unit spins backwards, and the former rear girls take the lead in the march back to the northeast corner.

After the Bees score in the second half, the Darts add two touchdowns but miss one extra-point kick. The Bees fail to score the rest of the second half. Final score: Darts 38, Bees 6.

The former antagonists march astride the midfield stripe and touch hands as they pass one another in the customary post-game sportsmanship ritual while Dan prepares to auction off the game football. After two deep breaths, the big voice in the sky speaks: **"It's time to raffle off the game ball. Bidding is open to anyone from either team. Please step into the aisle to make a bid. The**

tents in the stands can block our view. If you cannot see us in the press box, then we cannot see you. So, here we go. Who will give me $50?

"I see four guys waving their hands."

"Great! We have a lot of interest. Who will give me $100?"

All four pairs of hands still wave. Dan steadily increases the requested bid in fifty-dollar increments. When the bidding reaches three hundred dollars, only two bidders remain standing. From their ages, I guess a father versus a grandfather.

"I am asking for $300 now. Who will give me three hundred?"

One bidder makes a sweeping motion with his right hand and sits down. Granddad remains standing.

"I see you, sir, in the northern aisle near the 35-yard line. Do we have any other bidders? The current bid is $300, looking for $350. This game ball represents a lifetime memory. A football your boy touches in live action is a great keepsake. I have one myself...Going once...Going twice...Last call...Sold! Thank you, sir. Please pick up the football at the Darts table under the stands."

"Three hundred dollars. Not bad."

"Home crowd is in good mood after a big win."

"Nice win for this Sophomore Darts team," I comment.

"For sure, but I prefer a more challenging victory. A closer game is more fun to call. Maybe the Junior game will be more competitive. We shall see."

Chapter Four

Who They Sting

"I'm stepping outside for a quick break. Back in a minute."

From the top row outside the press box, I notice the evolving pattern of tents since early this morning. A quick count of the tarp colors indicates eleven blue, four maroon, three gray, two black, and one orange canopy scattered throughout the stands. The square and rectangular multi-colored tarps form a living, tiered mosaic that changes during the day's games as families erect and dismantle their protection from the sun. The parents determine the color palette.

Overhead engine roars divert my attention to the sky. Six jets packed into a triangle formation sweep over the stadium, from east to west to south to east. There must be a military air show at Ellington. I can't tell if they're the Blue Angels, the Navy air group I saw as a teen, since these planes fly too high for me to make out the plane colors or markings—I wish I had my binoculars on me. The overhead jets trigger a remembrance: blue jets with yellow markings streak across the sky in tight formations before peeling off in different directions, engine blasts overwhelm any sounds around you, streamers trail from the jets, apprehension for the pilots that appear to fly right at each other.

After the planes' roar fades to the east, a cacophony of horns and drums tells me the Deer Park High marching band practices in the west parking lot outside the stadium. Tubas peek out from outside the far stands. The high school football season starts soon, and the band needs to prepare for the Friday night lights. The parking lots, marked with white painted lines to simulate the full-scale yardage markers on a football field, provide the band with a wide-open space to practice. Band members dress in a variety of casual clothes rather than their uniforms, a good idea in this heat, as they march through their formations.

On the far side of the field, a blue-and-white uniformed mob of kids release their grating, high-pitched banshee screams as they streak through the inflated helmet at the south end zone area to their sideline tent.

The opposing visitors, clad in black and yellow jerseys, cluster under their near side tent.

The referees in their black-and-white striped shirts contrast against the green turf as they stride at a comfortable pace toward the center of the field.

A scraping door proclaims my re-entry to the press box. I stop for several seconds in front of the air conditioning vent, raise my arms to surrender to the cool air stream, and then twist into the announcer's booth.

"The officials are ready to get going," Dan tells me.

"I'm more than ready. Let's do it."

The pregame ritual starts when the lead official motions to the sidelines and two sets of team captains stride toward the center of the field. Their steady gait provides a clear view of their jersey numbers, which I scribble into the margins of the game logbook.

Before each game, two different trios stride to the middle of a stadium, the centers of attention, names called over stadium speakers. I never experienced such a moment at any point in my life.

"I hope you are ready for some footbaaall!" the voice in the sky declares. **"Welcome to Abshier Stadium on this picture-perfect fall day. We expect a great Junior football game today between our hometown Deer Park Darts and the visiting LaPorte Bumble Bees.**

"Here are our Junior Darts players:

Number 1. Dan 'Ghost' Scully, *Line*-man!

Number 3. Zeke 'Texas' Washburn, Wide receiver.

Number 4. Isiah 'Captain' Contrera, Wide receiver.

Number 9. Paul 'Gunner' Forster, Running back.

Number 10. Frank 'The Boom' Mulder, *Line*-man!"

The white-hatted official coordinates the handshakes between the two sets of team captains with their opposition. Then he shows the captains the ceremonial coin, flips the coin to head level and lets it fall to the ground. He picks up the coin and shows the exposed face to the captains.

"Number 15. Barry 'Beast' Ellis, *Line*-man!

Number 18. Sean 'Savage' Tam, *Line*-man!

Number 23, Owen 'Clutch' Pena, Running back.

Number 27. John 'Assassin' Archer, *Line*-man!

Number 30. Henry 'Mad Dog' Madden, *Line*-man!"

The lead official arranges the players face-to-face across the midfield stripe. The official taps the shoulder of a Bee captain, extends both arms in front of his torso, and draws his arms back into his chest.

"Number 33. Jake 'The Snake' Ramos, Quarterback.
Number 37. Joseph 'Happy Feet' Miller, Running back.
Number 50. Clive 'Tank' Bruckman, *Line*-man!
Number 66. Raylen 'Marine' Melendez, *Line*-man!
Number 70. Matthew 'Hammer' Guerra, *Line*-man!"

The team captains jog back to their respective sidelines. The special teams players filter onto the field.

"Number 77. Lucas 'Pac-Man' Picard, *Line*-man!
Number 88. Alvin 'Krusher' Kricek, *Line*-man!
Number 95. Sid 'Vicious' Anderson, *Line*-man!
Number 98. Douglas 'Bull' Jackson, *Line*-man!
Number 99. Calvin 'Rooster' Mann, Wide receiver."

"Ready?"

"Fire away."

"Darts captains are 33, 37 and 95. Bees captains are 7, 26 and 43. Bees won the toss and chose to receive."

Dan scans the rosters and relays: **"The Darts team captains are Jake 'The Snake' Ramos, Joseph 'Happy Feet' Miller and Sid 'Vicious' Anderson. The Bees captains are Eli 'The Missile' Weir, Terry 'Big Time' Emajan and Aiden 'The Force' Ford. The Bees won the toss and elected to receive the opening kick."**

"Welcome to the Jungle," a traditional lead-in song to combative sporting events, resounds through the stadium speakers as the players line up for the kickoff. The Darts line up along their 40-yard line with five players spaced on both sides of the kicker while the Bees return team threatens with six players at their 49-yard line, four players at their 40-yard line and one deep back at their 30-yard line.

"Raylen 'Marine' Melendez kicking off for the Darts."

"Do you know anything about these teams?"

"Never seen either one. The league standings show they won their first home game big. Our Junior team lost its opening game on the road."

The music stops once the lead official points to the kicker. Marine drives the football in a low arch, twenty feet high, to the Bees' 35-yard line.

A Bee receiver, Wild Thing, gathers the ball after one bounce.

The wave of blue-jersey Darts streams through the obstructing yellow-jerseys to meet him.

Wild Thing cuts left at the 40-yard line.

A Dart player, Pac-Man, sweeps from the middle and collides with him at the 42-yard line. Pac-Man, head up, impinges his facemask against Wild Thing's jersey number. Pac-Man wraps his arms around the runner's waist, keeps his legs pumping as though trying to run through the ball carrier, and drags the runner to the turf.

Wild Thing goes down.

Solid tackle by Pac-Man. Head up. No violent helmet-to-helmet contact. Nice job by whatever coach taught Pac-Man that tackle method.

This special teams play opens a time portal to dredge up another memory from my youth football. That tackle looks much different from the tackling technique I was taught. As the fastest player on my team, I play tailback, safety, and the attack "gunner" position on the kickoff "suicide squad." My assignment on kickoffs requires me to charge full speed—a living guided missile—at the football receiver, drive the crown of my helmet into his chest, reach both arms under his buttocks, yank his feet off the ground, and *piledrive* him into the turf.

"First and ten Bees from their 42-yard line."

Six Bee offensive linemen face off helmet-to-helmet against five crouched Dart defensive linemen. The rest of the Bee offensive configuration consists of two wide receivers, running backs Badger and Undertaker, and quarterback Missile. The remaining Dart defensive squad opposes the Bees with three linebackers, two cornerbacks and a deep safety.

At the same time, I record "49B" for ball location and "receive KO" at comments in the game logbook and then start the next line with "49" in the ball location column and "1/10" in the down/distance slot.

Meanwhile, the chain gang sets their poles per the far sideline referee's instructions. This chain gang is different. A slender mom, her shoulder-length blond hair stacked behind a brown cap, holds one yardage pole. The two male pole holders are conspicuous by their prominent beer guts that spill over the far side boundary.

"Split backs formation."

"The Bees open with a split backfield formation."

Before the center snaps the football, players collide in a tangled blue and yellow pile on the far side of the line of scrimmage. The far side official drops his yellow flag, rolls his fists over one another two times and points to the Bee side. The lead official faces the east press box, rolls his fists over one another and points to the Bee side. He picks up the football and steps it back five yards to the Bee's 37-yard line.

"Illegal procedure against the Bees. That makes it first and fifteen to go for a first down."

'Noculars are raised. Football is hiked. Play is run.

Hedgehog, the center, hikes the ball to his quarterback, Missile.

The Missile sprints right in a broad arc behind his tailbacks.

Undertaker and Badger, the two tailbacks, race to their right.

"Quarterback keeper around the right end..."

At the right side of their line, Badger cuts inside. He seals off the inner flow of Darts defenders.

Undertaker cuts outside against the Dart cornerback, Rooster.

Undertaker buries Rooster.

Missile fires between the Badger and the Undertaker.

Pure speeeed.

Missile dashes—untouched—into the end zone.

"He's free at the 50! To the 40...the 30...the 20...10...Touchdown!"

"My God. He's the fastest kid I've ever seen. There wasn't a blue jersey within twenty yards of him when he crossed the goal line."

"How many yards?"

"Sixty-three."

"No, that was not Hussein Bolt," the Big Voice declares. **"Eli 'The Missile' Weir with the touchdown run of 63 yards. Extra point try is coming up."**

I complete the active row, "TD" and "+6" circled in the comments section, and prep the next row for the extra point try.

The Bees form up with nine offensive linemen. A single player drops to one knee eight yards behind the line of scrimmage. The kicker, The Force, awaits the snap three yards behind the kneeler. Meanwhile, eleven pairs of cleats hop up and down on the Darts' side of the line of scrimmage while arms wave overhead. The kneeling holder, Ace, fumbles the snapped football from Hedgehog but picks it up and holds the ball on-tip in a vertical position on the tee. After the kicker takes three steps, he swings his right foot into the football and drives the wobbling football a few feet over the crossbar between the goalposts. The lead official turns to the press box and raises both arms skyward.

"Kick is good. Number 43, Aiden 'The Force' Ford. And that makes the score Bees 8, Darts 0."

"Not a pretty kick, but good enough," Dan says. "This team could be hard to beat."

While I update the game logbook for the two-point conversion, he provides the easiest scoring drive summary of the day.

"Scoring recap. One play. A 58-yard drive capped by a 63-yard touchdown run."

Dan triggers a pop song that encourages you to stand up for yourself, find what you're good at, work hard, persevere, become an "All Star."

For the ensuing kickoff, the Bees line up for a conventional kickoff from their 40-yard line. The Dart return team configures in a 5-4-2 pattern, with five players along their 49-yard line, four along their 40-yard line and two at their 30-yard line.

"Aiden 'The Force' Ford kicking off for the Bees."

The line-drive kick bounces on its tip end, rolls end-over-end, and skips upward at the Dart 42-yard line, where a Dart player corrals the football.

"Ball covered by Paul 'Gunner' Forster for the Darts. First and ten Darts from their own 42-yard line."

Offensive and defensive squads form up along their respective sides of the line of scrimmage. The Darts duplicate the Bee split backfield offensive formation. The Bees counter the Dart threat with five crouched defensive linemen, three linebackers as D-line reinforcements, two cornerbacks to cover the wide receivers and a deep safety to act as the last line of defense.

A first down run by The Snake gains one yard.

Happy Feet runs a sweep to the left that gains eight yards.

Dan revs up the crowd. **"Let's hear it for our boys, Darts fans! Big third and one coming up!"**

'Noculars are raised. Football is hiked. Play is run.

"Handoff to Owen 'Clutch' Pena up the middle. Gain of four yards. And that is enough for a Darts...First Dooown!"

The press box door scrapes open. A slender man in his early twenties, clad in a gray sweatshirt and dark blue Astros baseball cap, enters the observation room.

"Hey, Dan," he hollers.

"Hey, Jeremy," Dan yells back. To me, "Jeremy is the son of one of Cheryl's good friends." I nod to him through the plexiglass window between the booth and the observation room. Jeremy rolls a chair from the back wall to the front counter, anchors himself with elbows on the counter and hunches over his cell phone.

"Handoff to the tailback into the left side of the line. Fumble!" We each focus on the field as the referees unstack the players. **"Officials unpile the**

players...signal...Darts ball! Clive 'Tank' Bruckman on the recovery. Gain of four yards on the play. Second and six coming up."

"Let's not do that again, boys," I say.

"Jeremy, are you playing ball again this year?" Dan shouts.

"Yes. Wide receiver for a semi-pro squad in The Woodlands. We have our first game next week."

"Well, good luck to you," is shouted back.

"Quarterback Jake 'The Snake' Ramos with the keeper into the right side of the line. A tough gain of three yards."

"Hey, Dan," Jeremy hollers from the observation room.

"Yeah?" Dan yells back.

"I hope you didn't have any money down on the Longhorns. They're not doing so well right now."

"No, no gambling outside of casinos. But I am surprised about the 'Horns. They were a big road favorite today."

"Handoff to Joseph 'Happy Feet' Miller around left end. Gain of two yards on the play. That brings up a big fourth down play. Let our team hear you, Darts fans!"

"Hey, Dan."

"Yeah?"

"Did you see TCU won big today?" Jeremy shouts.

"They might be the best team in Texas this year," Dan yells back.

'Noculars are raised. Football...is not snapped.

Commotion along the line of scrimmage. The far side official drops a yellow flag to the turf and runs toward the football while pointing to the Dart side. He leans toward the lead official. The lead official faces the east press box, rolls his hands over one another two times and points to the Darts. He picks up the football and paces five yards back from the original line of scrimmage.

"Illegal procedure against the Darts. Still fourth down."

"That hurts. We need to stay on schedule to control the ball."

"Agreed," says Dan. "Not to mention that steady play on the field helps us maintain a steady rhythm in the booth."

True—under usual circumstances.

"Hey, Dan." Another round of hollering. "Did you catch the A&M score today?"

"Don't tell us! I'm recording the game," I scream back.

"Okay, but you'll like it."

Thanks a lot.

"The quarterback drops back to pass...Incomplete! Pass incomplete."

"Hey, Dan. I'm going to sit with the family for a while. Catch you later."

"Okay," is the return shout. Dan looks at me. "Jeremy is a fine young man, although a bit of a football lunatic. His heart condition caused him to fail the physical required to play high school football. Once he turned eighteen, he latched onto a semi-pro football team."

The press box door scrapes open and closes to celebrate his departure. Back to business.

"Did you see the jersey number of the intended receiver?" Dan asks.

"Sorry. I didn't catch the number."

"The ball goes over on downs to the Bees. First and ten Bees from their 43-yard line."

For their second possession, the Bees require three plays to score. The Missile runs around the right end and streaks, untouched, 35 yards to the end zone. The extra point pass attempt fails. At the end of the first quarter, the score is 14 to 0.

After the first quarter, the lead official relocates the football at the equivalent spot on the opposite side of midfield, a positional change allows each team the opportunity to attack from both north and south directions during the same half.

"That's the end of the first quarter. We will swap ends of the field and resume play with second and seven Darts."

"Birthdays?"

"Yes."

"We have some birthdays to announce. Players with birthdays near this date are Frank 'The Boom' Mulder and Sean 'Savage' Tam. Happy birthday, boys! Please give these young men a hand."

When play resumes, the Darts possess the ball for fourteen consecutive plays. The Bees keep us out of the end zone, and the ball turns over on downs at the Bee 12-yard line. This time, the Bees need four plays to score; their drive is capped by a 46-yard touchdown run by the Missile. The extra point pass attempt fails, so the scoreboard shows Bees 20, Darts 0.

The Darts receive the ensuing kickoff and continue to bleed down the clock until halftime, when the two teams jog off the field to regroup for the second half.

***

A few minutes before halftime, the press box door scrapes open. Two dark-haired women step into the observation room and wave to us as they stoop over and pant to catch their breath. I guesstimate one in her late-twenties and one in her late-thirties. The older woman wears an oversize, solid Royal blue, button-down shirt while the younger woman wears a pull-on shirt with alternating teal blue/black horizontal stripes. Solid Blue spends an extra minute hunched over.

"And that is the end of the first half: Bees 20, Darts trying to get on the board. Please stay in your seats. We have a great halftime show by the Deer Park Sparklers spirit team coming up!"

The girls line up in five groups along the east sideline. The lead girl in each line wears a sleeveless, single-piece uniform, what I expect a baton twirler to wear. Their uniforms feature a V-shaped golden belt line along the waist with three vertical golden lines from the waist to the shoulder. The other girls have blue pleated skirts with white tops. The blue "Darts" team name, trimmed in gold, spreads across each girl's chest. A mix of blue tinsel strands and gold tinsel strands dangles from each pom-pom.

"Hello, Dan," says Solid Blue from the announcer's booth doorway.

"Hi, Sarah," Dan replies after he stands and faces Solid Blue. To me, "This is Sarah Anderson, the girls' drill team manager." Back to Sarah, "This is my brother, Earl."

"Howdy," as I wave with my right hand. "Anderson..."

"Yes, her husband is Gabe, the organization manager you met this morning."

"And this is Julia, our choreography director," Sarah says as she lifts her right arm toward Stripe Shirt. I nod to her.

Dan and I squeeze past them for the ladies to enter the announcer's booth.

Solid Blue, I mean Sarah, drops into the chair in front of the mic. Dan rolls a second chair into the booth for Stripe Shirt and connects their phone cord to the stadium receiver system.

"Remember to press the mic button to talk. The music will go through the stadium speakers as soon as you start it from your phone," he tells them.

"I see. Thank you." Solid Blue continues: **"Good afternoon and welcome to Abshier Stadium. Please give a hand to our 2019 Deer Park Sparklers spirit drill team! Ladies, here is your music."**

The intro song, a snippet of pop with a touch of hip-hop, starts with a male vocalist declaring he feels tonight will be a good night, a female vocalist who follows with the same sentiment and then an additional male vocalist who cranks up the energy level.

The song triggers the girls to march from east to west, hands on hips while holding pom-poms, in five parallel lines. At midfield, the lines halt, and the girls spin to face the east press box. Most girls march-in-place as the lead girl in each line takes one step to their right and then advances toward the front of the formation nearest the east sideline. The music stops and the girls "freeze" in place.

The fans might pick up the marching band's practice session in the west parking lot. If so, the stadium music should soon drown out the sounds from outside the stadium. "That is one large squad. I count fifty-one girls. It's twice as large as the visitor drill team."

"Yeah, a combined team of eight-year-olds through eleven or twelve-year-old girls," Dan says.

Solid Blue activates the stadium mic. **"The Deer Park Sparklers manager is Sarah Anderson. The spirit team routine director is Julia Benes. First, the drill team leaders..."** She names the team captain, who introduces herself with an extra flourish of sideways kicks and leaps, followed by the lieutenants who identify themselves with a leap and pom-pom whirls. **"Allow me to introduce the rest of our team to you."** She announces each girl's name, and the girl responds with a leap and wave of her pom-poms.

Dan checks his phone. "Oh. I got a call from Cheryl." He replies, puts the phone to his ear and turns toward the wall. "You called....I keep my phone muted in the press box....We are busy nonstop. It's constant action in the booth. I don't have time to interrupt what I'm doing to answer the phone....Okay....Okay....If you text me, then I will"—extra emphasis on the "will"—"make a moment to text you back....Okay....Love you."

He didn't volunteer. I didn't ask.

I summarize the first half stats while Dan checks his phone. The Bees use three possessions to run 8 plays, gain 203 yards and score three touchdowns while the Darts have three possessions, run 25 plays, gain 79 yards and do not score. A couple of Bee penalties helped the Darts control the ball. Now, back to the halftime show.

Solid Blue starts the next song, and I was shocked I recognized one—a remixed version of the pop rock classic, "Beat It."

The routine starts with the front girl in each of the five columns leaping into the air while spreading pop-poms overhead and then dropping to one knee. Each subsequent girl in line performs the same routine. After each girl drops to her knee, they perform the routine in reverse from back to front. Once they stand, every other girl in each line takes a step to her left. Then they begin a synchronized sequence of repeated herky-jerky arm motions upward, outward, forward.

That's odd.

One girl near the end of the middle line appears to wave four arms, two with pom-poms and two without. Time to go to the binoculars. The tiniest girl on the field waves her empty hands behind the taller girl in front of her. A detailed look indicates one other smaller girl does not have pom-poms.

"Do the girls bring their own equipment?"

"They each have their own uniforms, of course, but I've seen the drill team manager pull pom-poms from a 55-gallon plastic drum at the practices," Dan replies. "The girls drill in the grassy area inside a track next to the junior high field where the boys practice."

"I see."

The next song, a twenty-first century mystery to me, features a female vocalist who proclaims to the listener that they are all beautiful, they are beautiful in every way.

The music change triggers movement into a new formation. The girls face east and form two parallel lines that extend from midfield toward each end zone, with the taller girls in the center of the lines to anchor the formation. After the girls toss their pom-poms behind them, they clasp shoulders and begin their leg kick routine, a synchronized sequence of leg kicks.

Only half the height of the team captains in the center of the formation, the two smallest girls stand at opposite ends of the line. The girls in the center exhibit rapid, smooth leg kicks, likely consistent with more experienced performers. The littlest girls only have one shoulder to clasp onto while they kick. Each of their faces shows the determined grimaces of ones trying to maintain pace with the taller girls. The kick routine proficiency may not match that of the high school spirit squad or cheerleaders, but I suspect these girl's efforts and physical exertions compare well to those of the high school girls.

The closing song's female vocalist cries out about this being her life, don't forget it; it's her life, and it lasts forever—huh, if you say so.

The girls retrieve their pom-poms and arrange themselves in a square formation within another square at the center of the field. At least, I presume they're squares even though a couple of the corners are a bit ragged. At some designated point in the music, the girls that comprise each square formation march along the square profile while they shake their pom-poms. The square carousel-within-a-carousel routine strikes me as being very ambitious for a squad that ranges from eight to twelve years old. Where are my two littlest girls without pom-poms? They are on opposite sides of the inner square and wave their arms to match the motion of the other girl's pom-poms. After the music ends, the block squares march to the east and collapse against the near sideline. As the girls cross the sideline, everyone in the stands applauds, with the more intense devotees of the routine offering them a standing ovation.

"Please give a hand to our 2019 Deer Park Sparklers spirit squad! Well done, ladies."

As the two women leave the announcer's booth, Dan tells them, "Great job, ladies. Very nice performance."

"I liked it too. It has so much movement to accompany the arm motions. Very impressive," I say. "I have a question. Why do taller girls have different uniforms than most of the team?"

"Oh, the team captain and her four lieutenants are the designated officers whose roles are to coach and inspire the other team members in each of their individual squads," says Solid Blue. "I expect us to get better as the season goes on. We intend to be ready for the drill team competition at the end of the year."

"We have the largest group of girls I've ever seen on a drill team."

"Our squad is larger than most, but you shouldn't be surprised. After all, as many children participate in cheerleading activities as in tackle football."

I lower my chin and raise an eyebrow. She must have noticed my "you're full of it" look.

"It's true. There's a website...oh, what is it...Aspen. The Aspen Institute. They're a nonprofit organization that monitors youth athletic participation in the country every year. You can look online and see how popular cheerleading activities are."

The two ladies wave "bye" and head for the exit. The door scrapes against the floor at the press box entrance to declare their departure.

Dan plops into the seat in front of the mic while I roll the unneeded chair from the announcer's booth. **"Please give another hand to the Deer Park Sparklers drill team! These young ladies do a great job! We will see them again at halftime of the Senior game."**

***

"The officials are on the field, and we will start the second half in a few minutes. First, some unofficial halftime statistics."

The Big Voice recounts the stats while both teams line up for the kickoff. Then he triggers a song I hear at some professional sporting events, but I do not know its official title, so I call it the "Hey" song—for the obvious reason the only lyric in the song is the repeated "Hey."

On the field, the Bees present the standard kickoff attack alignment of five players on each side of the kicker along their 40-yard line. The Darts stage their counterattack deployment with six players along their 49-yard line, four players at their 40-yard line and one player at the middle of their 30-yard line.

"The Darts receive the kickoff to open the second half. Aiden 'The Force' Ford is kicking off for the Bees."

The lead official points to the kicker, and the stadium's speakers cease their repetitious "hey." The Force sends the football bounding through the first two Dart lines and, while the deep return man tries to corral the ball, the Bees swarm to encircle the deep back. Clutch can't gather the bouncing football, so he falls on it at the Dart 32-yard line.

"The kick is covered by Owen 'Clutch' Pena at the Dart's 32-yard line. First and ten coming up."

In the booth, I sustain the game logbook bureaucracy by adding "32D" to ball location and "receive KO" to comments. I start the next row before the first play from the Darts.

Meanwhile, the Dart offense establishes the same configuration as the first half: six offensive linemen, two wide receivers, running backs Happy Feet and Clutch with quarterback Snake. Again, the Bees counter the Dart threat with five defensive linemen, three linebackers, two cornerbacks, and a lone deep safety.

As the players set their alignment, the far side official aligns the chain gang along the sideline to mark the ten yards needed for the first down, as well as the down marker at the line of scrimmage.

For the opening snap of the second half, Krusher hikes the ball to Snake.

Snake takes the snap. Spins right. Hands the ball to Happy Feet.

Happy Feet strangles the ball with both arms. He punches into the line between Beast and Mad Dog.

Pump those legs!

Yellow jerseys swallow Happy Feet.

"Handoff over the right side of the line. *Tough* run from Joseph 'Happy Feet' Miller. Gain of 2 yards."

'Noculars are raised. Football is hiked. Play is run.

"Pitch to the tailback toward the left sideline. Hit behind the line! Great defensive play from the Bees' linebackers, knifing through to bring the back down for a loss of four yards on the play. That brings up third and twelve to go."

The active row ends, the future row starts.

"The Bees swarmed over the runner as though they called the play themselves," Dan comments.

'Noculars are raised. Football is hiked. Play is run.

"Quarterback keeper up the middle...Fumble!"

Half the players on the field pile atop each other around the original football spot at the line of scrimmage.

"Bees got it."

"The officials unravel the players and signal...the Bees' ball. First and ten Bees from the Dart's 35-yard line."

I state the obvious. "Turn the ball over with the safest play you can run. That hurts."

"This game could go from one-sided to massacre in a hurry."

The two teams rotate their defensive and offensive squads. Meanwhile, I close out the active line in the Darts section of the game log and start the first row of the Bee column. The far sideline official has ten-yard-long-chain pole holders rotate responsibilities while the placard holder swaps to "1" on the ball marker pole.

The door scrapes open to announce a new visitor. A Dart player, jersey number 32, clops down the observation room in rubber-cleated shoes.

"Hello, Poppa," he says from the door of the announcer's booth. The young man at the doorway, tall enough to reach my shirt pocket, stands clad in his blue-and-gold Darts football uniform, damp hair mussed and flattened from sweating, helmet held in right hand.

I wave to him while Dan, without taking his gaze from the field, says, "Hello, Matthew. Nice game today."

"Yeah, we won. Can you help me take my pads off?"

"Sure." To me, Dan says, "Keep an eye on the field?"

"Can do."

Dan spins out of the chair as Matthew raises his arms in surrender. Groans and "ouch, ouch" emanate from behind me as he tugs Matthew's jersey above his shoulder pads through his raised arms.

"You can sit in the next room, but you need to be quiet," Dan tells him.

The quarterback pitches the football to the tailback, who runs around the right side of the offensive line. The Darts shove the Bee ball carrier out of bounds at the 23-yard line. Yellow flag at the 30-yard line.

"Toss sweep. Flag on the play," I tell him.

The lead official faces east, holds his right hand, palm open, in front of his face and clasps his right wrist with his left hand. He then points to the Bee side.

Dan sits down and asks, "What do we got?"

"I guess the official is signaling a block in the back."

"Illegal block by the Bees. That will back them up. It remains first down."

Matthew leans over the observation room counter and stares at the field for a minute. Then he grabs a chair and rolls it to the counter. Plop down. Lean back. Spin around. Push the rolling chair from the counter to the wall. Kick off the wall back toward the counter. Kick off the counter against the chairs piled against the wall—a metallic "clang" echoes through the press box.

"Matthew!"

"They weren't even backed up ten yards. Must be a spot foul stepped off from the point of the infraction."

"I'm going to sit with Cheryl," Matthew shouts from the observation room.

"All right. Take your helmet and pads with you," Dan yells back.

'Noculars are raised. Football is hiked. Play is run.

"Quarterback keeper around the left side...He's free down the sideline! The 30...the 20...the 10...Touchdown! Eli 'The Missile' Weir."

"Forty yards."

"Forty yards on the touchdown run."

"This game is 'officially' a rout now," I comment.

"Too bad. You can see this Junior team is solid, but we need playmakers. Speed. You have to have speed, especially when you go against a team with one or two speed demons."

"Scoring recap. Thirty-five-yard drive on two plays if you count the penalty."

"No recap this time," Dan says. "I don't want to rub in the score."

The game continues as the Darts run the ball to generate first downs to control the ball and consume the game clock. For the Bees, the quarterback focuses more on passing than running. The Missile completes four of his nine pass attempts. The game ends with a score of Bees 40, Darts 13. After the game, the former foes from the two teams walk in opposite directions along each side of the midfield stripe and touch hands in a traditional demonstration of sportsmanship.

Time to auction off the game football.

"All right, we're going to auction off the game ball now. Bidding is open to anyone from either team. Please step into the aisle to make a bid. We missed a bid earlier today because we could not see the bidder. If you cannot see us in the press box, then we cannot see you. Here we go. Who will give me $50?"

Dan progresses through the bids in fifty-dollar increments. Once bidding stalls, he appeals to the parents' sentimentality, interjects his personal experience, mentions this opportunity could be their last to ever get a game ball. The bids max out at $200.

Now looking for two hundred and fifty. Only $250 for a lifetime memory. Put the football in a trophy case. Put it on your fireplace mantle or on a bookshelf. I have a game ball myself...Going once...You may never have this opportunity again...Going twice...Last call...Sold! Thank you, sir. The game football will be available at the Darts organization table under the stands.

"Not as much as last game."

"I didn't expect as much," Dan says. "The bids are higher when the home team wins. I remember one game last year when two grandfathers got into a bidding war. That football sold for six hundred dollars."

"That's too much for a football."

"It's not so much about the ball as the memory, the tribute to the son or grandson."

"And maybe a little personal ego involved in trying to win the bid," I add.

"Maybe."

Dan pops another cherry sour into his mouth as the scraping door indicates another visitor to the press box. A twenty-something year old man with shoulder length dreadlocks and yellow T-shirt steps to the doorway of the announcer's booth. Man, *that* is a head of hair. I imagine having a head of locs like that the same way I think about running a marathon race. I do not want to run a marathon, but I sure wish I *could* run a marathon.

"Hey, guys," Dreadlocks says. "I came to apologize. There's no justification for passing late in the game with a big lead. I don't like the idea of running up the score at any level of play, especially in youth football where we are teaching sportsmanship principles to these boys."

I wave my hands back and forth in front of my chest while Dan gulps down a cherry sour while shaking his head side-to-side and responds, "No, no. Please do not give it a second thought. There are no hard feelings."

"Well, thanks. I wanted to tell you I didn't like it."

To change the conversation tone, I tell him, "You guys have one the fastest kids I've ever seen."

"Elijah—the head coach's son. Our coach has his boy's football career mapped out through the short-list of colleges he wants Eli to attend. He'll bend your ear for an hour about the coming payments for college players' names and images for endorsements. He believes his kid will be a millionaire when he enters college."

"I'll believe it when I see it," I tell him.

"His main consideration is which program best prepares Elijah for professional football."

"That seems a little extreme for a ten-year-old."

"Believe me, this guy is some kind of fanatic. Anyway, good luck the rest of the season," Dreadlocks says as he waves bye.

"You too," Dan says.

After the door slides closed, Dan comments, "It was nice of that guy to come by, but to be honest, I'm glad they switched to a passing game. If their quarterback kept running the ball, then the score could have been obscene—or butt up against the maximum allowable score difference."

"Agreed. At this age, passing the ball still has a lower probability of success. And the way that kid throws, it was obvious he needs a lot more practice in the passing game."

"Well, we've had one close game and two blowouts. I hope we get a close one for the last game of the day."

"To be determined," I conclude.

Chapter Five

'Scaped by Miracle

I use the idle time between games to cross the length of the hallway to the press box bathroom—again. After hair, bladder capacity goes next. The announcer's booth, with two occupants and a rear cabinet for stadium electronics, could fit into the bathroom, with its sink, toilet and mop bucket.

On my way out of the bathroom, I peek into the rear press box observation room. Video Teen sits spellbound. His smartphone's glow mesmerizes Video Teen like a visual siren's song. I leave him be.

As I re-enter the announcer's booth, "The officials are already on the field," Dan says.

"They're back in a hurry. Must be ready to get home."

The players for each squad mingle around their respective midfield sidelines. Three players clad in yellow and black stride from the east sideline to midfield to start the pregame coin toss ceremony while three players in blue and gold uniforms advance toward them from the opposing sideline. The two outer Dart captains interlock arms with the captain between them. I jot their jersey numbers in the margin of the game log sheet as they approach each other.

"I hope you are ready for some footbaaall! Darts football!" the Big Voice says. **"Welcome to the final game of the day. We expect a great game between the LaPorte Bumble Bees and the Deer Park Darts Senior squads. Allow me to introduce our Senior Darts roster.**

Number 7. Vincent 'Vinnie' Lopez, *Line*-man!
Number 9. John 'The Bear' Criton, *Line*-man!
Number 15. Marty 'Dominator' Addams, *Line*-man!
Number 17. Rich 'Superman' Lane, Wide receiver.
Number 20. Joe 'Crazy Legs' Grant, Wide receiver.
Number 21. Luis 'Prime Time' Garcia, Running back."

The lead official directs each captain to shake their opponents' hands in the pregame ritual. He shows each of them both sides of the ceremonial coin and flips the coin into the air to head level. After it settles on the turf, he picks up the coin and shows the exposed face to each captain.

"Number 25. Melvin 'Hammerhead' Frohan, *Line*-man!

Number 26. Raymond 'Shark Slayer' McKay, *Line*-man!

Number 28. Gabriel 'Big G' Alvarez, Quarterback.

Number 30. Arnold 'Rampage' Rhymer, Running back.

Number 34. Allen 'Speedy' Sun, Wide receiver.

Number 39. David 'Hulk' Banning, *Line*-man!"

The referee aligns each set of captains face-to-face against their adversary. Bees face south while Darts face north. The official taps the shoulder of the nearest Dart player, extends both arms in front of his body and draws his cupped hands toward his chest.

"Number 40. Tim 'Terminator' Tucker, *Line*-man!

Number 45. John 'Fresh' Matheson, *Line*-man!

Number 49. James 'The Wall' Koenig, *Line*-man!

Number 61. Samuel 'Hot Sauce' Benes, Running back.

Number 75. Wesley 'Steel' Cashman, *Line*-man!

Number 99. Jack 'Attack' McGee, *Line*-man!"

The captains jog back to their respective sidelines while their special team units take the field.

"Ready?"

"Fire away."

"Teams captains for the Darts are 21, 28, 75. Team captains for the Bees are 7, 12, 55. Darts won the toss and will receive."

"Got it."

After he scans the rosters, the Big Voice announces: **"Team captains for the Darts are Luis 'Prime Time' Garcia, Gabriel 'Big G' Alvarez, and Wesley 'Steel' Cashman. Captains for the Bees are Tom 'Iceman' Winters, Jeff 'Shredder' Sinclair and Mick 'Moose' Garibaldi. Darts won the toss and elected to receive the opening kickoff."**

Dan triggers "For Those About to Rock," another classic rocker sometimes played before aggressive professional sporting events, for the pre-kickoff music.

The Bees line up with five players on each side of the kicker along their 40-yard line. Meanwhile, the Darts set up in a 5-4-2 pattern, with five players along their 49-yard line, four players along their 40-yard line, and two players at the 30-yard line. The Darts attack from south to north or, from the press box perspective, from left to right.

"Al 'Viper' Bestow to kick off for the Bees."

The official points to the Viper, who sends the arching football to the 28-yard line, where Superman catches it. The Bees conduct their frontal assault against the line of blockers put up by the Darts. Three Bee players penetrate the blocker wall and force Superman out of bounds at the 35-yard line.

"Rich 'Superman' Lane on the return. First and ten Darts from their own 35-yard line."

"Do you know much about these teams?" I ask as I update the game log sheet with "35D" as ball location and "receive KO" under comments. The next line starts with "35" under ball location and "1/10" under "down/distance."

"One of Cheryl's cousins has a son playing in the game. That's why she and Matthew are still here."

"I meant the team's records."

"Oh. The league standings show both won their openers in low-scoring games."

The Darts open their attack configuration in a classic I-formation with quarterback Big G behind center Hulk, fullback Hot Sauce three yards behind the QB and tailback Rampage three yards behind the FB. A pair of wide receivers, Superman and Crazy Legs, split fifteen yards wide on either side of the football. The remaining players comprise the crouched offensive line.

The Bees counter with an unusual defensive line formation, three linemen in a three-point stance to maximize leverage against their direct opponent, with one lineman standing upright at each end of the D-line. Three linebackers stand several yards behind the linemen. Two defensive backs match up against the two wide receivers. One deep safety stands in a reserve position fifteen yards from the football.

'Noculars are raised. Football is hiked. Play is run.

Hulk hikes the football to quarterback Big G.

Big G wheels right. He slides the football into the "breadbasket" pocket formed from Rampage's open arms, right arm low over his belly, left arm over right arm, left elbow cocked upward.

Rampage clamps elbow down to trap the football. He follows Hot Sauce to the right offensive guard Shark Slayer.

No hole. No crease. No daylight.

Pump those legs!

It's futile.

The backsides of blue-and-gold jerseys form an involuntary wall. The onslaught of black helmets and yellow jerseys collapses the wall backwards.

Rampage falls on his back—smothered under a pile of several players from both teams. Forward motion gets the football back to the original line of scrimmage.

That play brings back some bad personal memories from my "meat grinder" days.

"Handoff to the fullback, Arnold 'Rampage' Rhymer into the right side of the line. Stout defense by the Bees. No gain on the play."

Document results in log sheet. Second down coming up.

"Quarterback keeper around the left end. Nice gain of five yards by Gabriel 'Big G' Alvarez. That brings up third down and five to go for the first down."

After each play, Dart players rotate onto the field and speak to the quarterback. The team huddles and then breaks toward the line of scrimmage. On third down, Big G hands the football to Prime Time around the left tackle Terminator for three yards. Fourth down coming up.

'Noculars are raised. Football...is not snapped.

Pre-snap contact along the line of scrimmage. The lead official faces the press box, places both hands on his hips and points to the Bees. He picks up the football, steps off five yards, and points his left arm at a 45-degree angle over the Bee linemen.

"Offsides on the Bees. The ball is advanced to the 45-yard line. And that is enough for a Darts...First Dooown!"

The side official waves the chain gang further downfield along the far sideline. The man with the rear rod places the pole even with the football while his forward rod teenage partner stretches the chain ten yards downfield. Another volunteer, the box man, aligns the pole even to the football and flips the down indicator from "4" to "1".

Rampage gains one yard on first down.

Hot Sauce goes nowhere on second down.

"Flag down."

"Penalty flag on the play."

The lead official faces the press box, grabs his left wrist with his right hand and points to the Dart side. He picks up the ball and paces ten yards back from the original line of scrimmage.

"Holding, Darts. That costs us ten yards and makes it second and long from the Darts 41-yard line."

"It hurts when you are driven off-schedule by penalties. I haven't seen much speed from our skill positions," Dan says.

"It's tough to make up yards if you don't have speed."

A quarterback keeper by Big G and a dive play by Rampage set the stage for a critical fourth down play.

"That brings up a big fourth down and four to go to reach the first down marker. Support our boys on the field. Raise your voices, Darts fans!"

'Noculars are raised. Football is hiked. Play is run.

"Quarterback hands off to 'Rampage' Rhymer into the line. Gang tackled near the first down mark!"

"We're short."

As the players unpile, the lead official points toward the south end zone.

"Bees' ball. The ball turns over on downs. The Bees take possession at their 46-yard line."

"Man down."

The lead official waves his arms overhead and taps his shoulders. Every player on the field drops to one knee. Two Dart coaches sprint to the prone blue jersey, hunch over the reclined figure and say I-don't-know-what to him. The player sits up, and the coaches help him to his feet. Rampage exhibits a steady, deliberate gait as he walks off the field under his own power with a coach on either flank.

"That's Number 30, the running back from the previous play. Can't tell what happened. He's walking okay, so I guess he got the wind knocked out of him."

"Please give that young man a hand," the Big Voice says. "I hope Rampage comes back. It looks like he's a critical part of this team."

The change of possession prompts the simultaneous pre-snap activities on the field like an automated machine with human components: the referees spot the football and return to their ready positions; the chain gang sets the yardage and down marker poles; the Bees offensive players huddle and then move to their assigned spots in the split backfield formation; the Darts defensive players form up in response. Meanwhile, I close out the last row of the game log sheet for the Dart possession and note the first line of the Bee possession.

On first down: **"Quarterback hands...no. He keeps the ball around right end. Down the sideline! Forced out of bounds at the Dart's 26-yard line!"**

"Twenty-three yards."

"Twenty-three yards on the run by Tom 'Iceman' Winters."

The officials pause an extra beat as the chain gang scrambles to the new football location.

"Nice fake handoff and roll out with the other halfback acting as lead blocker," Dan comments.

"The formation design helped set up the play. Looks like their coach prefers to use his wide receivers as decoys to pull defenders away from the side of the field where the sweep is directed. Not a vote of confidence in their ability to block."

"That's enough for a Bees...First Dooown!" a man screams from the top row of the stands outside the press box.

That holler fills the announcer's booth with laughter.

'Noculars are raised. Football is hiked. Play is run.

"Halfback dive into the teeth of the defense. Gang tackled after a short gain. That brings up second and seven from the Dart's 23-yard line."

The active row ends, the future row starts.

'Noculars are raised. Football is hiked. Play is run.

"Quarterback hands...tosses the football to a tailback around the left end."

"Uh-oh."

"Around the left end. He's down the sideline! To the 20...the 10...Touchdown! Jeff 'Shredder' Sinclair with a 23-yard touchdown run."

"Man, we have got to stop those sweeps," an exasperated Dan says.

I complete the active row with "TD" and "+6" circled for emphasis in the comments and start the next row. Meanwhile, the Bees line up at the three-yard line. The Darts counter the Bees with a condensed defense—all eleven players between the three-yard line and goal line.

For the extra point try: **"Handoff to the tailback...follows his fullback into the line...Pile at the goal line."**

The side referee sprints to the player pile and points both arms skyward.

"He is in for the score. Larry 'Slam' Molari. The extra point is good, so the score is Bees 7, Darts trying to get on the board."

"These teams look close talent-wise," I comment.

"We have a good chance if we don't shoot ourselves in the foot with penalties. And tighten up the defense to stop their sweeps."

The first half progresses with both teams chewing up game time with conservative running offenses. The halftime score: Bees 13, Darts 0.

"A quick reminder. Please remain in your seats for the halftime show. The Deer Park Sparklers spirit team puts on a fabulous performance.

Their show is well worth the price of admission. You do not want to miss it!"

Admission is free, but I won't mention that to Dan.

The press box door scrapes open a minute before the end of the first half. Solid Blue and Stripe Shirt re-enter. The two moms wave at us as they stoop over to recover their breath.

***

"Welcome back, ladies," Dan shouts.

Once we're out of their way, the women situate themselves in the announcer's booth. He rolls a second chair into the booth and elicits a "thank you" from Stripe Shirt. Solid Blue sits in front of the mic again. Dan and I roll chairs from the back wall to the observation room counter to watch the halftime performance.

"Good afternoon, ladies and gentlemen. Please give a hand for our 2019 Deer Park Sparklers spirit team!"

The pom-pom routine progresses as during the previous halftime. The same introductory music signals the girls' march, hands on hips while holding their pom-poms, in five parallel lines onto the field. Once the girls reach midfield, they spin to face the east press box.

Solid Blue speaks into the stadium mic: **"The Deer Park Sparklers manager is Sarah Anderson. The spirit routine director is Julia Benes. The drill team leaders are..."** She calls out the team captain and the four lieutenants, the designated officers whose roles are to coach and inspire the other team members in each of their individual squads. Then other drill team members respond with a leap and pom-pom shake as each one is highlighted through the stadium speakers. My two littlest girls also jump and wave their open arms.

During the spirit squad introductions, I summarize the basic first half stats. The Bees three possessions ran 11 plays, gained 125 yards and scored two touchdowns. The Darts four possessions ran 25 plays, gained 56 yards and failed to score. Can that be right? I recheck to confirm the results. When it comes to data, I'm my own harshest critic. Back to the halftime show.

The remixed version of the classic pop song "Beat It" again blares from the stadium speakers as the girls form into their initial set. They perform the same leaps and pom-pom actions as executed for the previous halftime show: jumps, drops to knees, sequence reversal, alternate arm motions. The two smallest girls, without pom-poms, wave their arms to match the motion of the others.

I hand the stats to Dan. "Is this right? We ran 25 plays and only got 56 yards?"

"I double checked. We ran a lot more plays and made more first downs. Penalties on our part knocked us back. Penalties on their part kept us going. We yo-yo between the twenty-yard lines during the first half."

"Okay," he says with a single shake of his head.

A female singer cries out that all of us are beautiful, beautiful in every way—a means to encourage a positive self-image among the young ladies. The girls again form two parallel lines centered near midfield, oriented in a north-south direction. They place their hands on each other's shoulders and perform the same synchronized leg kick routine from the Junior game. The littlest girls at each end of the line each hang off an adjacent shoulder while they struggle to maintain pace with the older girls. No quit in them. They each lag a beat behind the other girls, but do their best to keep up.

The press box door scrapes open, and an out-of-breath eight- or nine-year-old boy pants, "My mom sent me up here. She wants you to tell the crowd we found a phone in the stands." He holds out the pink-cased phone.

"No problem," Dan says as he takes the phone. "I'll do it after halftime."

Add "lost and found" duty to stadium announcer role.

The kid whirls around and sprints from the press box. He vanishes beyond the canopies.

Dan activates the phone and sees a screen-locked image of a 30-ish year-old woman with long dark hair and bright smile hugging a young boy. "Hmm. Reminds me. At the Senior team practices, a big topic of discussion involved one mom who divorced her husband and started going with a coach on the Senior team, the team her boy plays on. The ex-husband sits on his tailgate across the street from the practice field to watch his boy. He also comes to the boy's Saturday football games. Big topics of discussion are when the affair with the coach started and how far apart the former couple will sit in the stands."

More information than I needed.

The final routine again features a female vocalist who cries out about this being her life, you need to remember it's her life, and it lasts forever. The girls repeat their square-within-a-square at midfield. This time, the corners are sharper, less rounded than during the previous halftime show. Do drill team coaches make their own halftime adjustments? Could be that the kids' first performance in a ten-thousand-seat capacity stadium provides confidence for the next show. Regardless of the reason, the girls perform the pom-pom portion of the stationary portion of the routine—a crisp execution to my untrained eye. My two favorite girls are on opposite sides of the inner square and wave their arms to match the motion of the other girl's pom-poms until the music ends. The block squares keep their shape while the girls march eastward and crumble against the near sideline.

"Please give a hand to your 2019 Deer Park Sparkler spirit team!" Blue Shirt shouts.

Everyone in the stands applauds as the girls cross the near sideline. The more intense devotees stand and applaud.

"Great job, ladies! A fine performance from the girls," Dan tells the two women as they exit the announcer's booth.

"Thank you," says Sarah. "I expect us to get better over the course of the season." She turns to the exit, stops, and wheels around toward Dan. "Oh, the parents want me to thank you for all kind words before and after every performance."

"It's my pleasure. I see the girls train as hard as the boys at practice. These girls earn the extra acknowledgement."

"Thanks again. See you at the afternoon practices," Sarah says as the two women exit from the observation room. The door scrapes against the floor to declare their departure.

"That is a very entertaining way to spend several minutes."

"Agreed."

***

Dan eases down in front of the mic while I wheel the extra chair back to the observation room wall.

"Give our Deer Park spirit team another round of applause. Outstanding job, young ladies!"

The Big Voice sorts his notes and relays the halftime stats. Then Dan takes a swig from his orange sports drink and continues: **"The Darts kick off to start the second half. David 'Hulk' Banning kicking off for the Darts."**

As the special teams form into their respective kicking and receiving units, "Seven Nation Army," a song of defiance against overwhelming odds, emerges from the speakers. A song from this century I recognize. The Darts line up in the customary kickoff configuration of five players on each side of a kicker. The Bees align their return team with six players along their side of midfield, three players along their 40-yard line and two players at their 25-yard line.

"A lost phone has been turned in to the press box. If you lost your phone, please come up to the press box and retrieve it."

The lead official points to the kicker. Hulk sends the football into the air to the 30-yard line.

A Bee deep back, Iceman, catches the ball and cradles it under his left arm as he sprints up the far sideline.

A pair of Dart players, Hot Sauce and Rampage, elude the Bees' blockers and shove Iceman out of bounds at the Bee's 47-yard line.

"Nice return. Number 7."

"Ball advanced to the Bee's 47-yard line. Tom 'Iceman' Winters. Forced out of bounds by Samuel 'Hot Sauce' Benes and Arnold 'Rampage' Rhymer. First and ten Bees."

The Bees line up as they did in the first half in a split-backs formation. At the same time, the Darts respond with the same defensive configuration used in the first half—with one noticeable difference.

"Dan, do you see the change in our defense? The coach spread the two outside linebackers from inside his defensive tackles to outside the tackles. He's daring the Bees to run into the middle instead of those sweeps that killed us first half."

For first down: **"Handoff to the tailback into the left side of the line. He finds a hole...Into Darts territory. Jeff 'Shredder' Sinclair. Wesley 'Steel' Cashman with the tackle."**

"How many yards?"

"What yard line?"

"Ball spotted at the 39."

"Uh...15 yards."

"Fifteen yards on the carry. First down, Bees."

"Not looking too good for the home team."

"We need a turnover."

The pattern of play continues until a miscue a few plays later.

"Fumble on the snap! Pile up at the 30!"

The lead official dives into the melee of black and white helmeted players. He stands and points toward the Darts' side of the line of scrimmage to show the Bees retain possession.

"Who recovered?" asks Dan.

"I couldn't pick out a number from that pile. There must have been seven or eight guys on the ground wrestling for the football."

"Well, we almost got the break we needed."

"Yeah, the football gods are teasing us," I say.

The Bees execute a pass play on second down.

"Quarterback...drops back to pass!"

The football sails out of bounds near the 10-yard line at the far sideline. Every official on the field crosses their arms two or three times in front of their torso.

"Incomplete pass! Allen 'Speedy' Sun breaks up the pass."

"Breaks up the pass? Even Yao Ming wouldn't be able to touch a football thrown so high out of bounds."

"Just tossing our kid a little love."

"That brings up third and twelve to go from the Darts 28-yard line."

'Noculars are raised. Football is hiked. Play is run.

"Quarterback...fakes to the halfback into the line...pitches to the tailback. He's free around the right side! The 20...The 10...Touchdown! Twenty-eight yards for the score. Jeff 'Shredder' Sinclair."

"We still can't stop the sweep. Moving our linebackers further outside didn't solve the problem."

"Our linebackers attacked the middle of the line because of the fake handoff. Their quarterback may not be much of a passer, but he excels at fakes and tosses to his tailbacks," Dan says.

Twin guitar riffs from the classic rock genre blare from the stadium speakers as the lead male vocalist shouts "Don't Look Back" but look forward instead and make the most of the time you got.

As the music plays, the two combatant teams form along the Darts' three-yard line. The Bees employ a modified full-house backfield: quarter-back, fullback, and two tailbacks, while seven offensive linemen crouch in their three-point stance. No wide receivers on the field. Meanwhile, the Darts counter with seven defensive linemen and four linebackers clustered at the goal line near the football.

While the players line up, I close out the active row and start the next log sheet line for the extra point attempt.

"The quarterback hands off to the tailback. He follows his fullback into the meat grinder over the right guard. Pile up at the goal line! The officials signal...he's in. Extra point is good. That makes the score Bees 20, Darts 0."

"I hope the good guys get going soon."

"That makes two of us," Dan says as he clicks the remote controller to change the scoreboard.

While the teams line up for the kickoff, the voice in the sky speaks: **"As a reminder, we are responsible for picking up all the trash in the stadium**

at the end of the day. Please help us out by placing your trash in one of the barrels scattered throughout the stadium. Thanks in advance for your cooperation."

"Scoring recap?"

"Shoot," Dan says as he pulls out some scratch paper.

After I recount the plays and yards, the Big Voice relays: **"Scoring drive recap. Fifty-three yards on five plays and capped off by a touchdown run of 28 yards."** After a few sips of water, **"Al 'The Viper' Bestow kicking off for the Bees."**

Dan cues the classic rocker "Dream On," a song exhorting the listener to keep dreaming regardless of past travails, for the kickoff tune. The Bees line up along their 40-yard line in the customary kickoff formation while the Darts prepare to receive with five players along their 49-yard line, four at their 40-yard line and two at their 25-yard line.

The lead official points to Viper and the kicker drives the line-drive football to the Dart 40-yard line, where the smallest player on the field camps out while he waits for the football to descend.

Crazy Legs catches the football. He wraps both arms around it.

Charge! Straight downfield.

No subtlety in that move.

A swarm of black-helmeted Bees overwhelms Crazy Legs after he slices through a crease in the coverage to advance the football over the midfield stripe.

"Slick runback. Did you get the jersey number?"

"Number 20."

"Joe 'Crazy Legs' Grant with a fine return. It will be first and ten Darts from the Bees 46-yard line."

"Based on size, the young man looks as though he should play on the Sophomore squad instead of the Senior team," Dan comments. "The little guy showed no hesitation. He hurtled straight into the onrushing yellow jerseys and stayed low enough to avoid some head-high tackle attempts."

Again, the Darts start their possession in an I-formation with two wide receivers. The Bees fill out their defense with the same five linemen, three linebackers, two cornerbacks, and one deep safety.

First down does not go as planned.

"Quarterback keeper into the left side of the line. Gabriel 'Big G' Alvarez with the tough run up the middle."

"Flag down."

"Penalty flag on the play."

The lead official faces the east press box, taps his right hand on his cap and points to the Dart side.

"I think he signaled too many men on the field."

"Twelve players on the field against the Darts. That backs us up five yards and makes it first down and 15 yards to go."

"Ooh. That is so frustrating."

"I expect to see a penalty like this more often—a mistake that results from so many kids running on and off the field."

"I disagree. The coaches, the adults, send in the players," Dan says. "It was the first game of the year. I mean, the first home game. With one game under our belt and a Senior squad...No. We should not make this kind of mistake."

'Noculars are raised. Football is hiked. Play is run.

"Quarterback drops back to pass. Throws toward the side-line...Caught! Complete at the Bees 32-yard line. Joseph 'Crazy Legs' Grant with the reception. And that is enough for another Darts...First Dooown!"

"How many yards?"

"Uh...Call it 18 yards."

"Eighteen-yard gain on the play."

After a short run by Big G and an incomplete pass attempt to Superman, the Darts get on the board.

"Quarterback hands...drops back to pass. Complete over the middle! He breaks a tackle! At the 20...the 10...Touchdooown! Arnold 'Rampage' Rhymer with the touchdown catch and run!"

"Twenty-nine yards."

"Twenty-nine yards on the touchdown pass from Alvarez to Rhymer. Extra point try is coming up."

"The passing game is fun."

"As long as we complete the passes."

Active line is completed with "+6" circled with "pass TD" in the comments. Next row started for the extra point attempt. The Darts line up in their previous offensive formation. The Bees counter with two cornerbacks, three linebackers, and six defensive linemen.

"Quarterback keeper! He crosses the goal line! Gabriel 'Big G' Alvarez in from the three yard-line. The Darts are on the scoreboard. Bees 20, Darts 7."

"All right. We're back in it."

"Sure are. And nice job by the two running backs who ran into the middle of line and helped push the pile across the goal line."

The ensuing drives by each team consume the rest of the third quarter. To run down the game clock, the Bees emphasize a ground game. The Darts stress the aerial game to make chunk plays.

The press box door scrapes open, and a panting twenty-something year old woman moves to the announcer's booth doorway.

"You found a cell phone?"

Dan holds up the pink phone. She smiles, claps her hands once, and clutches the phone with both hands.

"Ooh, thank goodness. My life revolves around my phone, and I was afraid I lost it. Thank you," she shouts on her way out of the press box.

Our "lost and found" department operates on the honor system. I'm not sure that was the same woman we saw on the cell phone screen saver.

Late in the fourth quarter, the score sits at Bees 20, Darts 13. The Darts force a change of possession. Our coach uses two of the three allotted timeouts to stop the clock during the previous Bees possession.

Darts ball. Time bleeds away.

The lead official with the white cap, set behind the offensive unit, alternates his gaze between the timer tethered to his left wrist and the players before him.

"Man, I wish we the game clock on the scoreboard worked," Dan says. "I can't call out to the officials and ask for the remaining game time after every play."

"There can't be much time left." The lead official stares at the timer in his left hand with only an intermittent glance onto the field of play. "Our boys fought so hard to get back in the game, came from so far behind..."

"First and ten Darts from their own 47 yard-line."

The Darts line up with an empty backfield. The quarterback, Big G, sets seven yards behind the line of scrimmage, both arms extended forward to receive the football for a "shotgun" snap. Four wide receivers, two split to each side of the six players on the offensive line, lean forward to ready themselves to sprint downfield.

Meanwhile, the Bee's match four cornerbacks against the four wide receivers. Four defensive linemen face off against the six Dart offensive linemen. Two linebackers set ten yards behind the defensive line. One deep safety positions himself at the Bee 30-yard line.

I look at the scoreboard. Idiot! The game clock section of the board exhibits a stoic black rectangle. The clock won't start working because I want it to.

Is this the final play of the game?

"Alvarez to pass...Incomplete! Pass attempt to the streaking Rich 'Superman' Lane down the far sideline. Second and ten coming up."

"Mmh. That pass wasn't close," I say.

"Tough pass to complete. Thirty yards downfield. Moving target. Well covered. At least the incomplete pass stops the clock."

The lead official flashes fingers to each sideline. I presume he signals to the coaches on both teams the remaining seconds in the game.

"I sure wish we knew the game clock situation."

On the next play, two Dart wide receivers, Speedy and Prime Time, streak down the far sideline. Two Bee cornerbacks run with them. The Bee deep safety runs over to meet the four players.

On the near sideline, two Dart receivers, Crazy Legs and Superman, streak downfield twenty yards.

Superman continues to the corner of the end zone.

Crazy Legs cuts to the middle of the field.

Both Bee cornerbacks stay glued to Superman.

Crazy Legs stops. He spins to face his quarterback.

Big G tosses a low, arching pass in his direction.

Caught!

"Quarterback to pass...Complete! Free up the middle!"

Crazy Legs turns downfield.

Run! No zigzag. No angle. Run straight to the end zone.

Faster!

One Bee cornerback at the far sideline freezes and watches the Dart receiver. Two other Bee defensive backs run toward the spot where Crazy Legs caught the football. Their poor pursuit angle soon leaves them trailing the ball carrier.

"He's at the 30!"

Faster!

Two other Bee defenders, one from the far sideline and one from the near sideline, sprint to the goal line to intercept the streaking Dart receiver—their instinctive triangulation apparent from the press box. Three streaking players head for a common intersection point.

"The 20...the 10...Hit at the goal line!"

Both defenders hammer Crazy Legs at the goal line, and the three collapse in a tangled heap.

The referee who trails the play races downfield, dives down and gazes into the pile. He stands erect...in slow motion, he lifts both arms skyward.

"He's in! Touchdooown! 'Crazy Legs' Grant! Fifty-three yards on the catch-and-run. That makes the score Bees 20, Darts 19. Extra point coming up."

The lead official retrieves the football and waves it over his head. Game time has expired.

"Miracle! The last play of the game—and we score."

"Well-earned miracle," Dan says. "Three receivers ran deep and drew the cornerbacks with them. One receiver was left open in the middle, the smallest player on the field, and he made the play. Impressive execution for a bunch of eleven- and twelve-year-olds."

"Goes to show you can't judge a player's heart by his size. The young man shows a lot of grit."

I close out the active row in the game log sheet with "+6" circled and "pass TD" added to comments. I prep the next row for the upcoming extra point play.

Cheers and standing ovations emanate from the north side of the stands as the Senior offensive players huddle before the extra point attempt. Of all the huddles I've seen in youth tackle football for all the plays I've seen in youth tackle football for all the games I've seen in youth tackle football, I cannot remember huddled players wrapping their arms around each other's shoulders until this instance.

The northern stands grow quiet as the offense forms along the line of scrimmage. Meanwhile, the southern side of the stands exhibits the opposite behavior and cheers as loudly as they can to encourage the defenders. The Darts line up in the same offensive configuration they used for the touchdown. The Bees counter with four cornerbacks to match each wide receiver; two outside linebackers slant toward each pair of receivers while one middle linebacker and four defensive linemen attack the line of scrimmage.

"A quarterback draw might get us the score."

"One point gets us the tie. I'd gamble on two points for the win," Dan says.

Hulk hikes the football. Shotgun snap.

Big G receives the low, arching, ankle-high snap.

Blitz! The Bee middle linebacker bursts through the Dart offensive line.

Big G twists to evade the tackler. The linebacker grabs the quarterback near the head area and hurls Big G to the turf.

"Quarterback to pass...blitz! 'Big G' goes down."

"Facemask! Call it. Please, call it," I say.

A yellow flag rests at the 15-yard line.

The lead official faces the east press box. He puts his right hand in front of his face, makes a tugging motion and points to the Bees. Penalty—halve the distance to the goal.

"Facemask on the Bees. Repeat the down."

The lead official turns to the Dart side of the field and points both arms in their direction.

"Timeout Darts. This is their final timeout."

"Man, this is too stressful," I say as I complete the active line and start the next row in the log sheet.

Both squads huddle with their coaching staffs along their respective sidelines. The entire stands rise, applaud, and cheer as the players distribute themselves across the line of scrimmage. The Darts line up with Big G under center and Rampage set five yards behind him. Superman and Speedy split wide right and Crazy Legs splits wide left. The remaining six players man the offensive line. The Bees oppose them with three cornerbacks at the line of scrimmage to match the three wide receivers. One linebacker drifts toward the side with two wide receivers while two other linebackers set behind the five defensive linemen.

"The football is only a yard away. If we run the ball, then we'll likely get the tie. If we pass, then we have a much lower probability of getting the win. The coach went for the win last time. I bet he goes for the win again," Dan predicts.

Three Bee coaches, between their 35 and 40-yard sideline, drop to one knee and stare into the end zone. Across the field from them, five Dart coaches stand along their sideline. The players from both benches position themselves between their respective 40-yard lines, facing towards the end zone. Fans in the stands rise.

All eyes focus on the north end zone.

The Big Voice describes the play: **"The quarterback...fakes a handoff...under pressure...lobs the ball into the end zone...Caught! Caught! Arnold 'Rampage' Rhymer! Darts 21, Bees 20!"**

All three officials raise their arms skyward. The Darts reacted they just won their Super Bowl. Dart players on the field swarm on top of Rampage. Bee players on the field hang their heads and drift back to their sideline. Dart bench players stream onto the field to the north end zone. Most fans on the northern side of the stands jump and holler. Most fans on the southern side of the stands collapse to their seats. Dart coaches on the far side pound each other's shoulder, leap and shout. Coaches on the near sideline rise from their knees and applaud and pat the shoulder pads of their boys as the Bees trudge off the field. All fans at the southern end of the stands rise and applaud.

The lead official waves both arms overhead. The three officials stride off the field toward the northeast side of the stadium.

"Wow, what a game. Rampage got knocked out of the game in the first half but comes back to snag the game winning score."

"Games like this are rare, but when they happen, they are sooo fun to call," Dan says.

"Yeah, I don't know any of these families or kids other than Matthew. I still get wrapped up in their games, more so than I expected when we started this morning. I want them to all be winners."

Walking in opposite directions astride the midfield stripe, the Bees and Darts players touch hands in the ceremonial display of sportsmanship. The winning Darts peel off at the end of the line and sprint back to their far sideline. The losing Bees turn back and jog to their near sideline. Fans on both sides of the stands rise and applaud the two teams.

"Time to auction the game football. What can I get after a game like this?"

"What a game! It's time to auction off the game football. Bidding is open to anyone. Bidders, please make sure you see us in the press box when you bid. Now, who will give me $50 for this once-in-a-lifetime memento? Perhaps your last chance to get a game ball from your boy's final season in this youth tackle football program."

Dan and I scour the stands for bidders. Five adults wave their arms at us from various sections of the stands—more interest than normal for the start of bidding. Dan steadily increases the requested dollar amount as the bidders drop out. Five bidders stay in for $150. Three bidders remain at $250. Two bidders are left at $300. At $350, one bidder sees his competitor continue to wave to the press box and decides the price is excessive. He crosses both arms overhead once, shakes his head side-to-side and sits down. One bidder still stands.

"Will anyone give me $400? When you think about it, that's not much for a memory that lasts a lifetime. The game football is something you can put on your fireplace mantle...on your bookshelf...in your trophy case. I have a game ball myself, and I am thankful for it. Okay...Going once...Going twice...Last call...Sold! Thank you, sir. Please collect the game ball at the Darts organization table under the stands."

"Have you ever noticed it's only men who bid on the game footballs? At least half the people in the stands are women, but I've never seen a woman bid on a game ball. There must be some deep sociological reason."

"Huh. Now that you mention it, I haven't either. In my case, Cheryl would kill me if I tried to put a football in our living room. She tolerates one game ball as long as I keep it in my office."

"Anyway, a $350 bid is pretty good. All-in-all, a nice way to end the day," I conclude.

The stadium speakers blast an instrumental piece from a military band, a song I'm familiar with from my college days: "The Aggie War Hymn." **"I want to give a shout out to my brother, Earl,"** the big voice in the sky says. **"He volunteered his Saturday to help me out in the booth as a spotter and to provide the halftime statistics."**

I suspect Dan's words are hard to understand because his shoulders are being shaken from behind for as long as the tune fills the stadium.

Chapter Six

All is Well

Dan rises from his chair and stretches his arms high. "Man, I am so hungry," he says.

"Ditto that."

"What do you feel like?"

"Tex-Mex?"

"Sounds good. I'll buy," Dan offers.

"That *really* sounds good." I feel like chicken fajitas, flour tortillas with refried beans instead of charro beans. Need refried beans as a paste to hold the concoction together. Shredded cheese with a little guac and pico de gallo. Skip the sour cream. And fresh diced jalapeños on the side. Ooh, that sounds so good.

Dan polices the booth while I get off my feet for a few minutes. I lean back in a chair in the observation room and reflect on the last game. I envy those Dart players, especially the ones involved in the key moments that generated the victory. I never experienced such a moment, not on my winless youth football team. One play constitutes both my personal highlight and lowlight from that season over fifty years ago. I see it like it's happening to me now.

From my deep safety position, I run to my left and intercept a high, arching pass twenty yards down the sideline. Then sprint toward their goal line, break one tackle, juke another potential tackler who slows me enough for an opposing player to drag me down about forty yards from where I snared the football. Once I'm down, a half-dozen opposition players pile on top. An arm reaches under my chest and drags the football from beneath me. The officials award them the football. Tears stream down my cheeks. Why do they get the ball back? I was down. The only interception my team has that season accompanies the only fumble I lose that season. That trivial event, a meaningless thirty seconds from over fifty years ago, still haunts me—though maybe more for the tears than for the lost football.

The Big Voice leans over to the stadium mic for a final announcement. **"Thanks to everyone who attended today's game. I hope you had a positive gameday experience regardless of which team you rooted for. Please help us all have a positive experience by placing your trash in any of the receptacles located around the stadium. We are responsible for keeping this beautiful facility clean. Your help is appreciated. Please drive safe on your way home."**

"I'll text Cheryl to see if she wants to join us."

"Okay. I'll check on our buddy down the hall," I tell him as he slides the log sheets, roster notes, and binoculars into his leather pouch.

In the far observation room, Video Teen packs the camera equipment as though it's an Olympic speed event.

"Ready to get out of here, huh?" I ask.

He interrupts form-fitting the camera in its padded case to face me. "Yes, sir, I am sure ready to go. Once I leave here, I still need to load the video files into Dr. LePrince's online folder so he can edit them from wherever he is and then transfer them to the league folder locations."

"All right. I won't slow you down. Have a good evening." I suppose Dr. LePrince wants to provide coaches with access to game video as soon as possible to help them prepare for next week's practices.

"Thank you. And to you, too."

Dan greets me in the observation room, pouch in hand. "Ready?"

I pick up my notebook and binoculars. "Lead the way."

***

Dan quick-steps from the press box down the aisle on the southeast side of the stands. I keep up with him better than I did this morning on the climb to the press box. Our pace slows from interference by the adults who trickle onto the steps that lead to the exit ramp. Children run and hop down the stairs, so we stagger our pace to make sure we don't knock any of them down—and vice versa.

Spectators at the final game collapse their canopies like giant square umbrellas. At least, they try to collapse. One couple fumbles with a latch at one corner as they wrestle with a tarp. I wouldn't repeat in public the words the man spews about his problematic canopy.

The dozen members of the cleanup crew dive up and down between the stands. Several teens—I presume drafted by their parents—double-time their pace along each 90-yard-long row to collect plastic bottles, candy wrappers, plastic bags, plastic cups, and whatever else they find on the ground.

We're halfway down the stairs when a woman near my age waves at us from the edge of the steps. "We love your game announcements. It helps us keep up with what is going on," she tells us.

"Thank you."

"Are you guys paid for doing this?" she asks.

"Not a cent," Dan replies as I shake my head side-to-side.

"Well, you should be. You do a great job." She waves to us and moves down the row to be with her family.

Dan looks up at me, and we exchange smiles. "Glad you liked the game call," he shouts after her as we resume our descent.

At the base of the stairway, we spin around and tread flat-footed down the ramp to reach the area beneath the east stands. Dan and I pause to catch our breath. At least no repeat of the extended huff-and-puff experienced on the morning's upward climb to the press box.

"There they are, Cheryl and Matthew," he points out as we approach the gate.

Matthew stands next to his shoulder pads and helmet. His eyes wander around the ground in front of him, as though he searches for something to hold his attention. Cheryl smiles as we approach them. "Hi, Earl. I hope you did not mind spending your Saturday to help Dan out during the games," she says while Dan hugs her.

"No, no. No problem at all. I don't have a chance to do much with my younger brother anymore—we sure can't do anything athletic together these days—so I'm happy to help. I would have spent the day goofing off, watching college football, and swilling beer. Besides, how else can I catch up on the saga of the divorcee and the football coach."

Cheryl shoots her "what are you telling him?" look at Dan, who raises both eyebrows, shrugs his shoulders, and shakes his head a few times.

"We're here to support our boys, not gossip about who slept with who. She's a sweet person, and you guys shouldn't be saying anything bad about her." Her elbow into Dan's ribs elicits an exaggerated "Ouch."

"Anyway, the home crowd liked the broadcast, but the visitors around us grouched about it a few times," Cheryl comments as she turns toward me. "They claimed it was overly biased for the home team."

"They're right. This is the Dart home team broadcast. Dan gives visiting players shout-outs during the games to help provide some balance, but we are homers through-and-through. No apology."

"There were also the usual occasional complaints about Dan mispronouncing their names."

"Hey, I do the best I can."

"How did it go with Mom today?" I ask.

"Lee did fine. The weather is a bit hot and humid for her, but she made it through most of the first half. She saw her great grandson play, so the experience made her happy. She wants to take part in family activities while she can. I wish I got her some ice water from the concession stand. The heat and humidity are oppressive enough for all of us, more so for Lee."

"Well, I'm glad it worked out. Mom wants to be a part of family activities while she is still on this Earth," I say. "If we include Matthew, then I guess Mom makes the fourth generation to see a family member play youth tackle football."

"And your dad is okay." Cheryl continues, "Like usual, he sits in his wheelchair in front of the TV while he watches the all-Westerns channel. He keeps the volume so high it hurts my ears."

"Yeah, that sounds like Dad," Dan says. "After 60-plus years of marriage and 30 years in the same house, he's a creature of habit."

Cheryl giggles. "There was a tarp invasion issue. I erected a canopy before the game so Lee could be under shade as soon as we arrive in the stands. Four people squatted underneath our cover. I didn't recognize them, so I figured they were Bee supporters from LaPorte and didn't know what's what. One of them claimed they were under a public tent. I set him straight and shooed them away." The last comment draws a chuckle from Dan.

"And Sean sat with us too," Cheryl says. "He has a house now a few miles from your parents in an older subdivision in Deer Park. After months in a halfway house near Minute Maid Park and a year of living with us, Sean wanted his own house. We co-signed the note and installed new wood fence there for a housewarming gift so he can let Lori—the new love of his life, an energetic thirty-pound mixed breed dog—run around outside. Lori is a rescue dog that Sean adopted from the Houston Humane Society pet adoption center, located a few miles south of the Texans' football stadium. Sean told us that since he was given a second chance, he wants to provide a happier life for a dog who suffered some abuse or neglect. Lori's a great dog. She barks and shies away from strangers at first, but once you let her sniff your hand, she becomes your buddy. The biggest problem then is being smothered by a dog who wants to slobber all over you."

"A nobler way to get a pet dog than mine," I say. "In my case, a neighbor's lab had a litter of six pups, and she wanted to shed most of them. That's how I got Sandy." I remember my neighbor's backyard, where all but one of her lab puppies hop up and down out of control. This one pup nibbles and paws at my shoelaces, more curious about them than the stranger among them. She's the one who won me over. With her oversized paws and outrageous floppy ears, she was the ugliest pup of the litter. I wouldn't trade her for any other dog in the world.

Cheryl leans over to Matthew and asks, "Do you want to come home with me or go with Poppa for Mexican food?"

"I'll go with Poppa."

"All right," she says. "Take your football equipment with you."

"I parked outside the south end of the stadium, a good 100-yard walk from here," Dan tells me.

"We're in the same direction. I'm closer to seventy yards away."

Before I peel away from the sidewalk, Dan grabs my right hand. This time, my fingers only turn pink instead of purple after the handshake. "Thanks again. You helped me out a lot today."

"I'm glad to help. As a matter of fact, I am ready to go again. I want to stay and call another game. In fact, I demand we stay and call another game."

"Whoa, rein it in a bit. We'll be back here in two weeks for the next home game."

"Sounds good to me."

I head back to my truck through the thinning parking lot. Stop halfway. Flex legs to make sure nothing cramps. The old body held up pretty well after standing most the day. A long but satisfying day, now to be capped off with a free meal.

One learns more about the youth football culture by attending all the games instead of only one game, especially the support teammates show for one another. The Senior players clasp each other's shoulders in the huddle before the game-deciding play. The girl's spirit squad alters their music as a gesture of support to bolster the family of a soldier redeployed toward harm's way. I won't forget it.

The multiple games also provide the first opportunity to hear many roster calls—I love the nicknames—that also reveal the extensive Hispanic-Anglo integration in the community. Not as much mingling apparent with Black families yet. It'll come. I'm sure of it.

Football games are fun for the kids. The benefits—exercise, teamwork, socialization, mental resilience—must be weighed against the risk of long-term brain trauma. The parents choose. I hope it's an informed choice. I'm sure not going to mention the subject again during a youth football game.

Despite this potential dark cloud, the gameday experience satisfied all those involved with it. Boys get to play football. Girls conduct their cheer routines. Parents and relatives watch their children perform in an impressive sports venue. Dan's energetic stadium announcements, his conscious effort to call out as many names as he can over the stadium speakers, add to the overall adventure.

I climb into my truck. Start ignition. Turn on the running lights. Be careful. I don't want to risk hitting a kid on the way out. Man, I am so looking forward to the next gameday.

Opening Day 2020: Pandemic Year

Chapter Seven

Once More

I must be crazy. Self-sequestering at home since March, I only leave the house for periodic trips to the grocery store, occasional restaurant take-outs, essential doctor visits, and voluntary blood donations—not that I'm building a resume for my sainthood application. It's a way to get direct human contact during the COVID-19 pandemic.

Now, I'm again at the Deer Park High School stadium for the September start of the 2020 youth tackle football season. The other pickup trucks and SUVs meander through the stadium parking lot near the posted ten miles per hour speed limit. The ever-present children that dart between the parking spots near the main entrance warrant extra caution. After all, no one here intends to hurt a child.

I park my pickup about fifty yards from the east gate. No attempt to face the pedestrian traffic around the main stadium entrance. I intend to avoid a near-miss collision similar to what occurred last season.

A longer walk burns more calories, but a trek through drizzling rain holds no appeal to me. I shut off the engine and sit in the truck for a minute to soak in the sights and sounds. Rain patters on the metal roof of the cab and cascades down the windshield to distort the other vehicles' headlights and red brake lights, causing them to flare out and fade at the edges. Hazy figures of adults and children scramble through the rain to reach the cover of the concrete stands. The surreal image reminds me of the rainy city scenes from my favorite movie, *Blade Runner*.

Okay. I guess I have to get out of my truck. Hold my mask over my mouth-to-nose area with my right hand and slide the rubber band strap down the back of my head with the left. Slip my reading glasses into my shirt's chest pocket. Put on my gray cap with the maroon 'DP' letters. Hook left shoe under the open door, tug myself out of my truck.

Once outside my truck, I put on my trusted, tan-colored windbreaker. The jacket only zips up one third of the way—it's faded, it's flawed, but it's functional.

I pull the other items I need from the passenger side: binoculars, pens, notebook, roll of toilet paper, facial tissues (the kind that incorporates antivirals), roll of paper towels, Clorox wipes, Lysol disinfectant spray, alcohol prep pads, alcohol hand spray—all loaded into a green, cloth grocery bag. Double-time through the drizzle in a beeline to the main gate. My vision darts between the stationary yellow parking logs, vehicles that creep over the puddle-filled asphalt, and the people who splash past me to find cover beneath the concrete stands.

Noise emanates from the immediate area inside the main gate, more so than I remember from last season, perhaps because everyone clusters under cover to escape the rain. Nowhere for the noise to spread out. As the only person wearing a mask, I stand out in the crowd. I take that back—two women and the teenage boy who serve in the concession stand each wears a mask. Did someone rig a plastic shield along the concession area counter?

The line in front of the concession area curls into the path of the ramp to the stands. The home team youth football organization, the Deer Park Wildcatters, sets their table against the concrete back wall between the toilets to my right and the player dressing room to my far right. Boys in black jerseys carry their gray helmets through the crowd to the visitors' dressing room under the stands to the north. I zigzag through the crowd as best I can to minimize direct person-to-person contact to get to the ramp.

A deliberate, flat-footed walk up the damp ramp ensures secure footing to the stands.

Surprise.

The kids on the field play without helmets and pads—flag football. No time to dwell on field action now. I'll study the game once I reach the press box. After a Master Po *Kung-Fu Panda* moment to face an arch enemy, I take a deep breath and exhale while I ascend the fifty-two steps to get to the top of the stands. I pass the umbrellas that dot the stands and several tarps that shelter clusters of families and friends from the rain. After the climb, I lean against the chain-link fence that runs along the stadium's top wall and pant faster than my dog does after we play catch outside in the afternoon summer heat.

After a minute, the rain spurs me to scoot between the top row and press box wall to get to the entry door. The door scrapes open against the floor, and I ascend the remaining eight steps into the main observation room.

***

The unmasked dad in the announcer's booth and I wave at each other. While he describes the events on the field—number something got the ball, number something gained some yards, number something pulled a flag—I throw my jacket on a chair along the back wall and unload the cleaning supplies.

First order of business, clean the observation room vinyl countertop. I expend two Clorox disinfecting wipes, careful to drag the perforated six-inch-long sheets through the plastic tab that tears off individual sheets, to rub down the 12-foot long, vinyl counter. The armrests for the chairs that pile along the back wall also get a wipe down, and the cloth seats are swept with Lysol disinfectant spray. The lingering chlorine odor suggests a disinfected environment, or at least the main points likely to contact people are clean.

Time to attack the bathroom at the end of the hall.

The hallway channels me past the announcer's booth, a second booth of the same size, and second observation room. A slender young man in his mid-twenties—no mask—occupies the adjacent booth that remained empty throughout last season. Well-groomed, full head of dark hair with a long-sleeve blue dress shirt and dark brown slacks. We sure don't shop off the same Kohl's budget rack. I presume he dresses nicer than I do in my faded jeans, maroon polo-style shirt, and ratty tennis shoes since he's a paid professional and I'm a lowly volunteer.

"I see we have a professional music maker this season. I'm Earl."

"Good morning. I'm Martin. The Wildcatters organization hired me to provide the stadium music this season." A cord extends from his laptop computer through a seam in the wall into the announcer's booth.

No handshake. Even if I want to, both my hands clutch cleaning supplies.

"That's good news for Dan. He performed double duty last season: announce the game and trigger the music during lags in game action. Music adds a lot to the gameday experience, so, uh,"—I wobble my head side-to-side for a moment as I search for words in my typical articulate manner—"welcome to Abshier Stadium."

"Thanks, man. I hope to contribute as much as I can," the Music Man says.

I raise both hands toward him. "Would you like me to wipe down your area?"

He glances around the room and comes back to me, "Thanks, but I'm okay for now."

"All right, catch you later." Man, I never sported a head of hair like that at any time in my life—not that my barren scalp, which resembles a tan-colored mound of lumpy paper mâché surrounded by sagging gray dental floss on three sides, envies a full head of hair.

I linger for a moment at the doorway to the second observation room. A man near my age hunches over a camera mounted atop a tripod. How does he stay so thin?

"Good morning."

"Hello, there," he says before he even turns to face me. No mask.

"I'm Earl."

He twists toward me and shifts his glasses toward the top of his nose. "Harold LePrince, here."

"I remember. We met two seasons ago when Dan and I worked the Freshman home games. His grandson played on that Darts team." I nod toward the camera. "I see you're back on the video operation. What happened to the young man who handled the camera last season?"

"Oh, you mean Jon. Fine young man, from the same church I attend. When I get tied up on church business, like our overseas mission work, he stands in for me. No overseas travel allowed this year, so I am staying put and taking care of the video work myself."

"Adventures in youth football compared to an overseas church mission. Not the same gravitas, but glad you're back this season." I scan the countertop. "Would you like your room wiped down?"

Mr. LePrince runs his eyes across the room and faces me. "No, I am all right. But thank you anyway."

"Okay. Tell me if you change your mind."

He turns back to his camera while I move on to everyone's second-most important room in the press box, or in my case, the most important.

Kudos to the bathroom housekeeping service. Paper towels fill half of the metal canister on the wall. Full liquid soap bottle by the sink. I get to keep the roll of toilet paper I brought with me. Clorox wipes assault the light switch, sink handles, toilet handle, and toilet seat. I saturate the bathroom with Lysol spray and shut the door—double check to make sure the door remains unlocked before shutting it. That treatment should exterminate any virus; I'd have trouble surviving that atmosphere.

The chlorine odor still lingers in the main observation room. I hope others in the press box aren't bothered by the faint chlorine odor, but even if they are, the odor should dissipate over the next hour or so—a small price to pay for killing the virus. In the classic Vietnam era war movie, *Apocalypse Now*, an officer squats on a beach and tells us he loves the smell of napalm in the morning; it smells like victory. I don't love the smell of chlorine in the morning; however, at this point in the COVID-19 epidemic, chlorine smells like hope for victory on a real-world viral battlefield.

Time to check out the football field. The field below provides the illusion of being dry during the misting rain: no water puddles visible, no players slip, no water kicks up from cleated shoes. I admire the engineering incorporated into the field designed so rainwater leaves less of a sheen on the artificial turf than it does on my truck's overspray-laden windshield.

The four officials—each dressed in a white cap; black cloth mask with two ear straps; black-and-white vertical-striped shirts; black shorts—wear clear plastic jackets that bead raindrops that coalesce and drip to the turf. How do they use whistles while wearing a mask? I'll keep an eye on penalty calls and see how they handle the masks.

The door scrapes open to pronounce another visitor's entry to the press box. A thirty-something male in an orange cap and lightweight gray jacket rises into the observation room. No mask. He pants to catch his breath. "Hello. I have the rosters for our four tackle squads."

"Morning. I'll take them," I say as I extend my right arm outward from about five feet away. I sure won't mention potential head trauma with youth tackle football to him. "Any hard to pronounce names?"

"Beats me. I'm just dropping off the rosters."

"Okay. I'll be sure Dan gets the lists. He is a linguistics master, so I'm confident he can handle the proper pronunciation for anyone's name."

"All right. Later."

Thanks a lot for the help. Before press box door shuts, heavy footsteps clomp into the observation room.

"Dan, morning."

"Good morning, Earl." Dan, maskless, drops his leather pouch and plastic grocery bag onto the counter. "Give me a minute to catch my breath." He leans on the counter, closes his eyes for several seconds, gasps for air, and twists to extend his right hand toward me.

"You want us to shake hands? Are you trying to kill us?" I extend my right elbow toward him, and he does the same to me, and we whiff. The comedy act draws a smile from both of us.

"It may be hard to see, but I lost thirty-five pounds since last season," he tells me.

"That's great, man." Argh—I only dropped five pounds.

"I wish the weight loss helped my stamina, but it is what it is."

We each grab a chair and roll it to the counter. Feet on floor to keep the chair from rolling to the back wall.

"What's your magic formula?"

"I went cold turkey on fast food," Dan tells me. "Several times a week, I used to hit fast-food drive throughs." I remember the seasonal Jack in the Box Monster Tacos summon him like a clarion call to consume fast food. For me too.

"Now, Cheryl keeps me eating salads. And we walk around our neighborhood for an hour most evenings."

He points to the plastic bag on the counter. "I didn't bring any food, but I brought bottles of water and some sports drinks to last us through the day. No lunch, unless you want something from the concession stand." Apparently, no cherry sours this season.

"This'll do fine. I microwaved a frozen kolache for breakfast this morning. It was edible. That, and the thermos of coffee I drank on the hour-plus drive here, will get me through the day."

"Well, thanks for giving me a hand again this season. The league president spent an hour on the phone with me. He described the league merger, the uniforms, the policies, and how crucial our announcing is to a positive gameday experience. He laid it on thick," Dan says with a grin. "He didn't have to hard-sell me on doing it again. As long as Matthew plays youth football, I'm willing to announce the games from the booth. But only if you agree to help me out."

"No problem," I tell him. "I'll help my younger brother out in any way I can."

"Over the course of the daily practices, I've met most of the Wildcatters organization managers in person. The league president, who reports to a board of directors, manages the athletic director, drill team director, and equipment coordinator. The athletic director makes sure the teams are staffed with coaches and proper safety protocols are followed. An equipment director maintains the helmets and pads as necessary. At the end of the season, we return Matthew's helmet and shoulder pads back to the organization. Looks to me like women, mothers and grandmothers, manage administrative roles like league communications, record keeping and finances while the men focus on the nitty-gritty of football."

"Sounds like a pretty sophisticated set-up for youth football."

Dan describes the Wildcatter practices where all the boy's age groups work out on different sections of a junior high football field and the girl pom-pom team practices in the grassy area inside a nearby track.

"There was some friction between coaches after the merger between the two leagues. Our head coach with Matthew's team, the best boy's football coach I've seen, almost got into a fight with the linebacker coach drawn from the other league. Mr. Linebacker spewed profanity while he taught extra violent tackling methods to the boys, designed as much to inflict pain on their opponent as to tackle. Our coach hollers at the kids to make his point without using profanity and employs accepted tackling techniques to make the game safer for everyone. The Coach told Mr. Linebacker to tone it down. The linebacker coach refused, ranted at The Coach for several minutes and quit the team."

"Did he take his boy with him?"

Dan cocks his head and wrinkles his brow. "Pull his boy out? That must be a..."—Dan drops his head for a few seconds before he snaps his face toward mine—"rhetorical question. Of course not. League rosters are set. If you want your boy to play football, he must stay with his designated team. If the mom wanted to keep the boy out of tackle football, she would have decided before the season started."

The practice description triggers a memory from my old youth tackle football days, one I haven't thought of in decades. Coaches divide my Senior youth football team into two squads—the Spitfires and the Mustangs—so that each squad alternates play time for different quarters of every football game. At practice, the coaches select alternating players at random from each squad to face off from ten yards apart, one a designated ball carrier and one the tackler.

One practice, I'm the designated Spitfire tackler who pairs against the biggest player on the team, the Mustangs' center. After our squad coach sees the matchup, he asks me, "That's a pretty big boy. Do you want to match up against someone closer to your size?"

I wave him off. "I'll give it a try."

While I stare at the player ten yards in front of me, I rock back and forth from a prone position and fire off the line as soon as the coach tosses the football to the center. I strike the ball carrier waist-high with my shoulder pads, but cannot stop his lumbering gait. I reach behind him, grasp his hips and tug him backwards on top of me. He falls on my stomach, knocks the wind out of me and sits on top of me—laughing—while I gasp for air. Later, while I hunch over to catch my breath, the coach leans over my shoulder. "You made good contact, but slid off him. Next time you face a much larger opponent, dive for his knees. No matter how big a guy is, *you take his knees out and he is going down*."

"Oh, I talked to Gabe Anderson," Dan says. "You remember, the league president from last year. He participated in the league negotiations for the merger between the Darts and Wildcatters. He told me the top two demands from the Wildcatters organization were, first, everyone adopts the Wildcatters name and colors, and second, the game day stadium announcers come over with the Darts."

"Hah. They wanted us. We should've asked them to double our pay."

Dan laughs and says, "Love that Aggie math. Getting double nothing is much better than getting nothing." He nods out the window. "Sorry about the weather today. Not the best way to open the season."

"I promise not to blame you for the weather. Besides, playing in a little rough weather is good for the kids. The ordeal is part of their character-building experience."

"Oh, I brought you something." Dan twists around to retrieve a baseball cap from the pouch lying on the counter. He hands the cap, identical in design to the one he wears, to me. The front third exhibits a reddish color with white stitches with the rest of the cap gray in color. The front of the cap displays "Cats" in gold letters outlined in white to contrast against the maroon.

"Thanks, man." I fashion the cap's brim with both hands. I don't stress over clothes or shoes, but I care about my baseball caps. A flat brim screams "dork." An over-arched brim, one that blocks much of your peripheral vision, declares you're a tobacco-chewing redneck from the sketchy side of the trailer park. But a well-arched brim, one that centers at the forehead and extends downward to just above your outer eye sockets, proclaims: "Yeah, I know what I'm doing. I've played ball before." Perfect fit. The cap rides high enough to avoid the rubber strap that runs behind my head. After I finish the cap brim, "No mask, I see."

"I cannot wear a mask," Dan tells me as he looks me in the mask. "I don't see how you do it."

"Well, I'm in multiple high-risk health categories, so I have plenty of incentive to do whatever I can to avoid contracting COVID. And I'm fortunate to get this N95 mask. Our brother, James, got this one for me. Not sure how. According to the internet, it's not a real N95 because it has a single rubber strap that goes behind my head and real N95s have a pair of straps, one for each ear. But it's much better than my original mask. When masks weren't available, I made my own from a 20-inch-long section I cut from the leg of my old sweatpants. I tugged it halfway down over my head and pulled the open end down to below my eyes. A simple double-layer cloth to cover my mouth and nose. My mask wasn't stylish, but it got the job done."

"Hmm. So far, so good for us. Cheryl, Matthew and I have been fine. Kade and his mom's family have been okay. And Sean has also been clear of the virus so far. The remote homeschooling was a major pain, but Cheryl is retired now and at home to help Matthew as needed."

"The local news this morning reports Harris County COVID-19 positivity rate is at 8% and dropping. Maybe the pandemic situation is getting better," I speculate.

"Hope so. COVID sure didn't stop this restructured league from taking my money for Matthew to play this year. I wish more than four home dates were scheduled, but four is better than none."

"I won't feel comfortable in public until I get vaccinated—and when vaccinations are available to everyone. Between my age and ailments, I should be high on the authorized vaccine list. Early next year, I hope."

"I'm no fan of vaccinations," Dan says. "I'm sure the flu shot I got thirty years ago made me bad sick at the time. I missed a day of work because of it. No more flu shots, or any vaccinations, for me since then. But COVID looks pretty scary, enough for me to take the vaccine as soon as it's available."

"Oh my God! You missed a day of work!" I joke. Then I drop my smile. "But between COVID and the weather, I'm a bit surprised to see so many people at the stadium. Umbrellas and tarps are everywhere"—I scan the stands—"throughout the stands to protect people against the elements. Few masks. I thought the governor's mask mandate covers adults and children over nine years old when in public. I'm not sure if the mandate covers indoors only or also encompasses outdoor activities." I twist around to face Dan. "Maybe clustered family units are exempt. It's hard to keep up with all the rules. I believe churches are exempt from mask requirements."

"That explains it," Dan says with a smile. "Football is a religion in Texas. No masks needed in the football cathedral!"

"Whatever. I'm still a little surprised we're able to play this year. I'll emerge from isolation,"—arms up, spread beyond my chest—"but I wish others were more considerate of the most vulnerable."

"Thanks again for taking the risk to help me out. Like I told you on the phone, it took a lot of gyrations for two local leagues to merge to make sure there were enough players to complete the Pee-Wee through Senior football squads. Our league provided most of the players, but we made the most concessions. The Darts surrendered their organization and rolled into the Wildcatters program. The Darts were around forever. My son, Bryan, played in the Darts organization over thirty years ago."

"I'm glad the league keeps access to the high school stadium. A ten-thousand-person capacity venue provides plenty of room for different families to spread out, stay apart." I add, "I see one big change on the field—flag football."

"I was also surprised to about the flag football. The league manager told me the parents for the Pee-Wee team opted to go with it for the six- and seven-year-olds. The eight through twelve-year-old kids stick with tackle football."

"I suppose the parents for the youngest kids are concerned about potential head trauma?"

"Cost could also be a factor. The uniform costs must be a lot lower for flag football, with only jersey and shorts and cleats required, compared to tackle football. The helmet and shoulder pads for Matthew are covered by a three-hundred-dollar fee to the league. I buy his padded pants, jersey, and cleats. And Matthew grows so fast I need to replace much of the equipment every season."

"At least you don't have to buy the helmet and pads. Our Dad bought mine when I played," I tell Dan. A well-fitted helmet in good condition offers some protection against immediate, serious head or brain injuries—but does not guarantee protection against concussion or long-term adverse brain health effects.

I hope these kids' helmets fit better than my helmet when I played youth tackle football. I remember telling my dad that my helmet is too tight around the temples and too loose at the cheeks. My helmet wobbles a bit upon impact despite the tightened chin strap. No problem. He uses his pocketknife to gouge out the padding at the tight section. He cuts Styrofoam-like padding from a cardboard shipping box and glues it into the helmet from the ear holes to the front cheek area. My helmet doesn't wobble anymore.

"Most Dart parents are okay with paying for a new jersey this season because the new colors match the color scheme for the Deer Park High football team."

While Dan relates his football expenses, my eyes wander to the Pee-Wee flag football game in progress. I recognize the shape of the football, but not much else. Orange cones mark a quarter of the field for their game. Seven versus seven for the six- or seven-year-olds. Three offensive linemen at the line of scrimmage versus two rushers who set up several yards in front of the line of scrimmage. No blocking, but the game allows "impeding" side-steps with arms behind your back, for three offensive linemen. The game plan appears to be: (1) quarterback takes a shotgun snap, runs down the field and zigzags so the opposing players miss the flag on his waist, or (2) quarterback hands the ball off to a running back who runs down the field and zigzags so opposing players miss the flag on his waist, or (3) quarterback throws a wobbly forward pass, seldom complete in the light rain. It's a speed game.

I need a closer look.

Binoculars up. Oh, no. Exhaled breath during extended use of my binoculars escapes around the N95 mask seal at my nose and fogs up the binocular eyecups—the eyepiece keeps fogging over. I change my breathing technique to adapt to the mask. I prefer breathing through my mouth whenever I wear a mask, but after I breathe through my nose, the lens fogging stops.

I see clearly now.

The images through binoculars show smiling, laughing children along the sidelines. No laughter apparent on the field of play. All the players, especially the ball carriers, display a furrowed forehead with narrowed eyes, a squint that reveals their intensity during game action. Frequent substitutions allow all the participants to get balanced game time. Girls participate with the boys. I presume parents are more comfortable letting their girls play an organized game of chase with the boys rather than going head-to-head in helmets and pads. Overall, flag football strikes me as a fun experience for the kids. Do you need helmets and shoulder pads to learn the values of working hard, working as a team and developing camaraderie, demonstrating perseverance, and learning to deal with failure as well as with success?

"We have a game clock this season," I say and point to the scoreboard.

"Yes. Five officials regulate each home game for the Wildcatters organization. The league manager told me one official manages the scoreboard from a remote controller under a tent on the sidelines while the other four officials regulate activity on the field. They rotate clock control responsibilities during the day to make sure one of them always gets an extended break in the shade. I'm guessing, but the two sets of officials from each organization may have merged."

"That's smart. The officials spend a lot of time on their feet in Gulf Coast heat and humidity and, like today, in the rain. We don't want anyone to drop from heat exhaustion."

Dan passes me the logbook with extra-large spiral bound sheets to record game action. "I'm clueless about who we're playing," I say.

"The Pasadena Tiger Sharks. I also don't know much about their organization, except their Sophomore squad knocked Matthew's team out of the interleague playoffs last season."

"All right," I say under a masked smile. "Some extra juice for the Junior game today."

Dan focuses on my masked face and says, "I need to ask something else of you."

"You got it."

"You better hear the request first. All the parents, everyone I talk to, love the halftime stats. Nobody ever heard that being done before at youth football games, but some parents asked me if we can break out the performance stats for individual players."

"Ooh. That's tougher," I tell him. "Last season, I recorded the yards, down and distance, and a comment to describe the type of play. I'll have to focus on the field a beat longer to get a specific jersey number, record it with the yardage situation for each row, and total the stats on a player-by-player basis. I'll look at the game log sheets and see what I can work with."

While I scan the log sheet form, the lone male announcer in the booth concludes the Pee-Wee game with the pronouncement through the stadium speakers: **"The Pee-Wee game is over. The final score is Wildcatters 38 and Tiger Sharks 27."**

A man stands at the near-side 50-yard line and raises the football skyward. The soggy orange Astros T-shirt clings to his chest, and water drips from the brim of his Cats cap while he scans the stands.

"The game ball is going to be auctioned off now."

"Game over."

The Music Man enters the observation room before we stand up.

"The bidding starts at $50. Please wave to the league director on the field, and he will acknowledge your bid."

While the press box occupants conduct their conversations, the Freshman game announcer conducts his impassive auction of the game ball over the stadium speakers.

"Good morning. I'm Martin. Call me Marty. I'll be providing the music for today's games."

Dan rises, and his chair turtle-creeps toward the back wall. No handshake. Both men exchange nods accompanied by awkward waves.

"Glad to meet you. The league manager told me there's a professional to handle the music this season. I enjoyed what I heard during the Pee-Wee game. A lot more polished and timelier than what I did last season. Is that the kind of music you plan to play today?"

"I play many styles of music, classic rock or classic country or modern pop or hip hop or today's country, in many settings: bars, graduations, group outings.

For the diverse family crowd in this stadium venue, I'll play classic rock with an occasional country song thrown in."

I rocket both arms from the chair armrests toward the ceiling with a thumbs-up from each hand.

On the field, the person holding the ball overhead points to a spot halfway up the stands across from the north 20-yard line.

"We have a $50 bid. The next bid needs to be for $75."

"Sounds great," Dan says. "You must have a larger music selection than I played last year—snippets of songs for kickoffs or at the end of quarters. Oh, we need to play the anthem before the start of the Freshman game."

"Got it covered. I have an instrumental version I call up."

"We'll also need some birthday music. I make birthday announcements during the day, usually after the first quarter."

The adult male lifting the football skyward, the Ball Bearer, points to his right at a man who waves from the bottom of the stands near the south 40-yard line.

"There is a $75 bid. The next bid needs to be for $100."

"Got it covered. I have a Beatles song I can play during the announcement. I set the relative volumes so the mic in your booth talks over the music that plays through the stadium speakers. Holler whenever you're ready so I can queue it up."

"Sounds good. Also, it's rare, but if a boy on the field gets hurt, we go silent from the stadium speakers. All the boys on the field drop to one knee, and two coaches run out to tend to the injured kid. As the coaches escort the player off the field, I'll ask the crowd to give him a hand, and we restart from where we left off. The game keeps on keeping on."

Football Bearer swaps the ball from his left hand to his right hand. He gestures back toward the north 20-yard line.

"We have $100. We are now aiming for $125."

"Understood," the Music Man says. "Dead air is against my instincts, but I'll go mute during any injury timeout."

Football Bearer points to another person at the bottom of the stands near midfield.

"One hundred twenty-five. The next bid needs to be $150."

Football Bearer swings his head in slow motion across the stands, from left to right, from right to left. He raises both arms to the press box.

"Good," Dan says. "Again, glad you're here. If you need anything, let me know."

"Will do. Likewise, if you need special music at any point in the game, please give me a shout. Otherwise, I'll do my thing and enthrall the masses," Marty says with a smile.

"Sold! Thank you for your winning bid. Please pick up the game ball at the Wildcatters' table under the stands."

The Freshman squads, in their helmets and pads, congregate under the tents erected along their respective sidelines.

"Time to roll," Dan says.

"And to rock-n-roll," the Music Man yells as he returns to his booth.

The dad who announced the Pee-Wee game exits the announcer's booth. "Is Dan here?"

"Here."

"Morning. Everything in the booth is working fine. I have to find my wife and collect my boy," says Mystery Announcer. He shouts "good luck" as he exits the press box.

I watch him double-time it out the door. "I wonder if he's in a hurry." Then, to Dan, "Give me a second to wipe down the booth?"

"Go for it."

I race one Clorox wipe across the countertop and chair arms. Peel open a lined alcohol packet and use an alcohol wipe on the stadium microphone. A plastic zip-lock bag with several alcohol wipe packets is set next to the mic.

"That's good enough. Thanks."

Argh—I forgot to spray the cloth seat.

Dan plops into the chair in front of the mic, takes two deep breaths. **"I hope you are ready for some footbaaall! Wildcatters football! Welcome to Abshier Stadium on this rainy morning. Regardless of the weather, we have an impressive lineup of games today between the visiting Pasadena Tiger Sharks and our Deer Park Wildcatters. Thank you for being out here today to show your support for these young men. Playing in these conditions is all part of their character-building experience."**

Two girls from the Wildcatters spirit squad, each clasping a pole topped by the American flag, high-step from the near sideline toward the west along the midfield stripe. Ten yards in, they rotate 180 degrees in unison until they face the east stands.

"Before we start, I ask you to stand and remove your hats for our national anthem."

Dan rises to match my standing position. Caps off.

The Music Man sends the national anthem through the stadium speakers. The crowd rises as one, except for a single figure, a twenty-something years old woman who cuts across an empty row in front of my field of vision. Her fixed gaze to the north leads her next to a slender, bearded Black male of similar age. She sits beside him, and they rifle through an oversized faux-straw purse, the kind you might see at the beach. On the row in front of them, three Black children, all smaller than any kid who played in the Pee-Wee game, stand and face the flag. Two older Black gentlemen near my age stand along the row behind the young couple and focus their gaze to the American flag.

After the anthem ends, the crowd applauds and sits down. Dan follows suit and offers a personal message: **"Thank you for standing for our national anthem. It has a special meaning for me. My father served overseas during the Korean War. I have a brother who fought in Desert Storm. My son, an officer in active service in the army, serves overseas. Thank you again for showing your appreciation for those who served and those who serve now."**

The crack in Dan's voice draws my hand to his shoulder.

"Before the next game, I'm getting the names of those flag bearers. I want to give those girls a shout out for being here early in this drizzling rain and holding the flag during the anthem."

He looks down onto the field and refocuses on the mission objective. Parents tell us they love the enthusiastic broadcast and player name shout-outs from the voice in the sky. So do the boys on the field. We want to entertain all of them. Our inaugural COVID-19 game is coming up for this new, reformed league. I sure hope it goes well. We'll see.

Chapter Eight

Do Deeds of Youth

The Wildcatters along the far sideline—clad in maroon helmets, maroon jerseys with white gold-trimmed numbers, white padded pants—bob up and down like mismatched pistons in a revved-up engine, as though they each consumed varying amounts of pure sugar for breakfast. The rain and wind eliminate the inflatable helmet for the kids to charge through today, so the players jog straight from warm-ups to the sideline area near their maroon team canopy. Five maskless coaches, all with Wildcatter T-shirts and caps, cluster under the maroon team tent.

On the near sideline, the Tiger Shark players are also animated in their silver-gray helmets with jagged black stripes, black jerseys with gray numbers, and gray padded pants. Three maskless coaches squeeze between the kids and talk to separate groups of players about I-have-no-idea-what. Two other coaches face a third coach, all under the gray Tiger Shark tarp, as he addresses them.

I take a quick survey of the canopies and wonder what drives the color selections: a favorite color, the color of the current youth team you support, the color of your favorite pro team, the color of an alma mater, or the color associated with whatever tarp happens to be on sale. The count for the start of the Freshman game shows four gray, four maroon, four blue, one red and one white tarp erected. No pattern to canopy color and placement in the stands. Four times the number of umbrellas to tarps are scattered throughout the stands. Most umbrellas are idle, folded and leaning against the metal seat next to their owner.

Four officials, all in traditional shirts with vertical black and white stripes, black caps and black shorts with a vertical white stripe down each leg, stride to the center of the field. Each official wears a black cloth mask with a strap around each ear. None of the officials wear their clear see-through rain jackets. One official points to each sideline. The pre-game coin toss ritual begins once three players from each sideline reach the officials.

Most of these kids have "fake" bodies. The shoulder pads extend outside the frames of their eight-year-old bodies so much that their tucked-in jerseys fold inward like an under-tensioned sail. The jersey numbers scrunch together to make the individual digits difficult to identify.

"Keep an eye on the coin toss?" Dan asks.

"You got it." I watch the field and listen to nicknames for this Freshman squad as I hear them for the first time.

"Ladies and gentlemen, allow me to introduce our 2020 Freshman Wildcatter roster.

Number 2. George 'Chaos' Karr, *Line*-man!

Number 4. Walt 'Snake' Skinner, Wide receiver.

Number 10. Rylan 'Bull' Montoya, *Line*-man!

Number 11. Billy 'Killer B' Riker, *Line*-man!

Number 13. Joseph 'Golden' Shephard, *Line*-man!

Number 17. Ross 'Texas Terror' Taylor, *Line*-man!"

I focus my binoculars on the coin toss ceremony and record each captain's number in the margin of the game log sheet as they stride to the center of the field. The lead official lines up the captains to face one another. No handshakes. The player head bobs represent the verbal greeting between the captains. The official shows each captain the ceremonial coin and tosses the coin to his chest level. He retrieves it from the ground and shows the up-facing side to each hunched-over captain.

"Number 20. Tommy 'El Titi' Torres, Wide receiver.

Number 22. Herb 'The Hammer' Thaut, *Line*-man!

Number 23. James 'Angry Bird' Cobb, Quarterback.

Number 24. Robert 'Bulldozer' Dex, Running back.

Number 33. Mark 'Rhino' Reed, Running back.

Number 34. John 'Doomsday' Doggert, Running back."

The masked official aligns the team captains face-to-face: three Cat captains stand at the north 49-yard-line and face south, while three Tiger Shark captains stand at the south 49-yard line and face north. The lead official stands next to the nearest Cat captain, taps him on the shoulder pads and waves his arms, palms down, in front of his torso one time. He steps alongside the nearest Tiger Shark captain, extends both arms in front of his chest and draws his arms back to his body. The official claps his hands, and the captains jog to their respective sidelines.

"Number 35. Max 'Punisher' Guerra, *Line*-man!

Number 39. Andrew 'Hit Man' Reyes, *Line*-man!

Number 45. Paul 'Megatron' Morrow, Wide receiver.
Number 76. Jacob 'Attack' O'Neil, Quarterback.
Number 88. Victor 'Viper' Bergman, Wide receiver.
Number 99. Diego 'Destroyer' Barojas, *Line*-man!"

"Ready?"

"Fire away."

"Cat captains are 4, 23, and 76. Shark captains are 20, 45, and 61. We won the toss and deferred."

Dan jots the numbers on scratch paper as I relay them. "Got it."

He checks the roster sheet next to his mic and matches the jersey numbers to player names.

"Team captains for the Cats are Walt 'Snake' Skinner, James 'Angry Bird' Cobb, and Jacob 'Attack' O'Neil. Team captains for the Tiger Sharks are Carson 'Crackers' Bennett, Eddie 'E-Man' Ford, and Paul 'Iron Man' Zahn. The Cats won the toss and deferred their choice to the second half."

A traditional pre-game rocker, "Welcome to the Jungle," a song that threatens those who enter their jungle lair, blares from the stadium speakers.

"By the way, the normal pronunciation for 'j' in Hispanic names is an 'h' sound. I bet that last name is pronounced 'Bar-o-haus' instead of 'Bar-o-jas'."

"Hmm."

The Wildcatters form their kickoff unit with five players on each side of the kicker. The Tiger Sharks return team positions seven players along their 49-yard line, three players along their 40-yard line, and one player at the 30-yard line.

"Andrew 'Hit Man' Reyes kicking off for the Cats."

The stadium music stops when the lead official raises his right arm and draws it down to his side. Hit Man steps into the tee-mounted football and sends it bouncing past the midfield stripe. The erratic football ricochets among the Tiger Shark players like an imaginary self-awareness that refuses to be corralled. A trio of Tiger Sharks traps the football, and Bam Bam covers it.

"First and ten Tiger Sharks from their 43-yard line."

Independent, simultaneous activities prepare for the onset of conflict. In the booth, I record "43T" for ball location and "receive KO" under comments in the Tiger Shark section of the game log sheet, and I start the next line in the game log sheet line with "43" in the ball location cell and "1/10" in the down/distance cell.

On the field, the maskless chain gang sets up along the far sideline per the side judge's instructions. The rear pole sets at the starting football location on the 43 yard-line and the attached chain on the forward rod stretches ten yards to mark the first down line-to-make. The adult holding the box pole aligns it even with the ball position, with "1" shown in the box at the top of the pole.

Meanwhile, the Tiger Sharks form their attack unit with six offensive linemen, all crouched in the customary three-point stance to maximize leverage against their counterparts. The Cat defense employs five crouched linemen to combat the Tiger Shark line. Three linebackers stand several yards behind the linemen to reinforce them at the point of attack.

The center, Knuckles, anchors the offensive line. The Tiger Shark quarterback, E-Man, sets under center while two running backs, Machine Gun and Bam Bam, set seven yards behind the quarterback.

Two Tiger Shark wide receivers, each set fifteen yards on each side of the football, threaten the defense with the forward pass. Two Cat cornerbacks match against the wide receivers to counter the possible pass attempt while a Cat deep safety, set fifteen yards downfield, guards against potential explosive plays. One Cat cornerback, El Titi, locates twenty yards from the football, kneels into a three-point crouching position and leans toward the football. I smile at the faux pas.

"A 'split backs' formation, two wideouts."

"The Tiger Sharks open in a 'split backs' formation with two wide receivers."

Knuckles, the center, hikes the ball to his quarterback, E-Man.

E-Man spins left. Cradles the football in his left arm.

The Texas Terror slices through the offensive line. He strikes the quarterback mid-thigh.

E-Man spins away. He lunges forward behind his guard, Iron Man.

Iron Man leads E-Man into the heart of the Dart maroon jerseys.

Punisher and Chaos overwhelm E-Man.

"Quarterback keeper into the line. Stout defense! No gain on the play."

I close out the active line by inserting "20" into the player number cell and "0" in the yards gained cell. The next line starts with "43" in ball location cell and "2/10" under down/distance.

The Tiger Sharks conduct two more running plays to get into a fourth and long situation.

"Okay, Cats fans. That brings up a big fourth and eight to go for the first down. Let our dee-fense hear you!"

'Noculars are raised. Football is hiked. Play is run.

"Handoff to the tailback. Sweep around the left side. Stopped dead in his tracks! Great tackle! Diego 'The Destroyer' Barojas. The ball goes over on downs to the Cats."

"Well done, young man," I comment.

The active row ends, the future row starts.

"The Boys Are Back in Town," a song about wild young men causing mayhem when they get back into town, blasts from the stadium speakers.

Meanwhile, each team swaps out several players for their respective defensive and offensive squads. The Cats configure their offense: six linemen, two wide receivers, quarterback Angry Bird, fullback Bulldozer, and tailback Doomsday. The Tiger Sharks respond to the Cats with their defensive formation: five defensive linemen, three linebackers, two cornerbacks, and one deep safety.

At the same time, I close out the active row for the Tiger Sharks with a tick mark in the margin to note the end of the possession and start the next line, the first row of the Wildcatter's section of the log sheet, with "48T" for ball location and "1/10" for down/distance.

Before the snap, the far sideline official drops his yellow flag, unhooks his mask loop from one ear to blow his whistle, and then resets his mask. He puts his hands on his waist and points to the Cat side.

"We jumped."

"A penalty is a bad way to start our first possession," Dan says.

The lead official and the side judge confer. The lead official faces the press box, puts both hands on his hips, points to the Cat side, and moves the ball five yards backwards.

"False start by the Cats. That costs us five yards and brings up first and fifteen."

"One dad on Matthew's team—he used to be a high school football referee—told me last year we screwed up by calling out illegal procedure instead of 'encroachment' for the defense and 'false start' for the offense. I told him I'd get it right this year."

"Aah. That makes all the difference in the world," I say as I update the game log sheet. "Encroachment. False start. I'm all for being precise, but this always sounded to me like some committee got together to develop fancy language to describe a simple event to look smarter and more sophisticated than us commoners. 'Jumped early'"—as I flick my hands outward—"sounds fine to me. Whatever." Back to the field.

"Handoff to the tailback. John 'Doomsday' Doggert follows his full-back into the meat grinder over the right guard. Tough running picks up five yards on the play. Second and ten coming up."

The Cats exchange running backs for the offensive huddle. Meanwhile, I finish the active row and start the future row.

During the next play, "Problem with the snap."

"Fumble! Quarterback drops on the ball. That brings up third and eleven."

"Man, if we can't even snap the ball to the quarterback, then it will be one long game." I state the obvious as I complete the active line and start the next line in the game log sheet. One Cat player, Megatron, sprints to the offensive huddle from the far sideline while one player, Viper, sprints off in a reverse race between the huddle and sideline.

'Noculars are raised. Football is hiked. Play is run.

"Handoff to the tailback. Sweep right...Dragged down at the 35-yard line. Robert 'Bulldozer' Dex with the carry."

The active row is finished, the future row is started.

Again, two Cat players, Rhino and Doomsday, race past each other as though they are running a 40-yard dash in opposite directions. After the substitute player huddles with the rest of his teammates, the group breaks apart into their offensive formation.

"Handoff to the tailback around the left side."

"He's got some room."

"He turns the corner! Shoved out of bounds inside the 20-yard line. Fine run by John 'Doomsday' Doggert."

"How many yards?"

"Sixteen."

"Sixteen yards on the play. And that is enough for another Cats...First Dooown!"

The officials wait an extra beat to give the chain gang a chance to re-spot the yards-to-make poles between the 19 and 9-yard lines. The box pole holder, with the pole set at the 19-yard line, flips the down indicator from "3" to "1."

"This Tiger Shark defense doesn't look well coached," I comment.

"Oh?"

"On every play, only the players in the direct path of the ball carrier react. Everyone else stands around and watches."

"These are a bunch of eight-year-old kids. You can cut them some slack," Dan says.

"Heck, no. Swarm to the ball. Swarm! Swarm!"

"Hah."

The next play features a quarterback keeper by Angry Bird behind Hammer and Punisher into the right side of the line.

"Quarterback keeper over the right side. Fighting for every yard...He refuses to go down...James 'Angry Bird' Cobb. Gain of 13 yards on the play. And that is enough for another Cats...First Dooown!"

"Impressive run," I say. "The kid fought through three tacklers to get to a first-and-goal situation from the six-yard line."

A Tiger Shark coach yells from the near sideline toward his kids at the south end zone, raises his left arm and swats at the air across the front of his face. The three Tiger Shark linebackers creep toward the line of scrimmage.

"Oooh." A low, steady groan seeps from under my mask as I exhale.

"Fumble on the snap! The ball is...officials signal...Tiger Shark ball. First and ten Tiger Sharks from their own five-yard line."

One black jersey raises the ball over his head and hands it to the official. His teammates slap his shoulder pads while the Cats players trudge back to their far sideline.

An up-tempo, blues-based song, "Black Betty"—with stanzas that each end with a verbal expression of a firearm discharge—blasts from the stadium speakers.

I close out the active line with the turnover noted in the comment section as the two squads reverse rolls and the Tiger Sharks become the attackers against the Cats defenders. Start the next row of the Tiger Shark section of the game log sheet to document their possession of the football.

I shake my head a few times. "Drive down the field and turn the ball over...on the brink of a touchdown."

"On the positive side," Dan says, "hold them here and we'll be in prime field position for another chance to score. In this case, I'm glad the teams aren't allowed an elective punt declaration to move the ball 30 yards downfield like the Pee-Wee teams. The Tiger Sharks have four plays to make a first down, or we get the ball back in the 'red zone' inside their 20-yard line."

"Assuming they don't have a real punter, which is not likely at this age."

The Tiger Sharks quarterback, E-Man, dives into the Cats defensive line for three plays for a net yardage of minus one. The fourth down play starts at the Tiger Shark 3-yard line.

"Come on, Cats fans! On your feet! Let our defense hear you!"

The lead official waves his hands overhead, turns to the end zone behind the Tiger Shark offense and extends both arms outward.

"Odd time for a timeout. You can't stall. The game clock drives you to run a play."

"Beats me," I say. "Their timeout chokes off the crowd enthusiasm, so you need to wind them up again."

"Okay, Cats fans! Get wound up again! For our boys—shout it out: Dee-fense! Dee-fense!"

The Tiger Sharks run another quarterback keeper. E-Man turns away from the offensive line, runs five yards into the end zone and drops to one knee. The official next to the quarterback raises both arms skyward and presses his palms together.

"Safety! Two points for the Cats. The Tiger Sharks will kick off to the Cats."

"I didn't see that one coming," Dan says. "I should have. The Tigers surrender two sure points now instead of an almost certain six points a minute from now."

After the Tiger Sharks kick from their 20-yard line, the Cats force their way across the Tiger Shark end zone a score of Wildcatters 9, Tiger Sharks 0. Both teams conduct run-heavy game plans and keep the game clock rolling down to halftime.

The press box door scrapes open a few minutes before halftime and two women climb into the main observation room. They wave at us through the plexiglass window between the observation room and announcer's booth. Each one wears a cloth mask. One mask mirrors the Tiger Shark uniform motif, white cloth with a gray border and jagged gray stripes from the ears to the mouth. The other mask consists of a light gray cloth with a pink border, decorated by multi-sized, multicolor dots stitched across the face. Both masks puff out and deflate like bellows as the two women exhale and inhale to catch their breath. The shorter of the two, Tiger Mask, calls to in gasps us from the doorway. "Hello. We're here to direct the Tiger Shark ladies' spirit team."

Dan twists around. "This is the right spot. We will be out of here in..."—he glances back to the scoreboard—"sixty-eight seconds."

"Whew. It's quite a climb," she comments as the pace of her mask inflations drops to the point where they aren't noticeable.

We nod our heads in agreement.

"I may need some help with our music. I have it loaded on my phone, but I don't know how to send music through the stadium speakers."

"You're in luck," I tell her. "We have an audio expert in the booth next door." She slides to the adjacent doorway and converses with the Music Man.

"And that is the end of the first half. The halftime score is our home Wildcatters 9 and the visitor Tiger Sharks 0. Please stay in your seats for the upcoming spirit team halftime show."

***

The lead official collects the football, and all four officials stride to a designated, covered area under the northeast side of the stadium. Meanwhile, both teams jog to their respective dressing rooms to regroup for the second half, the Cats to the southwest home dressing team room under the stands and the Tiger Sharks to their northeast visitor dressing room.

We exit single file through the booth doorway so the two women can enter. Polka Dot Mask drops into the chair in front of the mic. Dan rolls a second chair into the booth for Tiger Mask and receives a "thank you." The Music Man steps into the booth as soon as Dan exits. He attaches a three-foot long cord from the phone to a second port on the stadium electronics receiver. Polka Dot Mask gives him an appreciative nod and turns her attention to the field. Music Man lingers at the doorway until Polka Dot Mask triggers the drill team music.

"Good morning, ladies and gentlemen. We are happy to be here today and hope our performance brings sunshine to this gray day."

I have to smile at an introduction that cheesy.

"Please give a warm welcome to the 2020 Pasadena Spirit."

I roll a chair to the observation room counter and concentrate on the game log sheets in front of me. Dan, engrossed by the glow from his cell phone, stands in the middle of the observation room and stabs his fingers into the phone as fast as a professional stenographer types.

"Ladies, here is your music."

A youthful male voice croons from the stadium speakers, a song where he tells a girl how she's beautiful, more than she realizes. I've never heard this song, so it must be a twenty-first century tune.

Two lines of girls, eight to a line, march hands-on-hips from the near sideline along the north and south 45-yard lines. Each girl—in a white pleated skirt with gold trim at the bottom and along the waist, a light gray top with "Spirit" written in black—clutches two black-and-silver tinseled pom-poms. After the lead girl reaches the middle of the field, the girls in the two parallel lines march-in-place for several seconds, stop, and spin in unison to face the east press box. Every other girl in each line takes a stretch-step to her side so each figure is visible from the east stands. The ladies freeze in place with pom-poms on their hips. This squad exhibits less variation in height compared to most of the teams I've seen.

"Here are the ladies of our 2020 Pasadena Spirit squad."

Polka Dot Mask calls out the names of each girl on the field. At every name pronouncement, a girl raises both arms overhead, shakes her pom-poms, and returns to a hands-on-hips ready position. Each girl has a pink ribbon attached to their hair. One girl's ribbon flaps several inches off her head in the stiff southerly breeze.

I tackle the game statistics summary while the name introductions are in progress. For team performance, look at each team's possession and total the differences between starting position and the final ball location. List the jersey number of every player who carried the football and total each player's yardage.

Dan sets his phone on the counter. "I want to wipe down the outside of the windows. Between the inside air conditioning and the outside humidity, the bottoms of the windows are fogging up."

Nodding toward the bag of cleaning supplies on the counter, I tell Dan: "I brought some paper towels if you need them."

"I might. Let me check to see if we have anything else here that I can use." He trudges down the hall while I compile the individual player yardage. He returns within a minute. "Look what I found," he says while his right hand grasps "a squeegee." The words "Press Box" are marked along the three-foot long wood handle. "I found it in a closet in the far observation room." Dan tears a few paper towels off the roll and scrapes open the press box door.

The next song, by a dynamic female vocalist who cries out she's a champion, not going to be held down, ready to roar, triggers the girls to reconfigure into their original two lines that face the east press box. I like the song, but I have no idea of the song's title or singer.

The synchronized arm motions suggest a mechanical device with eight pistons along a single rod. The girls bend their elbows to hold both pom-poms together in front of them, arms level with shoulder. They rotate through a series of flying "V" and "T" and "I" figures. After two minutes, the girls rest with pom-poms on their hips.

"Clomp!"

The rubber blade of the squeegee slaps against the observation room window. The visible top of Dan's cap anchors the view of the squeegee as it squeals down the window to drag the droplets away. He steps two feet to his left and repeats the process to capture more of the unwiped window.

"Clomp!"

He slides outside my field of vision in under a minute. While Dan's outside, I total the number of carries and yards gained for every ball carrier.

A hip-hoppish song, where multiple male and female singers throw out "boom" and "pow" vocals, sends the girls into a single-line formation that faces the press box. Another twenty-first century song I can't recognize.

The girls toss their pom-poms to the turf behind them and clasp shoulders for a synchronized leg kick routine. The loose ribbon from one girl's bow flaps against the adjacent girl's cheek. If she wanted to, the downwind girl could grab the flapper with her teeth. To her credit, the girl downwind of the fluttering ribbon maintains focus and conducts the routine in sync with the others.

Behind the line of girls, several pom-poms roll like black-and-silver tumbleweeds across the green turf toward the north end of the field. Meanwhile, each girl alternates her legs in a sequence of front kicks—man, I couldn't make those kicks at any age. After the kick sequence, they return to arms to hips. The girls' chests heave as they catch their breath after the exertion, but less so than the occupants of the announcer's booth after a climb to the press box.

Their return to ready position corresponds to the start of a song I recognize, a remixed version of the classic rocker, "While You See a Chance."

The press box door scrapes open as Dan re-enters the observation room. "All right, that takes care of the windows down the press box."

I stand to hand him a list of individual and team stats from a page torn from my record book. My chair creeps back to the wall as he tosses the squeegee on the counter and scans the info.

"Thanks, man. This is great."

"No problem."

Several girls scramble downfield to retrieve their pom-poms and reposition themselves into one of two groups. Four girls squat down in a diamond pattern at midfield and pile their pom-poms in the center. Other girls surround the central group to represent the hour markings around a clockface. The interior group reclines to perform synchronized leg movements. The outside group performs arm motions that hurl the pom-poms upward or outward in a sequential pattern that rotates clockwise and then counterclockwise.

"FYI—the team total yardage doesn't match the sum of the player yards. Penalty yards account for the offset."

"Got it."

After the music ends, the girls scream and charge off to the east sideline en masse. The entire crowd applauds, while the ardent devotees stand, clap, and cheer to honor the performance.

One adult male leans against the railing that borders the sideline area behind the Tiger Shark tarp with a camcorder the size of a football to record the girl's performance. The position puts him about ten feet above field level. I presume he wants to get as close a view as possible instead of a more general view from higher in the stands. The camcorder surprises me since I haven't seen one in decades.

Four masked game officials stride from the northeast side of the stadium toward midfield. The Cat players snake from the southwest corner of the stadium to their gray canopy on the west sideline. The Tiger Shark players, in groups of two to four, meander along the east sideline to their tent near the midfield stripe.

"Nice job, ladies," Dan says to the two women after they exit the announcer's booth.

Two nods and a "thank you" from Polka Dot Mask and Tiger Mask are the replies.

"And thank you for wearing masks," I add.

"Of course. We want everyone to be safe. See you at the next halftime." The press box door scrapes against the floor as they depart.

***

Dan plops down in his customary spot in front of the mic. He sneezes twice in rapid succession.

“Bless you.”

"What is that scent? A dull, minty odor...lavender? I sure hope I'm not allergic," Dan says.

“I smell nothing. I bet the exposure to Clorox this morning knocked out my nose receptors. I always take an allergy pill when I spend several hours away from home, so I brought some extras if you need one,” I say while nudging the box of anti-viral tissues toward the mic.

"No, the tissues are fine."

I return the extra chair to the back wall and reclaim my spot to Dan's left.

"Please give another round of applause to the Pasadena Spirit drill team. Excellent job, ladies!

"Now, some unofficial halftime stats for you. The Cats had three possessions with 16 plays for 134 yards and one touchdown. Quarterback James 'Angry Bird' Cobb led the way with six carries for 70 yards and one touchdown. John 'Doomsday' Doggert with four carries for 28 yards, Robert 'Bulldozer' Dex with three carries for 15 yards, Mark 'Rhino' Reed

with two carries for 17 yards, and Jacob 'Attack' O'Neil with one carry for 4 yards."

Dan swigs down a few gulps of water. **"For the visiting Tiger Sharks, they had three possessions with 14 plays and 42 yards. Leading rushers were Carson 'Crackers' Bennett with six carries for 12 yards, Eddie 'E-Man' Ford with four carries for 18 yards, Bill 'Bam-Bam' Adams with three carries for 11 yards, and Caleb 'Machine Gun' Hobbes with one carry for 7 yards."**

The kickoff music, "Ridin' the Storm Out," a song about inclement weather with the allegorical theme of resistance to hard times, fills the stadium.

"I'm glad the rain's held off. Almost nothing since this morning."

"Clouds still hang heavy around the stadium, but so far, so good," Dan says.

The Cats send out five players along their 49-yard line, four to their 40-yard line and two at their 30-yard line for the kick return squad. The Tiger Shark kickoff unit uses the conventional five players on either side of the kicker.

"Cats to receive the second half kickoff."

"Can you see who's kicking?"

"Number 38."

Dan scans the visitor roster. "There is no thirty-eight."

I take another look through the binoculars. "The kicker's jersey number is squished together. Maybe...thirty-six?"

"Perry 'Flash' Brown kicking off for the Tiger Sharks."

After the lead referee rotates his right arm to signal the start of game play, the music stops and Flash punches the football across the ground past midfield. The ball bounces off a Cats' maroon jersey and falls to the turf a few feet in front of him. Punisher pounces on the ball at the 39-yard line before two black jerseys hurl themselves on top of him.

"Max 'Punisher' Guerra on the ball. First and ten Cats from their 39-yard line."

Eleven Cats players huddle at their 30-yard line. The Cats break from their huddle and jog to the line of scrimmage to form the same I-formation attack configuration as in the first half. The Tiger Sharks counter the Cats' formation with five crouching defensive linemen, three linebackers, two cornerbacks, and one deep safety. At the same time, I update the game log sheet to reflect that the Cats recovered the kick at their 39-yard line and start the next line for the upcoming play. Per referee instructions, the chain gang sets their poles to mark ball location and distance to make the first down.

On first down, the quarterback Angry Bird takes the opening snap of the second half. Cradles the ball in both arms. He curls behind the two running backs, Doomsday and Rhino, toward the right side of the line of scrimmage.

The defensive end penetrates the line and strikes the quarterback on his left shoulder. The blow spins Angry Bird around, but he regains his balance and continues forward.

Doomsday peels to the right to block the cornerback.

Rhino peels to his left to sort-of block the linebacker.

Angry Bird slants toward the sideline until the free safety shoves him out of bounds—a well-executed play for a bunch of eight-year-old boys.

"Quarterback keeper around the right side. He breaks a tackle! James 'Angry Bird' Cobb."

"How many yards?"

"I can't tell what yard line."

"Spotted at the Tiger...forty-seven," he says.

"That's 14 yards."

"Fourteen yards on the play. Enough for a Cats'...First Dooown!"

The portly dads who manipulate the yardage chains scramble downfield to set their pole markers per referee directions before the ball is snapped.

"What the ...?"

A mishmash of several black jerseys, maroon helmets, gray helmets, and maroon jerseys form a pile at the middle of the 47-yard line. The sideline referees wave their hands overhead while they sprint toward the pile. The official who spots himself behind the defense runs to the pile and drops to his knees to determine which color jersey has the ball. He points north.

"Fumble. Recovered by the Cats."

"There must have been a fumble on the snap," Dan says.

"Beats me. I plain missed it."

After Rhino gains six yards and Angry Bird gets stuffed at the line of scrimmage, Dan asks, "Is it fourth down now?"

"Yes."

"Thought so. The down indicator shows third down."

I train my binoculars to the far sideline chain gang. "C'mon dad. Show some snap. Change the card to fourth down." The side judge notices the error and holds up four fingers to the placard holder, who flips the indicator to "4."

"Big fourth down play coming up for our Cats. Four yards needed. Let our boys hear you, Cats fans!"

The Tiger Shark linemen, down in a three-point crouch, each rock their extended leg back-and-forth. The three linebackers creep closer to the line of scrimmage.

"Quarterback dive into the right side. He has a hole! Gain of eight yards on the play. That is enough for another Cats...First Dooown!"

"Good blocking on that run," I comment.

"Sure was. Oh...I got too excited and forgot to call out the quarterback's name."

"I suspect you'll have more chances."

Before the next play, collision along the line of scrimmage. The masked far side official drops his yellow flag and waves his arms overhead as he runs toward the ball. He leans over to the masked lead official, who turns to the press box, puts both hands on his hips, and points to the Tiger Shark side.

"Encroachment, defense. That will cost the Tiger Sharks five yards. First down and five to go for the Cats from the 28-yard line."

'Noculars are raised. Football is hiked. Play is run.

"Handoff to the tailback around right end. Gain of 11 yards! John 'Doomsday' Doggert! And that is enough for another Cats...First Dooown!"

The active row ends, the future row starts.

'Noculars are raised. Football is hiked. Play is run.

"Quarterback sweep to the right."

"Ooh. Nowhere to run, so he runs backward. We lost...what...12 yards," I comment.

"Fine defense by the Tiger Sharks. That brings up second and long."

"I'm sure not going to shout out a player after a big negative play," Dan says.

Two members of the chain gang stay at the first down ball location. The rear post stands at the original first down ball location at the 20-yard line and the forward post at the 10-yard line. The far sideline official directs the football location/down marker post to the 32-yard line with "2" showing on the down placard. Meanwhile, I finish the active line and start the future line.

After a short gain by fullback Bulldozer, the Cat coach calls for a quarterback keeper.

Bull hikes the football to quarterback Angry Bird.

Angry Bird sweeps left along the line of scrimmage.

Run! Don't wait for Hot Wheels to lead the way, just run.

Megatron blocks the cornerback while Destroyer makes a pile to slow the interior Tiger Shark defense.

Angry Bird cuts between Megatron and Destroyer.

He streaks down the sideline!

E-Man and the other Tiger Sharks can't catch Angry Bird.

"Quarterback sweep around the left end. Free down the sideline! He's at the 20...the 10...Touchdooown! James 'Angry Bird' Cobb! Thirty yards on the play."

"This can be an amazing game," Dan says. "A kid makes a bonehead play two plays earlier and atones for it with a touchdown run his next chance to carry the football."

"That's the way to finish a drive. We hold the football for most the quarter, overcome penalties and negative plays, and cap off the drive with a touchdown."

The special team units trot onto the field for the extra point attempt under the celebratory song from the stadium speakers. "Rock and Roll All Nite" promises to make everyone shout and drive us all crazy.

The Cats form up with eight offensive linemen, a quarterback, and two running backs. The Tiger Sharks counter the Cats with eight defensive linemen and three linebackers behind the middle players in their line. At the same time, I complete the active line in the game log sheet with "+6" circled for emphasis and start the next log sheet line for the upcoming extra point attempt.

"Recap?"

"Hit me."

"Excluding penalties, 9 plays, 61 yards, 28 yards on the TD run."

"Got it," Dan says after he jots down the numbers. The Big Voice relays the scoring drive recap while the players align in their standard offensive formation before the extra point attempt.

"Quarterback sneak. Pile at the goal line. Officials indicate...in for the score! That makes the score Cats 16, Tiger Sharks 0."

The relentless guitars from "Long Train Runnin'" fill the stadium while I complete the active log sheet row with "+1" circled for emphasis. Players from each squad jog back to their respective sidelines and crisscross with those who jog onto the field for the kickoff.

"Andrew 'Hit Man' Reyes kicking off for the Cats."

The music stops as the referee at midfield lifts his right arm high and tugs it down. Dan and I focus our binoculars on the field to see Hit Man bounce the football past the midfield stripe.

A Tiger Shark player, Machine Gun, scoops up the ball and hurtles toward the onrushing Cats.

The Texas Terror and Doomsday drag down Machine Gun short of midfield.

"Nice return by Caleb 'Machine Gun' Hobbs. First and ten Tiger Sharks from their own 49-yard line."

"These guys don't have any speed. Hard to see them catching us now."

"Agreed," Dan says. "But the game can be unpredictable at this age, and we still have more than a quarter left."

The Tiger Sharks arrange their offense in a split backfield formation with two wide receivers. The Cats counter with five crouched defensive linemen, three linebackers, two cornerbacks, and a lone deep safety.

"Handoff to the tailback. Driven down at the line of scrimmage! Tackle by Diego 'The Destroyer' Barojas."

Dan still pronounces the "j."

Two more short runs lead to fourth down.

"Quarterback keeper. Gang tackled at the 45-yard line. And that brings up fourth down and four yards to go. Come on, Cats fans. Stand up! Yell! Clap your hands! Pound those metal seats you are sitting on! Let our Cat defense hear you!"

The mask stifles my chuckles.

"Handoff to the tailback. Stopped! Stopped short! The official signals...Cat's ball!"

I complete the active line for the Tiger Shark section of the second half log sheet and start the next line for the beginning of the Cat's possession.

The rest of the contest proceeds in a similar grind-it-out manner. The final score: Cats 16, Tiger Sharks 0.

"Okay, a fun game to watch," I say. "Our Cat Freshman squad doesn't have any speed burners, but they did all right."

"Yeah. Fumbles made it frustrating at times, but the wet weather had a hand in it. The unpredictability keeps me interested in every play."

The Freshman players march along each side of the 50-yard line in the customary display of sportsmanship. Helmets bob toward the other side of the midfield stripe. No hands touch.

One of the more recognizable opening guitar riffs in classic rock introduces an eerie song of eternal love and death. "Don't Fear the Reaper" streams from the stadium speakers.

Dan looks at me and bobs his head to the tune. "I recognize that song. It has to be twenty years, at least, since I last heard it."

"BOC is one of my all-time favorite groups. When I lived in Louisiana, I caught them whenever they rolled through Baton Rouge. It's great to listen to them again."

Dan's phone vibration informs him of a text message. "Time to auction off the game ball."

"We hope you enjoyed watching the Freshman Tiger Sharks versus the Freshman Wildcatters. We're going to auction off the game ball now. Please signal to our league manager waving the football overhead at the near-side 50-yard line. Remember, bidding is open to anyone from either team. Who will give us $50?"

A man at the near-side, 50-yard line raises the football skyward. He's easy to spot since his orange Astros T-shirt and Cats cap contrasts against the green artificial turf. The football bearer scans the stands before he shouts and points into the stands at his lower left.

"I have $50 at the lower north 20-yard line. Looking for $100 now."

The Ball Bearer shouts and points to the stands above the initial bidder.

"We have $100 from the middle, north 30-yard line. Who will give us $150? Only one fifty for this lifetime memory."

Another shout and point, this time, to the upper right area of the stands under the press box.

"We have one hundred fifty from the upper, north 40-yard line. Looking for $200 now. Only $200 for a lifelong memory. I have one myself and I have never regretted owning my game football."

The Ball Bearer yells and points back to the original bidder.

"We have $200. Looking for two fifty now. Will anyone give us $250? A small amount for a lifetime memory. Going once...Put it on your mantle. Put it on your bookshelf. Put it in your trophy case. Going twice...Last call for the game ball..."

The Ball Bearer shouts and lifts both arms skyward.

"Sold! Thank you, sir. You can collect the football at the Cats organization table under the stands."

"All right. Time to get ready for the Sophomore game," Dan says. "I hope it goes as smoothly as this one."

"Don't they all?"

Chapter Nine

Of Thunder and Lightning Heard

The most recognizable opening guitar riffs for any song in the classic rock genre thunder from the stadium speakers. Twelve distinct chords—enhanced as an additional guitar layers over the initial guitar, followed by drums that pound into the mix—introduce the male vocalist who recounts the fiery destruction of a concert venue, highlighted by the song's title "Smoke on the Water."

Four officials stride to midfield beneath the guitar onslaught.

"What can you tell me about these teams?" I ask.

"We wouldn't have a Sophomore team without a league merger. The Wildcatter roster shows only sixteen players, and half are from last year's Dart team. The Freshman Darts fielded a weak team. They ended last season with a losing record, so I hope the combined Sophomore team with the Wildcatters is stronger."

The Sophomore Cats, in their maroon helmets and jerseys, assemble in front of their tent between the forty-yard lines on the far side of the field. Several players bounce on the balls of their feet while others sway from side-to-side against their neighbors. A quick headcount confirms sixteen players. The visiting Tiger Sharks, clad in gray and black, form a mass at the near sideline between the field boundary to under their tent. I estimate twenty-two players in uniform.

At the official's signal, three players emerge from each sideline and stride to the center of the field for the ceremonial coin toss. Their jersey numbers, when exposed to the press box, are easy to make out. I record the numbers in the margin of the game log sheet.

The music fades as Dan depresses the mic button to begin the game announcement. **"I hope you are ready for some footbaaall! Wildcatters football! Welcome to Abshier Stadium for today's Sophomore game between the Pasadena Tiger Sharks and the Deer Park Wildcatters. Fingers crossed,**

the weather will cooperate as we expect to see a great game between these two squads."

The lead official lines each trio across from one another. No handshakes, but head bobs are visible among the team captains.

"Allow me to introduce our 2020 Sophomore Cat roster."

As Dan starts the roster roll call, many names are unrecognizable to me. I mean, they are cool nicknames—Predator, Cheetah, The Blade, Blitz, Bone Crusher—but I don't recall them from last season. Most are likely associated with the original Cats Freshman team.

The official shows both sides of the ceremonial coin to each team captain. A visiting captain calls "heads" or "tails." The official flips the coin to head level and lets it fall to the turf. He picks up the coin and shows its exposed face to each captain.

As Dan proceeds down the roster, I recognize some nicknames: Prime Time, Hot Wheels, Hot Sauce, Dynamite, and Gorilla. I'm glad to hear Prime Time's name for quarterback. I hope the Cats contributed some dynamic players to work with him this season.

The official lines up the Tiger Shark captains along the south 49-yard line and has them face north. Opposing team captains align at the north 49-yard line and face south. The official taps the nearest Cat captain on the shoulder pads and gives a single arm-wave parallel to the ground. He moves beside a Tiger Shark captain, extends his arms in front of his body, and draws them back to his torso. The official claps his hands and says something to the boys, who then jog off the field.

The official unfastens his mask from one ear after the boys head back to their respective sidelines.

"Ready?"

"Shoot."

"Team captains for Cats are 10, 72, 90. Captains for Sharks are 17, 34, 44. Cats won the toss and deferred."

"Got it."

Dan scans the rosters. **"Team captains for our Cats are Dave 'Prime Time' Nunez, Isaac 'Bone Crusher' Martinez, and Will 'Gorilla' Robbins. Captains for the Tiger Sharks are Carl 'Ace' Throme, Lee 'Lockdown' Lassiter and Eric 'Bullrush' Evans. The Cats won the toss and deferred their choice to the second half. Tiger Sharks will receive the opening kickoff."**

A song honoring those about to take part in a communal event, such as a rock concert or, in this case, a sporting event, echoes throughout the stadium: "For Those About to Rock."

A Tiger Shark coach stands at the near 40-yard sideline marker and taps the shoulder of each of his eleven special team players as they jog past him, single-file, onto the field. The Tiger Sharks tactical alignment places five players along their 49-yard line, four along their 40-yard line, and two at their 30-yard line. The Cat kickoff unit displays the traditional alignment of five players spaced on each side of the kicker.

"Cooper 'Monster' Hawks kicking off for the Cats."

The official at midfield points to Monster. He propels the football in a line-drive to a Tiger Shark receiver.

Bullrush knocks the ball down with his chest, scoops it off the green carpet and charges up the field.

The Cats charge at Bullrush.

Predator and Monster knock Bullrush to the turf.

"Eric 'Bullrush' Evans returns the ball for the Tiger Sharks. First and ten from their 48-yard line."

For their part of the simultaneous activities for game play, the Tiger Shark offense configures their attack in a standard double-wing formation: seven crouched offensive linemen, two receivers or wingbacks offset behind each outer end of the line, tailback Bullrush and quarterback Ace. The Cats organize their defense behind five defensive linemen with three linebackers set several yards behind the linemen. The two cornerbacks line up opposite the two receivers. One deep safety positions himself fifteen yards in front of the football. While the teams line up, the chain gang sets their poles along the far sideline per referee instructions to complete pre-snap preparations. In the booth, I record the kickoff in the first row of the game log sheet and note ball location and down/distance for the upcoming play.

"Handoff to the tailback. Stopped in the backfield! John 'Hollywood' Archer with the *crushing* tackle for the Cats. Second and long coming up."

The active row ends, the future row starts.

'Noculars are raised. Football is hiked. Play is run.

"Quarterback keeper around the left end. Pushed out of bounds across midfield."

"Their quarterback looks as quick as a startled squirrel," I comment.

"How many yards?"

"Let's see...spotted at the Cats 43 yard-line. That's 11 yards."

"Gain of 11 yards on the play. Carl 'Ace' Throme the ball carrier. Third down and two for the Tiger Sharks."

Two Tiger Shark players streak past each other, one to the huddle and one to the sideline. For third down, the Tiger Sharks quarterback rolls out and throws an incomplete pass twenty yards down the sideline. Fourth down coming up.

"Make some noise, Cats' fans. It's fourth down. Let our defense hear you!"

On fourth down, Golden Boy hikes the football to Ace.

Ace wheels right in a broad arc behind tailback Bullrush.

Ace plants right leg and cuts hard left. He swings around the right end.

"Quarterback keeper around the right end."

Bullrush blows into Smash, the Cat linebacker.

Ninja, the Tiger Shark wide receiver, battles Red Rocket, the Wildcatter cornerback.

Ace splits the gap.

"Oh, no."

Ace outraces the free safety. Nothing but alternating shades of green turf to the end zone.

"He's free down the sideline! The 30...the 20...10...Touchdown! Carl 'Ace' Throme. Forty-three yards for the score."

"Man, that kid is fast," Dan says. "Our defense doesn't have anyone on the field who can keep up with him."

"I take it back. He's closer to speedy cheetah than a quick squirrel."

The Tiger Sharks line up for the extra point attempt from the three-yard line. The Sharks deploy a trips left formation: six offensive linemen, three wide receivers split to the same left side, one quarterback and a lone running back. To oppose them, the Cats form up with six defensive linemen, two linebackers along the goal line and three cornerbacks to match the wide receivers.

Curious. One Sharks crouched lineman—line person—has a single braid of hair that extends from the helmet along the back to the waist.

"Girls are allowed to enroll in tackle football. Right?"

"Of course."

"I see a girl on the special teams line. Two to the left of the center."

Dan grabs his binoculars. "You're right. Number 70 with the ponytail." He scans the roster: "Sarah 'El Jefe' Herrera. I hope she makes a play so we can give her a shout out."

"You mean 'Heff-ay' not 'Jeff-ee'. I'll keep an extra eye out for their Number 70." Since I need to focus on the ball carrier, I doubt I can follow a specific offensive line player. I'll try.

"Quarterback...drops back to pass. Throw to his left...Incomplete! The extra point is no good. The score is Tiger Sharks 6 and Cats 0, with the Cats' turn with the football coming up."

"I'm glad he threw the ball. He could have walked around the right end for the score."

"Seems like their coach wants to work on the passing game. I wish I got the number of the nearest Cat cornerback. I would have given him a shout out."

"Recap?"

"Shoot."

"Four plays, 52 yards, 43 yards on the TD."

"Scoring drive summary. Fifty-two yards on four plays, capped off by a 43-yard touchdown run."

The best-ever rock cover of a Dylan song, featuring a dynamic guitarist with allegorical lyrics on the turmoil of social change, erupts from the stadium speakers as the Music Man plays "All Along the Watchtower."

While each side sends out their special team players for the upcoming kick-off, Dan yells to the adjacent booth, "Hey, Marty. We have a couple of birthday announcements. I want to do them at the end of the first quarter."

"I'll be ready," the Music Man hollers back.

"A public service reminder," the Big Voice declares. **"We are responsible for keeping the stadium clean today. Please help us out by putting your trash in one of the receptacles located at the entry ramps and under the stadium stands. Thank you in advance for your cooperation."**

The Tiger Sharks align five players on either side of the kicker along the south 40-yard line. In contrast, the Cats deploy five players at the north 49-yard line, four at the 40-yard line, and two at the 30-yard line.

"Lee 'Lockdown' Lassiter kicking off for the Tiger Sharks."

The lead official points to the kicker. Lockdown quick-steps to the football and drives it into the ground toward the near sideline. The football bounces once at the 42-yard-line, once at the 47-yard line and pops several feet high as it angles toward the near midfield sideline.

"Onside kick!"

The Wildcatter in front of the bouncing ball, The Ringer, drops to both knees to corral the ground ball. As the second bounce lifts the football above his head level, he raises both arms skyward, imploring the football to drop into his open hands. He does not extend his arms across the midfield stripe. As soon as the ball meets the 50-yard line, the Ringer's fingers clip the football, and two onrushing Tiger Sharks, Ninja and Be Nice, slam into him. The ball pops free. Be Nice crawls on the rolling football.

"And the Tiger Sharks recover the football!"

"Onside kicks never work. They executed that kick to perfection," Dan says.

"I feel for our Cat in front of the ball. He showed discipline by focusing on the football while the black jerseys bore down on him. The players and football converged at the same time. Splat"—I slap my hands together—"and ball loose."

"Fine special teams play from the Tiger Sharks. Gary 'Be Nice' Boltar recovered the football. First and ten Tiger Sharks from the Cats' 48-yard line."

The rout is on. At halftime, the scoreboard shows Tiger Sharks 26, Cats 0. The score could have been more lopsided except the Tiger Sharks insert offensive linemen as running backs late in the second quarter. Their final possession ends inside the Cats' 10-yard line.

Two minutes before halftime, the press box door scrapes open and draws our attention to the two women who step into the observation room. Tiger Mask and Polka Dot Mask wave to us. Their masks blow outward and suck inward as they exhale and inhale to catch their breath. I return their waves as the game clock ticks down in one second increments to zero.

***

"And that is the end of the first half. The score is Tiger Sharks 26 and our Cats trying to get on the scoreboard."

Dan and I grab our paraphernalia—the log sheets, cell phone, record book, binoculars—and shift to the observation room. We each roll a chair from the back wall to the front counter. As I summarize the stats, I can already tell this will be a rough season for our Sophomore squad. Regardless of age, fighting the good fight side-by-side with your teammates should be expected from any self-respecting competitor. An honorable lesson to learn for any team sport.

Polka Dot Mask sits in Dan's chair while Tiger Mask rolls a second chair into the booth. After they are seated, the Music Man steps behind the ladies and connects their phone to the appropriate receiver port for the stadium speakers.

Polka Dot Mask depresses the mic button. **"Good morning, ladies and gentlemen. Please give a warm welcome to your 2020 Pasadena Spirit team!"**

As performed during the Freshman halftime show, the stadium speakers send out a song whereby a youthful male voice promotes a positive self-image for the young ladies by telling them they are each beautiful, more than they realize.

Two parallel lines of girls march hands-on-hips from the near sideline along the northern and southern 45-yard lines. Each girl's uniform displays a black "Spirit" across their top to contrast against the gray tops and pleated skirts. Each grasps a pair of black-and-silver tinsel pom-poms. Once the line reaches midfield, the lines march in place until the music reaches a specific point. The girls stop and spin around to face the east press box. After the music stops, the group freezes in-place with pom-poms on hips. All their pink hair ribbons are in place.

"These are the ladies of our 2020 Pasadena Spirit squad."

Polka Dot Mask calls out the names of each girl on the field, and the girl identifies herself by shaking her pom-poms overhead. As the introductions proceed, Dan punches out text messages while I compile the team and individual player stats. The Tiger Sharks had five possessions, ran 19 plays, accumulated 188 yards and scored four touchdowns. Seven different players carried the football, and one player caught two passes. The Tiger Shark "super-player" carried the ball seven times for 144 yards and three touchdowns. In comparison, our Cats had four possessions, ran 14 plays and generated 27 yards of total offense. Ouch.

The girls form into their original two lines as the music changes to a female vocalist who declares she'll overcome being figuratively knocked down and come back stronger than ever. The girls conduct their stationary pom-pom routine as during the previous halftime.

Several rows below the press box, a girl as tall as the row she stands on scrambles on top of a metal seat. Her floral dress, pastel yellow covered by sunflower images, contrasts from the bland solid colors that most people around her wear—excluding the intermittent orange stars on dark blue baseball caps. The top of the dress, light gray top with ruffled short sleeves, suggests which team her parents support. She wears lavender and pink canvas tennis shoes, white laces, white toes with multicolored images of butterflies dotting the surface. To me, she looks too young to tie her own shoes.

The toddler stands and turns to face the field. She waves her arms overhead and to each side to mimic the pom-pom arm action on the field. The Spirit girls on the field drop their arms to their sides at the end of their set. The little girl on the seat also slaps her arms to her sides for a few seconds. Then the child starts to flap her arms against her sides, causing her brunette twin ponytails to swing about her head as she tries to fly. I smile at the toddler playing Spirit girl, but also squirm in my seat. She stands over the concrete floor on a metal seat as high as she is tall. I am not her parent, but...no. She looks sort of steady. Sort of. I hope.

I refocus, tear the stat summary page out of my record book and hand it to Dan. "Halftime stats for you. This may be the most lopsided I've ever seen."

"There is no way I can call out these numbers," he says as he scans the stats. "I want to give the kids a shout-out, but this is terrible. I'll come up with a different slant to the recap."

A hip-hoppy boom pow song from this century signals the girls to form into a single-line formation that faces the press box. As during the earlier halftime, they clasp shoulders for the leg kick routine. As before, the wind drives several pom-poms downfield across the turf.

My eyes drift back to the toddler standing on the metal seat. She kicks her right leg out once in a lavender flash of butterflies. Then she plops flat, face down on top of the metal seat. She crawls off the edge and hops down the aisle stairway as her two ponytails flop behind her like puppy dog tails. I lose sight of her behind the tarps erected in the stands.

A remixed version of “While You See a Chance” triggers the girls to rotate into their next formation. Several girls hurry downfield to collect their pom-poms and rejoin the group, but that delay disrupts their timing as they move into the final set. After the music ends, the girls rise and scream and charge off the field to the east sideline. The entire crowd applauds with many of those spaced throughout the stands standing, clapping, and cheering in appreciation.

Our chairs roll to the back wall as Dan and I stand. Tiger Mask rolls her chair from the announcer's booth to the back wall, and Polka Dot mask exits behind her.

"Excellent job, ladies," Dan compliments. "Your girls look very polished, as though you practice every day for the Saturday performance."

"Thank you," Polka Dot Mask says. "The girls work hard. We practice at the same time the boys practice."

"The hard work shows on the field," I say. "And congratulations on the dominant team. It has one of the fastest kids I've seen."

"You mean Carl. He's unstoppable. The Freshman team made it to the interleague super bowl last season. Based on that performance, the Tiger Shark organization expects big things from this Sophomore team."

"Well, good luck to you for the rest of the season," Dan says.

"And to you."

"Oh...Thank you for wearing masks," I shout after them.

"Of course," Polka Dot Mask hollers back.

"Let me do a quick wipe down." I tear open an alcohol pad packet and use the wipe on the stadium microphone.

"Thanks," he says. "This time around, the lavender smell doesn't overwhelm me."

***

Dan eases down before the mic and the Big Voice speaks: **"Please give another hand to the Pasadena Spirit. Fine job, ladies.**

"Now, here are the unofficial halftime stats. Leading rusher for the Tiger Sharks, 'Ace' Throme with seven carries for 144 yards and three touchdowns. 'The Bull' Valentine led all receivers with two receptions for 13 yards and one touchdown. Leading ball carriers for the Cats were 'Prime Time' Nunez, 'Hot Wheels' Sinclair and 'Dynamite' Lester."

The officials wait at midfield as the two special team squads jog onto the field for the second half kickoff.

BTO's classic rocker, with lyrics that describe the mundane tasks people perform in their daily lives as they are "Takin' Care of Business," plays from the stadium speakers.

The Cats kickoff return team positions six players along their 49-yard line, four players along the 40-yard line, and one who sets in the middle of the 30-yard line. Meanwhile, the Tiger Sharks prepare to charge from their south 40-yard line with five players on each side of the kicker.

"Well, I sure hope we can make enough first downs to control the ball. We need to chew up some clock."

"If the score difference becomes greater than thirty points during the second half, the officials keep a running game clock," Dan says. "I'm not sure of the exact number, but I think more than a forty-two-point difference in the score triggers an automatic suspension of the winning coach for the next game."

"Lee 'Lockdown' Lassiter kicking off for the Tiger Sharks."

Once the lead official points to the kicker, the music stops. We raise our binoculars to the field as Lockdown drives the football in a low-lined kick across midfield. The six maroon jerseys across the front line collide with the onrushing black jerseys. The Cat's deep back, Red Rocket, gathers the bounding football and charges straight up the field. Three Tiger Shark players penetrate the wall of blockers and tackle the Red Rocket at the Cat 44-yard line.

"George 'Red Rocket' LaForge with the return. First and ten Cats from the 44-yard line."

The Cat offense assaults the Tiger Sharks in a split-backs formation with a pair of wide receivers positioned to either side of the offensive line. To oppose the Cats, the Tiger Sharks set up with five defensive linemen, three linebackers, and two cornerbacks. The fastest player on the field stands twenty yards downfield as a deep sentry.

While the players set up, the sideline chain gang sets the yard marker poles along the far sideline per referee instructions.

In the booth, I document the results of the kickoff and note ball location and down/distance on the next row of the game log sheet for the upcoming play.

On first down, Prime Time accepts the snap. He steps right. Plunges into the line behind Bone Crusher, the right guard.

Two halfbacks, Predator and Dynamite, drive into the offensive line to help propel their line forward.

The defensive lineman opposite Bone Crusher sprawls at the quarterback's ankles.

The Tiger Shark inside linebacker, Be Nice, drives his shoulders into Prime Time's ribcage.

"Quarterback keeper over the right side. Hard fought gain of two yards by Dave 'Prime Time' Nunez."

On second down, Prime Time hands the football to Predator over left tackle Gorilla for no gain.

"Handoff to the tailback over left tackle. Sean 'Predator' Zelany. Stacked up at the line of scrimmage. That brings up third and...call it eight to go."

'Noculars are raised. Football...is not snapped.

"Ooh," I cry in exasperation. "A maroon jersey on the far side of the line fired into the Shark across from him."

The lead official rolls his hands over each other and points to the Cats. He paces five yards to the south to re-spot the ball.

"False start against the Cats. That backs us up five yards."

"Man, this Cat team cannot survive negative plays."

Dan looks across the field. "The down indicator on the far sideline shows fourth down."

"No, no. It's still third down after the penalty."

"Third down and thirteen to go for the Cats."

Prime Time takes the snap from under center. He drops back to pass, fires an arching pass down the far sideline to Cheetah.

"Quarterback...drops back to pass. Incomplete! Pass intended for Shane 'Cheetah' Vansen. Fourth down coming up. Come on, Cats fans! Stand and clap to inspire our boys!"

'Noculars are raised. Football is hiked. Play is run.

"Fumble! Fumble on the snap! Cats recover. But the ball goes over on downs. First and ten Tiger Sharks from the Cats' 41-yard line."

"Runnin' Down A Dream," a song that evokes images of a highway drive in bright sunshine after days of heavy rain, fills the stadium while the two teams reverse their combat roles.

The Tiger Sharks assemble their offensive formation while the Wildcatters establish their defensive position while the chain movers organize their down-distance locations. At the same time, I close out the Cat possession in the game log and start the log sheet for the Tiger Shark possession for the upcoming play.

Ace attempts a pass to the sideline on first down. The spiraling football skips off the wet artificial turf like a hurled flat stone skips across a smooth water pond.

"Quarterback...rolls out to the left...pass toward the sideline...Incomplete!"

"Our cornerback over there?"

"Uh...Number 8."

"Shane 'Cheetah' Vansen defending on the play. Second down coming up."

"I hope they stick with passing. I prefer their quarterback throw rather than run," Dan says.

"Handoff to the tailback, Gary 'Be Nice' Boltar, up the middle. Gain of four on the play. Brought down by 'Prime Time' Nunez and 'Hollywood' Archer. Third and six coming up."

For third down, one split wide receiver shifts to the far side of their offensive formation before the snap to put both receivers on the same side.

The quarterback drops back to pass. He hurls the football toward halfback Be Nice, who rounds the line of scrimmage and trails after his two wide receivers.

"Quarterback pass...Incomplete! That brings up fourth down. Okay, Cats fans. Let out a holler for our defense!"

"If their quarterback connected with the back, then the play would have gone the distance," I say.

"Big fourth down play coming up, Cats fans. Let our defense hear you!"

'Noculars are raised. Football is hiked. Play is run.

"Quarterback sweep around the left side."

"Jesus."

"He turns the corner! At the 30...to the 20...10...Touchdown! Carl 'Ace' Throme. Thirty-eight yards on the touchdown run."

"Sweet Child O' Mine," the classic hard rocker in which the male vocalist recalls pleasant memories, expresses his affection and desire to provide refuge from the elements, blares from the stadium speakers.

I update the log sheet as each team exchanges personnel for the extra point try. The Tiger Sharks align for a kick attempt. Nine Tiger Sharks crouch in a three-point stance at the line of scrimmage. All eleven Cat players bunch side-by-side across from the football, leap up-and-down, and flail their arms overhead. The hiker, Golden Boy, bounces the football backwards to the kneeling ball holder, Ace. He picks up the football and supports it with tip against the turf. The kicker, Lockdown, takes two strides, swings his right foot into the football, and drives the ball into the butt of his forward lineman.

"The kick is short. No good. The score is Tiger Sharks 32, Cats trying to get on the board."

"This is going to be a long season for the good guys, but I expect they'll soldier through it," I say.

"On the bright side, they get plenty of exercise, especially with this short roster."

Our kids may suffer the same level of success my team, my winless team, experienced during my year of youth tackle football. I remember how we practice hard, and we play hard, but not much to show for it record-wise. No participation trophies for that league—fine by me. The memento I appreciate from the season: my white helmet. Most teams have helmets painted to match their jerseys: red, green, brown, whatever. Each direct helmet collision adds another scar to my original pure white helmet surface. After the season, I admire the multi-colored smudges and streaks that speckle my helmet, a testament to physical play, the violent helmet-to-helmet collisions.

The rest of the half proceeds in the expected manner. The Cats run thirteen plays with their three possessions and do not score. They attempt four more passes and complete none. Incomplete passes do not stop the running game clock. On offense, the Tiger Sharks alternate linemen to the "skill positions" and run them up the middle. The dispassionate game clock counts down in one second increments until it freezes at one minute, fourteen seconds.

The lead official waves his arms overhead, picks up the football and leads the other officials toward the northeast stands. Both teams jog off the field to their respective sidelines.

"What's going on?" I ask.

"You got me." Dan's buzzing phone vibrates against the counter to signal a text message. He scans the message and leans back in his chair. "From the Cats organization manager. Weather delay."

"You're kidding. Dark clouds have surrounded the stadium all day, but we haven't had any rain since this morning."

"Could be a lightning strike detected near the stadium. The pole outside the north end of the stadium is topped by an alert horn that activates for one minute when lightning strikes are detected. Safety first."

I have to check it out. As soon as I scrape open the press box door, the continuous blare from a horn to the north slaps me in the face. The players from both teams troop to their respective dressing rooms. As they march down the sideline, the Tiger Shark kids below me shout in unison: "Tor-na-do! Tor-na-do!"

Good grief.

No lightning flashes. No thunderclaps. The clouds east of the stadium are darker than the silvery gray on the Tiger Shark uniforms. Streamers pour from the dark clouds to hammer LaPorte.

The garbled voice from the stadium speakers fades in and out. Back inside the press box, I tell Dan, "Your voice tapers up and down so much that I have trouble understanding what you say."

"Marty," he hollers. "The speakers are fading in and out."

"Don't turn your mouth away from the mic when you speak into it," he shouts.

"Ah, good tip." Dan yells in return, "Thanks!"

Dan repositions his phone to the base of the mic. **"Sorry about the technical difficulties. From the Wildcatters organization manager: A lightning strike has been detected near the stadium. The strike detection protocol requires a minimum thirty-minute delay. If lightning is detected again, the thirty-minute delay restarts. During the delay, we *strongly recommend* that fans vacate the stands. We will announce when conditions are met that allow us to resume. Thank you for your understanding."**

Dan leans back in his chair. "I left out the game's potential two-hour delay before being called. I hope we never reach that point."

Most individuals and families, including those with tarps, relocate for shelter under the stands. I count six blue, five maroon, three gray, one white, and one red tarp. No correlation between tent color and occupancy. One stubborn cuss sits by himself under an umbrella halfway up the stands, not another soul within twenty yards of him. Dan points at him and quips, "Maybe he wants to save his spot."

"Oh, man. The game progressed well, you conducted play descriptions in your typical brilliant manner, and I kept up with log entries," I say with a sigh. "This delay"—head bob accompanies every word—"sucks big time."

"We had a good rhythm in the booth. This delay throws everything off, makes it feel like we're staring over." We vacate the booth so we can spread out in the observation room.

***

After Dan rolls a chair to the counter and collapses into it, he says, "Oh, I need to text Cheryl and tell her about the weather delay. She and Matthew don't need to be as early as usual for the next game." Dan's phone buzzes before he can set it on the counter. "They're already here. Tent erected. She's under the stands now, visiting with friends."

"She erects the tarp herself?" I ask.

"She can handle it. But Matthew should have helped her."

As I lower my mask to my chin to swig a berry-flavored sports drink, the Music Man enters the observation room, brow furrowed, eyes fixed to the floor tile. No mask.

"Great tunes today," I tell him.

"Thanks. I'm glad you think so," Marty says as he looks up to us. "The organization manager, the person who hired me, sent me a text. He got a complaint from a parent who claimed one song I played was too sexually suggestive."

"What?!"

"You have got to be kidding," Dan says.

"They didn't identify the song, so I have no idea what the problem is."

"You've been doing great," I tell him. "Every song you've played got plenty of open airtime back in the day. I wish I knew what song they objected to."

"I promise I did not send the text," Dr. LePrince says as he strides into the observation room. A pleated, pale blue, made-in-China mask, the type that online websites always list as being on back order, covers his mouth and nose.

"Dr. LePrince, join us," Dan bellows.

"Call me Harold, please," he says as he sinks into a chair along the back wall.

"Have you met Marty?"

"Yes, we have met." Harold and Marty nod at each other.

The foursome conduct two independent conversations: Dan and Harold discuss the video recording job and church missionary work, while Marty and I talk about music and his DJ role.

"Looks like you picked a bad day to videorecord," Dan says.

"No, not at all," Harold says. "After I retired, my wife ordered me to find something to get me out of our house. This little video business accomplishes that...and generates a little extra income. She does not complain about that."

On the opposite side of the observation room: "Well, Marty, I hope you are paid by the hour."

"I often am. For this job, though, it's a lump sum to cover five games."

"Everyone with a cell phone is their own video recorder. I'm a bit surprised to see much demand for professional video recording," Dan says.

"Oh, much more than you might think," Harold says. "I am hired when someone wants an extended video package, often edited to show the highlights of an event. I film weddings, graduations, parties and youth football games. With all these COVID concerns, indoor jobs are rare now."

"I want to play tunes now, but the boss asked me not to," Marty says. "He wants people out of the stands, so no music to entertain the masses in the stadium."

"Hanging around all day on a Saturday can't be fun."

"Fun is irrelevant. I want it to be engaging. I have over five dozen possible tunes queued for gameday to match the different circumstances on the field. Extended delays destroy the overall rhythm, the flow of the music."

"Huh. Dan and I commented earlier that the delay hurts our rhythm in the booth, the descriptions of the game action. I thought you store songs in a computer folder and play whatever you feel like at the time."

"Do you get paid by event or by hour?" Dan asks Dr. LePrince.

"The event. The Wildcatters hired me to record each of the five games today. I transfer the videos to my website so coaches can access and view the gameday action. For an extra charge, I send an edited game video, one that focuses on their child's jersey number, to any parent who requests it. Not the most lucrative job, but it more than pays the expenses."

Marty elaborates on today's DJ job. "No, no. It's much more complicated than that, I pay a license fee to access and use a music library for different events, so I have to plan ahead. Every event can have a much different musical requirement."

"So, youth football games are not the pinnacle of your profession?"

"Hah. Not quite. I have a challenging gig in a few weeks for a wedding reception at an outdoor venue north of Houston—an open bar situation with a county music theme. The bride's father told me he wants more people dancing than drinking. I have to read the room, see what gets the crowd energized and respond with the necessary music."

"Open bar. I'd camp out at that spot as long as they have plenty of Shiner Bock." If I'm not driving, of course. Otherwise, old-man-me has a self-imposed three beer limit. That's my drinking name: "Three Beers" Jordan.

"I am guessing no church mission trip this year," Dan says.

"COVID made sure of that," Dr. LePrince says. "Since I retired, I have gone over there for a few weeks during late summers for much of the last decade, but not this year."

"Where is 'there'?"

"Ghana. Ghana is a predominantly Christian country on the African west coast," Dr. LePrince continues through his mask. "We partner with a po—I mean, under resourced Christian community in Awamtwi, a town about an hour from the large Kumasi metro area. Very friendly people. In no time, we are all 'Charlie' to them."

"Club owners have a different attitude. The challenge there is to read the crowd and see what gets them energized on the dance floor. But you also need to change the pace. A slower track lowers the energy level and gives clubbers a chance to catch their breath, drink, and buy more booze—what the manager wants to see. I'm afraid demand for indoor music collapsed during COVID. Without a professional agent, I have to scramble for my jobs."

The Music Man relates happier DJ bar memories. "The sight of a happy, boisterous crowd on the dance floor is the most fulfilling part of the job. Sometimes circumstances just don't work out." He tells of one job where the manager doesn't like the crowd response to the tunes, so he chews Marty out, hollers at him, curses him, and fires him on the spot. The manager takes over DJ duties and meets the same level of unsuccess. Marty smiles at the recollection.

"They often have their own playlist," Marty tells me. "I need to familiarize myself with what they have, equipment and music, ahead of time."

"You're giving me new respect for DJs," I say. "Or are you called something else now? I presume there are no more vinyl disc jockeys."

"Hah. No, DJ is fine. I invest a lot of work into the DJ role even though it's part time while I attend school. A lot of DJs at higher end clubs do still handle the vinyl. I'm a 'ham-and-egger' compared to the high-end pros."

The Music Man recounts a previous outdoor gig for a local fair. The summer heat, even under a tent, is oppressive. He drinks plenty of water to stay hydrated but can't go to the bathroom because he can't leave his equipment unattended. Then someone runs an extension cord for a large area fan and blows the circuit breaker—no music and no fan.

While Marty and I discuss music and DJ work, Dan and Harold talk about church missions and public service.

"I admire you for it," says Dan. "We are not devout church goers but respect those who are. Cheryl and I both believe in service to others in need. Cheryl is especially giving of her time across a broad social circle of friends and their families."

"Service provided to others is its own reward, whether such service is religious or secular in nature," says Dr. LePrince. "I hope I am not sounding too preachy." Harold recounts the issues associated with the young missionaries adapting to a different culture for their three-week experience. No one gets used to the starch-heavy diet. Most appreciate the food but want to hit their favorite barbeque or Tex-Mex places as soon as they get back to the states. No cell phone use allowed except in emergency situations—on the honor system. No online activity allowed except late Sunday nights, when they can visit with family and friends back home after their church service.

"Do they go into withdrawal without a cell phone or internet?"

"That's not the most difficult challenge." Dr. LePrince recounts the bum wash toilet training. "It never fails. Directions to always spray rinse water from forward to backward, never from backward toward the front, always elicit a few 'ooh, that's gross' comments. No matter what, someone forgets and tosses the 'for-drying only' toilet paper into the commode and risks gumming up the works." Harold's mask crinkles enough to indicate a broad smile behind his mask.

"What school?" I ask.

"San Jac," Marty replies. "Fortunately, they kept the operations technology program going through remote learning. I want to get a degree, latch on at a chemical plant. Since the lack of indoor gatherings during COVID squashed my DJ business, I need a steadier income to support my family."

"What about language problems?" Dan asks. "I would expect language to be a major issue on a church mission to Africa."

"Not really. English is the official language. There are tribal dialects, but English is the language of business. Besides, I taught English literature in college, and my background proves useful to help our hosts resolve the occasional language translation issue. Plus, apps are getting better at translating different languages. One day soon, we will all be able to communicate with others anywhere in the world, regardless of personal language limitations."

The vibrating phone smacks against the vinyl countertop to quiet the room. Three pairs of eyes follow Dan's motion while he scrolls through the text message. The chair creaks reverberate across the room as he leans back in his chair and sighs. "Do you want the good news or the bad news?"

"Good news, please."

"Well," Dan says, "both Sophomore coaches confirmed their kids got in the minimum required number of plays. They agreed to call the game as it stands. No need to return, go through pre-game warmups, and play out the final minute plus."

Three heads nod in unison.

"But."

Three heads freeze in a stare.

"More lightning strikes were detected during the original delay. The delay window has been extended."

A chorus of groans greets the news as everyone rocks backwards as much as their chairs allow. Their separate conversations resume.

I turn back to Marty. "I know working and going to college isn't easy. My folks couldn't pay for college for any of their sons. I found out decades later how much they stressed over it. Anyway, I stumbled into a co-op program that let me alternate work and school semesters. For my senior year, I needed a loan and got a little scholarship money. It took five years, but I got it done."

"How many of you go overseas?" Dan asks.

"Ten to fifteen youths, high school seniors or college students."

"Sounds like a lot of young people to keep track of."

"I suppose that's where you got into music," Marty says.

"In fact, my music preferences formed in high school. My friends and I all liked rock, while others liked country or R&B. Some liked disco,"—at which I give an exaggerated shudder. "In high school, I used a hand-me-down AM radio to listen to the mainstream rock pop of the day. Before I left for college, my parents gave me an FM radio," I recall with a smile. "I got to listen to music without the annoying static associated with AM broadcasts."

"Oh, I am not the only adult on church missions," Harold says. "Plus, our hosts are quite attentive. And this is no tourist trip around the country. Our kids team up with other young Christians and travel door-to-door to spread the word of God, and we hope gather some potential converts to the church. A Western face among the Black members of the congregation opens more doors to them, even if only out of curiosity. Hard to imagine a substitute for going from one stranger's house to another to help you get over being shy."

"That sounds exhausting," Dan says.

"Of course, the radio stations I listened to in my younger days have all changed formats," I tell Marty. "One swapped to country music. Another changed to some urban, Hispanic hip-hop sound. More proof that I'm in a fading demographic."

"I go online for my music," Marty tells me. "Pick the right website, call up a song or video you like, let the algorithm cycle through similar songs. You can either listen or skip as you like."

"No! Just the opposite! The work is invigorating," Dr. LePrince exclaims as he leans toward Dan, bobbing his hands chest in rhythm as he speaks. "Being around a team of young Christians working in service to others, I find the missionary work acts as a fountain of youth. At the age of eighteen, I went on my first church mission. It changed my life. The experience set me on a path to follow Christ, and my life is more fulfilled because of my Faith. I cannot perform the physical activities of my youth, but I try to help others however I can."

"Sounds like one hell of an experience."

"For my music," I tell Marty, "I tried to keep track of classic rock through the *Rolling Stone*. The magazine often included articles on aging rockers and their current music activities. Then they got hep and edgy and used multicolored, multi-sized, mixed fonts for the titles for the major articles. Honest to God, I could not read the article titles. At that point, I said to myself, 'screw it,' and let my subscription lapse. Now, I subscribe to satellite radio to get rock from the 60s through 80s, especially one station dedicated to those deeper album tracks that never got much airplay. One of my greatest music pleasures is finding favorite cuts, deep tracks that never received much radio airplay, buried in an album."

"Hah! I would not use the word 'hell' to describe my missionary experience, but I agree with the sentiment." Harold leans back as far as his chair allows and discusses the forested area outside the town, the timber business that employs most of the local population, the nearby pottery factory that allows the visiting kids to mold and glaze their own clay pot in a side room off the main factory floor. The young missionaries also get a Saturday trip to the largest open-air market in sub-Saharan Africa. One surprise—more broad spread use of solar panels there than where we live here.

"Given the music you are playing today, you must have a favorite classic rock group?" I ask.

"Right now, I'm getting into Deep Purple."

"Ooh. Good call. *Machine Head* is one of my top ten favorite albums." I raise one finger for each group I list. "Let's see," as I look to the ceiling. "Three other personal favorite albums belong to Led Zeppelin. And Blue Oyster Cult, Journey, Bad Company, Uriah Heep, Fairport Convention—don't ask why—and..."—as I swing my gaze back to the Music Man—"Black Sabbath."

"Do kids today feel the same way you did after your first church mission?" Dan asks.

"Some do. Others do not. But they are all better off for the experience. They step outside their comfort zones, associate with people of a different race, a different culture, and eat together, work together, pray together." Harold adds, "I get a great deal of satisfaction from seeing their spiritual and emotional metamorphosis: youngsters climb off the bus and meet their hosts with smiles and fears, but depart on the bus with smiles and tears."

"I can't point to a life-changing experience out of the state, much less out of the country," Dan says. "I'm one hundred percent Texan. The periodic trip to

Galveston beach or the now-defunct Astroworld amusement park provided some relief from the normal grind of school and after-school work." Dan describes how the annual family car drive to Indiana to visit grandparents for Christmas provided the longest times he remembered being out of the state. "Those childhood experiences," he recalls with a smile, "were the only times I ever got to play in the snow."

"Nothing wrong with that. Sounds like fun," Harold says through his mask.

"You can update your music taste with newer groups. I bet you'll get into their sounds." Marty discusses several of his favorite groups, including Muse or the Von Hertzen Brothers.

"I'm not familiar with either group. I'll give them a listen."

"The COVID epidemic creates some amazing situations," Dan opines. "COVID stifles your noble church mission trip and all kinds of more mundane, day-to-day jobs that require indoor contact. But youth football barrels along no matter what. Maybe parents like the idea that football provides kids with some normality in a stressful time. I'm sure glad Matthew gets to play this season. It seems like nothing can derail the passion behind the game—except the uncontrollable weather."

Dr. LePrince adds, "Whether as a kid or teen, a common thread in our experiences is the human contact that occurs outside the home, outside the local classroom. Online meetings and virtual social networks provide interactions but cannot develop meaningful relationships. In a world more superficial than ever, video meetings cannot substitute for positive, direct human connection, direct human interaction to feed the soul. I hope human contact returns to normal, or even increases, after COVID."

Amazing. Someone young enough to be my grandson likes much of the same music I do. "No matter how much rock I ever listen to, Led Zeppelin will always be the king," I tell Marty.

"Amen to that."

The vibrating phone raps against the countertop to silence the room. We glue our eyes to Dan as he hunches over his phone and smiles. "The Junior game starts in fifteen minutes."

"Hallelujah!"

We rise as one and deploy to our separate duty stations.

"Marty, do you have a tune planned to start the warm-up period?" I ask.

"I haven't decided yet which one I'll play."

After scribbling a song title on scrap paper, I hand it to Marty.

"I'm not familiar with it, but I'll see if the tune is available and check it out."

"It's an adrenaline pumper. I think you'll approve."

In the announcer's booth, Dan plops down in front of the mic and makes the announcement: **"Good news. The Junior game starts in fifteen minutes. I repeat, the Junior game starts in fifteen minutes. I'm certain it will prove worth the wait."**

Chapter Ten

Well Avenged

Dan sorts through his roster notes while I focus on the maroon Cats squad warming up at the south end zone. Two coaches direct the players through their calisthenics, through voice commands and hand motions, not by example.

The players start by running in place as though they're in a major hurry to get nowhere. Then, alternate knees rise to hip level and drop back. High kicks follow, more waist level than chest level. Bend at waist, legs straight, and touch toes—I wish I could do that one. One long leg stride forward is followed by one stride backward. Repeat for opposite leg. Quad stretches for each leg, where a kid bends a knee and grabs his ankle. Execute forward alternate calf extensions for each leg. The boys perform jumping jacks in as mismatched a manner as possible for two dozen kids. I couldn't find any three in sync.

Meanwhile, the stadium speakers explode with guitars and drums to introduce a male vocalist who screams how lightning depresses him since its power dwarfs his own. Defiant, he wants to release his own potential—he must become a "Rainbow in the Dark."

The Coach claps his hands four times to interrupt the exercises and signal the players to split into two groups. His group of offensive linemen, with quarterback and running backs, runs through a few handoffs against an imaginary defensive line. Jersey 32 occupies the left tackle position. After the center snaps the football to the quarterback, he hands off to the running back who charges through the line. Each running back gets multiple carries to burst through the line. The offensive linemen fire off at invisible defensive linemen at each snap.

The other squad forms parallel lines in groups of four that each face to the west. An assistant coach for this group impersonates the Statue of Liberty with a football torch. The Statue points the football to his right, and his players follow as-one to their left. The football points left, and the players hop sideways to their right. Football points forward toward the squad and the players quick-step backwards. Repeat several times. Does he enjoy increasing the pace at which he swings the football back-and-forth? I would.

The Coach with the offensive unit nods to Statue, who points his football behind his head. His defensive players tear past him to the west side of the end zone with the offensive squad at their heels.

The players drop to one knee and form a semicircle as The Coach strides among them. He rotates to make sure every player sees him pound his right fist into the palm of his left hand while he yells instructions to them. Then, The Coach stiffens, removes his cap and bows his head. The assistant coaches follow his lead. Each player bows his head toward the ground. After a minute, The Coach dons his cap, claps his hands, and the group hops up and down and collides together like trapped popcorn kernels. One kid picks up a maroon Wildcatters flag and charges in front of the screaming mob to their tent along the far sideline.

"Our head coach looks extra intense today," I comment.

"I talk to him during the daily practices. The Tiger Sharks knocked our Darts squad out of the playoffs last year—three turnovers cost us the game. The Coach wants this one bad.

"Oh, Sean's here today. He's manning a yardage marker with the chain gang."

"Got him."

A short, wiry, 40-ish man wearing sunglasses holds one end of the ten-yard pole chain.

"I'm not sure if he's off all day or goes into the port this evening."

Dan takes a deep breath and presses the mic button. **"I hope you are ready for some footbaaall! Cats football! We expect a great game today between the Pasadena Tiger Sharks and the Deer Park Wildcatters Junior squads—well worth the wait. Allow me to introduce our Junior Wildcatters team."**

The masked lead official signals to each sideline. Three player-captains from each team stride to midfield for the traditional coin toss. Each trio stands face-to-face, nodding to each other. No handshakes. I record their jersey numbers in the margin of the game log sheet and keep an ear tuned to the roster names from the stadium speakers.

For Matthew's team, the team I'm most familiar with, I recognize most of the names, or at least the nicknames, from last season. J-Dawg, the quarterback, the head coach's son, nexus of activity for each offensive play. Decent runner, improving passer, takes care of the football.

Beast Mode, the big fullback guaranteed to get positive yards on every handoff. Nobody runs far up the middle when he's at linebacker.

And Goose—the best combination of speed and quickness on the field. The maximum allowable scoring difference that league rules allow sets the limit to his football touches, yardage and touchdowns.

I recognize Demik. Above average player on both sides of the ball. Does he have a different nickname this season?

Shucks. Where's the Kraken? He was the best kicker I've seen in youth football at any age level. Did we lose our star kicker from last season?

The lead official shows the captains both sides of the ceremonial coin. He tosses the coin to head level and lets it fall to the ground. He picks up the coin and reveals the exposed coin face to each captain.

Dan provides a little extra emphasis when he calls out one name in particular:

"Number 32. Matthew 'Hit Man' Castillo, *Line*-man!"

Officials align the opposing captains face-to-face. The Cat's captains stand at the north 49-yard line to face south, while the Tiger Shark's captains stand at the south 49-yard line to face north. The official taps the shoulder pads of the nearest Cat captain, extends his arms in front of his chest, and draws them back to his torso.

For others, I recognize their nicknames rather than the specific player: Hammerhead, Need for Speed, Slam, Blue Thunder, Lights Out, Terminator, Freight Train, T-Bone.

Several nicknames are unfamiliar but still entertaining: Skittles, Superman, Dirty Thirty (to match his jersey number), Shazam, The Boss. These must be new team members from the Cats Sophomore team.

The rite completed, the team captains jog back to their respective sidelines.

"Ready," Dan says.

"Okay. Cat captains are 6, 9, 39. Shark captains are 24, 34, 60. We won the toss and will receive."

"Got it."

"Team captains for the Cats are John 'Pan' Demik, Jules 'J-Dawg' Bass, and Samuel 'Slam' Torres. Captains for the Tiger Sharks are Karl 'Machete' Aguerra, Phil 'Griffin' Colter, and Larry 'Hurricane' Roslin. Cats won the toss and will receive the opening kickoff."

The two special teams jog onto the field while multiple, simultaneous hand claps and foot stomps blare from the stadium speakers; the lead singer joins in with a defiant declaration, repeating the title refrain, "We Will Rock You."

The Tiger Sharks use the conventional alignment of five players on each side of their kicker. Their kicker positions the tee at the near hash 40-yard line. The

Cats prepare to receive the football with five players across the 49-yard line, four at their 40-yard line, and two at their 25-yard line. Six of the eleven Cats shift to between the near hash and the sideline.

"John 'Hot Shot' Sherman kicking off for the Tiger Sharks."

We both raise our binoculars to the field. "Matthew is on the 49-yard line, near the far sideline," Dan tells me.

The music stops when the official points at the kicker, who sends the football in an arc to the 30-yard line.

Hot Shot kicks the football to Goose—not the smartest decision. Goose draws the ball into his chest and sprints toward the near sideline as he transfers the football to his left arm.

The black-and-gray line of players funnels toward the returner's direction against the maroon blockers. Two Tiger Shark players, Hot Shot and Hurricane, shove Goose out of bounds near the midfield stripe.

"Fine return by Kyle 'Goose' Frye. First and ten Cats from their 49-yard line."

"For a second, it looked like he might make the corner and break free," I comment.

"If they keep kicking to Goose, I bet he takes one back all the way."

Offensive and defensive squads filter between the special team units that jog off the field. The Cats configure their attack offense in a "trips left" formation with three players split wide left. The Tiger Sharks counter the Cats with four defensive linemen, three linebackers, and one deep safety stands about fifteen yards behind the line of scrimmage. Three Tiger Shark cornerbacks split wide to their right to match the three Cat wide receivers.

As the players establish their formations, the far sideline official aligns the chain gang with the ball location and first down distance.

Meanwhile, I document the kickoff and note the ball's starting spot with down/distance for the upcoming play.

"That's weird," I say.

"What?"

"Trips left formation with our fullback clustered beside the two wide receivers close to the sideline." The fullback, half-again as large as the diminutive wide receivers, stands out in the mix.

"Maybe The Coach wants to open the middle or far sideline for Goose to operate from the tailback spot."

"The Cats open with a 'trips left' formation and a single tailback."

Skittles hikes the football to J-Dawg.

J-Dawg—quick step back. He hurls a tight spiral to the sideline.

"The quarterback...snap throw to the sideline."

Caught!

Beast Mode shrugs off a would-be tackler.

"Caught! He breaks a tackle!"

Run!

"He's down the sideline! To the 30...the 20...the 10...Touchdooown! Touchdown by 'Beast Mode' Bannon! Fifty-one yards on the Cat's first play of the game!"

"Wow. I haven't seen that play before."

"Me neither," Dan says. "There were more passes to the fullback during practice, but not that particular play. I bet The Coach wanted the ball first so he could spring the play on the Tigers before they even worked up a sweat."

"I had no idea the big guy could run like that. He left the Shark cornerbacks behind him in a hurry."

"Beast Mode was pickin'-'em-up and puttin'-'em-down. He may not be the zigzag master Goose is, but Beast Mode has impressive straight-ahead speed."

The stadium speakers blast a classic hard rocker that epitomizes primal power. The song begins with a lead guitar solo and background chants, continues until drums pound into the mix in synchronization with the lead singer's thunderous shouts, moving to descriptions of high-stress situations to culminate with the title refrain "Thunderstruck."

For the extra point attempt, the Cats use an I-formation. No wide receivers. The Tiger Sharks respond with eleven players bunched between the goal line and the three-yard line. The speakers fall silent as the official signals for the extra point play to start.

"Quarterback keeper into the meat grinder over right guard. Pile up at the goal line."

A mass of gray and maroon jerseys tangle at the goal line. Both outside officials sprint to the player pile. The far side masked official raises both arms skyward as soon as he gains sight of the football.

"Good! The extra point is good! 'J-Dawg' with the carry. That makes the score Cats 7, Tiger Sharks 0."

I update the score in the logbook while Dan provides the scoring drive summary.

"Scoring drive recap. One play, 51 yards on a touchdown reception by 'Beast Mode' Bannon on a pass from 'J-Dawg' Bass."

The special teams jog onto the field for the kickoff as "Enter Sandman," a solid rocker with vocals that depict childhood fears and nightmares, screams from the stadium speakers.

"Lonnie 'Skittles' Molari kicking off for the Cats."

The lead official points to Skittles. He drives the football in a line drive that bounces into the arms of the Tiger Shark deep back, the Griffin.

The maroon wave filters through the first line of black jerseys to attack the ball carrier from the front and both sides.

Griffin cradles the football in both arms. He runs straight up the field—face down, helmet directed at the onrushing Cats.

J-Dawg and Hammerhead sandwich Griffin at the Tiger Shark 45-yard line.

"Did you see who ran the ball back?"

"Number 34."

"Phil 'Griffin' Coulter with the return for the Tiger Sharks. First and ten from the 45-yard line."

"Do you remember anything about their team from last year?"

"Not much. No super standout players," Dan replies. "And with COVID affecting the rosters, I don't know if they got better players or lost good players or changed coaching staffs. My recollection is that they were a solid team. No speed demons, but a bunch of defenders who swarm to the football. Since we earned an off-week bye before our initial playoff game, our boys may have been rusty before some full-speed hard contact."

Six Tiger Shark offensive linemen crouch helmet-to-helmet against the maroon defense. Two wide receivers flank to opposite sides of the offensive line, and a pair of running backs set several yards behind the quarterback to form the split backs formation. The Cat defense opposes them with five crouched linemen, three linebackers, two cornerbacks, and one deep safety.

"Our quarterback J-Dawg and fullback Beast Mode are at two of the linebacker spots with Goose at deep safety," I say.

"Yeah, our coach has all his best players on both sides of the ball to start this game. The Demik kid at the other linebacker spot is also solid—a real standout at the team practices. He may also get some time at halfback."

"Does Matthew get time on defense?"

"Sometimes. He plays most often along the offensive line," Dan says.

"Handoff to the tailback. Sweep left. 'J-Dawg' slices through the line! Tackled behind the line of scrimmage for a two-yard loss on the play."

Two more running plays, one from Ghost and one from Machete, lead to a fourth and short for the Tiger Sharks.

"Big fourth down coming up. C'mon Cats Nation! Let our defense hear you!"

'Noculars are raised. Football is hiked. Play is run.

"Another handoff into the line. Gang tackled! Near the line to gain."

The lead official dashes toward the players on the ground, notes the relative position of the forward chain pole and football, and raises his right arm toward the north end zone. The far side official directs the chain gang to reposition the down marker and ten-yard distance poles. I update the log sheet.

"First down for the Tiger Sharks. First and ten from the Cat's 45-yard line."

"Their offense doesn't look like anything special," I comment.

"They lack the firepower the Cats have. I bet they grind the clock on offense and try to get turnovers on defense."

"Quarterback...drops back to pass...throws deep down the left sideline...Incomplete! 'Goose' Frye and 'Need for Speed' Carter break up the pass."

"As soon as I say that they'll grind the clock, they throw a bomb downfield. Anyway, that wobbly throw never had a chance, but I wanted to give our kids a shout out," Dan says. "And 'Goose' is my favorite nickname."

"The nicknames are fun. Most boys have dynamic, aggressive nicknames, but the best player on the team has an amusing one. I wish I knew why."

The Cats play solid defense and spectacular offense for the rest of the half. The Tiger Sharks grind out first downs as best they can to keep the football away from the Cats.

Two minutes before the end of the first half, the press box door scrapes open, and footsteps, one pair of clomping boots and one pair of squeaky tennis shoes, climb the steps into the observation room. Two masked women emerge.

Clomper hunches over with her flower-themed mask puffing in and out as a pendant swings from her neck. Her curled black hair, not quite full enough to hide the ear straps from her mask, remains undisturbed by the wind outside. Squeaker, a college coed in vibrant pink tennis shoes, stands upright beside Clomper. Squeaker's shoulder-length hair, not quite blonde and not quite brown—a deep golden color resembling darker cane left longer in the fields under the sun to boost sugar content before harvest—looks frazzled enough to reflect the effect of a windy day. Squeaker's pink mask shows no sign of strained breathing as she casts a stoic stare toward Clomper's head. Does Squeaker have a smirk on her face under her mask? Nah.

A minute later, "Hello, Dan," comes from a voice behind us.

Dan twists around in his chair. "Hello, Deb." To me, "This is Deborah Bass, Nate-Dawg's mom. And one of Cheryl's friends."

"Nice to meet you," I tell her one mask to another.

Back to Deb, "How long have you known Cheryl?" Dan asks.

"At least twenty years. Oh, this is my niece. She is helping us out with the drill team this season."

"Hello," from the waving hand behind Clomper.

Dan turns back to the field. "Oh, we missed a play." I mark "?" in the game sheet comments and note the football location and down/distance in the game log sheet. The game clock rolls down to zero, and both teams jog to their respective dressing rooms to regroup for the second half.

The Big Voice speaks: **"The halftime score is our Wildcatters 20, the visiting Tiger Sharks yet to get on the board.**

"Coming up at halftime, the Deer Park Golden Hearts drill team. Please stay in your seats to watch their outstanding halftime show. Their performance alone is worth the trip to the stadium today."

***

Clomper's brown leather boots sit below her black knee-length skirt with a winding floral design that climbs through her associated tan blouse to the shear, loose scarf that wraps around her neck—I bet it waves like a burgundy banner in this breeze— while a pendant dangles to a spot where I dare not stare. I consider telling her the press box doesn't have a dress code, but I'm not sure if she'll take it as a compliment or an insult, so I keep my mouth shut.

Dan and I grab our binoculars and notes and squeeze single file from the press box. Deb sits down in front of the mic. The Music Man follows behind her to connect the cord from her phone to the stadium speaker system.

In the observation room, Squeaker rolls a chair from the back wall to the counter. She flips the chair around so the back butts against the counter, kneels on the seat and stretches forward in her form-hugging jeans and pink racer-back tank top as both hands press over the countertop to lift her upper body. She stares onto the field as though the drill team performance depends on her unblinking gaze.

Oo-kay. Time to focus on the halftime stats. I dig into the game log sheets while Dan punches into his cell phone.

Clomper announces the drill team performance: **"Good afternoon, ladies and gentlemen. Please give a warm welcome to your 2020 Deer Park Wildcatters Golden Hearts! Ladies, your music starts now."**

A remixed version of a classic pop song, "Girls Just Want to Have Fun,"—I recognized this one—streams from the speakers as the female vocalist tells us you can't restrain her free will.

Thirty girls in five parallel lines set five yards apart skip from the near sideline while they swing their gold and their maroon pom-poms by their sides. Once they reach their designated spot near midfield, the girls stop, place hands on hips and spin to face the east press box. Each wears a pleated maroon skirt and sleeveless top with gold trim at the base of the skirt, across the waist, along the neck and each arm opening. A golden "Cats" adorns each of their tops. One of the taller girls in front has a bandaged left knee. Did she injure it during practice or perhaps when she played another sport? Regardless, the injury doesn't keep her off the field.

Deb the Clomper silences the music and announces the organization's adult leaders. She calls out each girl, who responds with a leap and overhead pom-pom shake at her name mention.

The music restarts and, of course, I don't recognize the tune; it's from this century. A female vocalist declares she will ignore those who put her down by shake, shaking off those who criticize her and moving to her own beat.

The girls form into two parallel lines along both 45-yard lines. The line undulates from front to back as the girls wave their pom-poms overhead. They repeat the motion in reverse. Then the girls begin a series of pom-pom movements from a stationary position. I have trouble following the rapidity of the motions.

One song morphs into the next. This one I recognize from an animated movie made by a studio that, once upon a time, made competent, family friendly cinema. The female vocalist cries out she has lost, been knocked down, but always gets up, will never quit trying; she will "Try Everything."

The music change triggers the girls to skip-hop to the next formation, a single line across midfield that faces the east press box. They drop their pom-poms, clasp shoulders, and begin a sequence of synchronized leg kicks. The two smallest girls abandon the routine. Instead, the pair hunches behind the line of kickers and performs pom-pom wrangler duty to corral the pom-poms before the wind scatters them northward. The girl with the bandaged knee winces every time she kicks her left leg. When the set ends, her knee has a slight forward bend, but her leg still supports her weight. Even without binoculars, I can see the girls panting from their physical exertion.

I see Squeaker's focused stare onto the field. "What do you look for in the routine? It seems fine to me."

"There is always room for improvement," she tells me without turning her gaze from the field. "From this height, I see the visuals associated with the group, the synchronization, the efficiency of changeover between the sets. And how well the girls perform under public scrutiny. Some girls do well in practice but crater before a crowd. I was a Golden Heart myself, and this experience did wonders for my self-confidence. I want it to do the same for these girls."

"You were Golden Heart and now you're back to help younger girls. That's cool." I hope "cool" is not a dated term. I don't keep up with the latest slang.

"My dream was to dance, any kind of dance, but not likely to earn a living that way. Right now, I attend U of H on a double major—fine arts that emphasize dance choreography and a minor in business. Once I graduate, I intend to open my own dance studio. If I can't make it happen, then I have a business degree to fall back on."

Sounds smart to me. I took extra courses toward a secondary English degree, but not enough to yield a practical benefit.

Back on the field, the strain of the girls' physical effort does not deter them from a smooth roll into the final formation to the accompaniment of a classic rocker that still gets airplay after forty years: "Don't Stop Believin'." No remixed version needed for this song.

The girls cluster into two square patterns at midfield. Both squares display a solid block of trembling maroon pom-poms to the stands. The square to my left flashes a "D" from gold pom-poms amidst the maroon pom-poms. The square to my right flashes "P" in gold amidst the maroon. After perhaps fifteen or twenty seconds, the color scheme inverts to maroon D and P amidst the gold. They cycle the colors back and forth a couple more times. At a designated point in the music, the girls rise and skip to the near sideline. Many in the stands also rise to send their standing ovation to the girls.

Deb shuts off the music and closes the performance: **"Your 2020 Deer Park Wildcatters Golden Hearts drill team!"**

Uh-oh. I got distracted by the halftime show and haven't finished the player stats—every ball carrier, receiver, scorer, associated jersey number, yards for every carry, total the yards. Repeat for the other team.

Deb twists out of the announcer's booth into the observation room. "What do you think?" she asks her niece.

Squeaker slides off the chair and replies in a monotone voice, "Same problem area as before."

“Well, I thought it looked great,” Dan says. “I see the girls drill as hard as the boys at the weekly practices, and their hard work shows with a fantastic performance on the field.”

"Thank you. But I want us to get smoother in transition between the sets. And some girls need to be sharper in their individual execution of arm and leg angles as well as synchronization within the group. I expect us to be ready to compete at the drill team playoffs at the end of the season. It's nice to perform for the crowd, but we're in it to win it all."

If I were a betting man, I would bet Deb the Clomper shows no smile under her mask.

As they turn to leave, "Thank you for wearing your masks inside the press box," I tell them.

Clomper brakes so fast that Squeaker bumps into her backside. "Glad to. We want everyone to be safe," Deb says. To Dan, "Thanks again for the kind compliments from the stadium speakers. I know the parents appreciate it."

Dan nods as the ladies clomp and squeak out of the press box.

"See you next halftime," Deb shouts as the door scrapes closed.

***

Why do all the female visitors to the press box wear masks while none of the male visitors wear masks? There must be some deep sociological reason that escapes me. Whatever. I compile the stats and interrupt a conversation between Dan and the Music man. "Here you go, Dan. Strong stats for the good guys."

"Great tunes," I tell Marty.

"Thanks. I try."

To both, "My new favorite nickname belongs to the Demik kid." Two blank stares greet my comment. "John 'Pan' Demik...as in global pandemic."

"Oh, I missed it."

"Me too. That is clever," Dan says.

The officials stride to midfield, a reminder for me to hurry with my bio-break. Thank goodness there's a toilet in the press box.

The Big Voice addresses the stadium crowd: **"Please give another hand to the Deer Park Wildcatters Golden Hearts drill team! These young ladies do an outstanding job!**

"Now, some unofficial halftime stats. The visiting Tiger Sharks had four possessions, ran 19 plays for 77 yards. Leading ball carriers were John

'Hot Shot' Sherman with seven carries for 18 yards, Phil 'Griffin' Coulter with five carries for 38 yards, and Karl 'Machete' Aguerra with five carries for 21 yards."

After a swig of water and a deep breath, the Big Voice states: **"Our home team Cats had five series, ran 15 plays for 141 yards and three touchdowns. Jules 'J-Dawg' Bass had six carries for 25 yards, one rushing touchdown, two pass completions. Miles 'Beast Mode' Bannon added four carries for 21 yards and one reception for 51 yards and a touchdown. Kyle 'Goose' Frye with three carries for 30 yards and one touchdown. John 'Pan' Demik with two carries, and Simon 'Superman' Tam with one reception."**

The Music Man triggers an iconic theme song from a classic underdog movie, a song that urges the listener to battle to keep dreams alive, to rise to the challenge, to survive against the odds, to display the "Eye of the Tiger."

The Cats set five attackers on each side of the kicker at the south 40-yard line while the Tiger Shark's return team disperses players along their 49-, 40- and 25-yard lines.

Dan's cell phone rattles against the vinyl countertop. He glances at the phone to identify the sender, deems the person important enough to interrupt the booth activity, and reads the text. Dan smiles and shouts, "Hey, Marty!"

"Yo!" Marty hollers back.

"It's our coach. He asks that 'Eye of the Tiger' not be played while his team battles a visiting team with 'Tiger' in its name," Dan yells.

"My bad. I should have thought of that. It won't happen again." The stadium music fades to silence.

Man, is there anything The Coach doesn't consider for his football game?

"Lonnie 'Skittles' Molari kicking off for the Cats to start the second half."

The lead official points to the kicker. Skittles double times his half-steps to the football and drives the ball off the tee.

The football bounces at the 33-yard line, where a deep back, Machete, snags it and sprints toward the near sideline.

The maroon wave crashes into the black wall of Tiger Sharks. Two Cat attackers infiltrate the semi-porous wall of blockers.

X-Man and Hit Man knock Machete out of bounds at the 40-yard line.

"Forced out of bounds by Xavier 'X-Man' Gonzales and Matthew 'Hit Man' Castillo. First and ten Tiger Sharks."

Okay, Matthew got his stadium shout out.

The opposing offensive and defensive squads jog onto the field. Both teams align in the same offensive or defensive formation they ended with in the first half. The far side official sets the chain gang to display ball location and distance to the next first down. In the booth, I close out the active row of the game log sheet to document the kickoff and start the next row for the upcoming play.

"A lot of new jersey numbers on defense," I say.

"We have a long roster. The Coach is trying to get everyone their required minimum number of plays. You don't want to play your subs late if the game is on the line." Dan adds, "He plays the same core players, like sergeants on the field, to maintain overall squad discipline."

The first down play is an adventure.

"Fumble! Fumble on the play!"

The interior players, their arms and legs projecting from maroon jerseys and black jerseys, white pants and gray pants, intertwine in a pile as though they collapse during a game of Twister. All four officials converge on the pile. The lead official points his arm over the Cat defense. The far sideline official directs the chain gang down marker to anchor his pole at the 39-yard line and flip the placards from "1" to "2" to indicate the change in downs. I update the log sheet.

"Tiger Sharks recover. Second and ten coming up."

The Great One hikes the football to the quarterback, Hurricane.

Hurricane wheels left. He tosses the ball to Machete.

Machete sprints left behind Hot Shot.

Argh. No maroon jerseys at the point of attack.

Machete turns the corner. Down the sideline.

Bullet and Shazam shove Machete out of bounds.

"Handoff around the left side. Some room down the sideline. Forced out of bounds in Cats territory."

"Who was the ball carrier?"

"Number 24."

"Karl 'Machete' Aguerra with a fine run."

"Fourteen yards."

"Gain of 14 yards on the play. First and ten Tiger Sharks from the Cats 47-yard line."

"That was an impressive run," Dan says.

"Yeah, don't do it again."

On the next play: **"Quarterback dive into the right side of the line. Stuffed! Crushed at the line of scrimmage! Travis 'Terminator' Weathers**

and Miles 'Beast Mode' Bannon with the stop. Second and long coming up."

On second down: **"Pitch to the tailback to the right..."**

"Reverse."

"He hands off to the wide receiver running to left. Hit behind the line! Loss of eight yards! Jules 'J-Dawg' Bass! Third and eighteen to go."

"Man, J-Dawg shot through their line as though he heard the play called in the Shark huddle," I comment.

An incomplete pass results from the third down play.

"That brings up fourth and long for the Tiger Sharks. Come on, Cats fans. Give a yell. Dee-fense!. Dee-fense!"

'Noculars are raised. Football is hiked. Play is run.

"Quarterback drops back to pass...Caught! Pass is caught."

"What number?"

"Thirty-four."

"Phil 'Griffin' Colter with the catch. Dragged down short of the first down mark. Great tackle by 'Goose' Frye. The ball goes over on downs. First and ten Cats. Give a hand to our defense!"

"Oh, man, they almost made the first down," I say.

I complete the active line in the logbook to close out the Tiger Shark possession and start the next line for the Cat's possession.

"Dream On," a classic rock anthem that tells us life is short, so strive now to achieve your dreams, blares from the stadium speakers.

As the song plays, the Cats prepare to attack with a full-house backfield: quarterback, fullback, two halfbacks. One wide receiver splits fifteen yards to the left of the offensive line.

"Full house backfield. One wideout."

After hearing all this classic rock today, I could sure go for some Led Zeppelin.

"The Cats open in their full-house backfield."

To counter, the Tiger Sharks mount their defense with five defensive linemen, three linebackers, one cornerback, and one deep safety.

"I see Matthew at right tackle. I want to focus on him. Keep an eye on the play for me?"

"You got it."

'Noculars are raised. Football is hiked. Play is run.

"Quarterback for two yards."

"Quarterback keeper up the middle. Jules 'J-Dawg' Bass with the carry."

The active row ends, the future row starts.

'Noculars are raised. Football...is not snapped.

The near side official drops his yellow penalty flag, unhooks a mask strap, blows his whistle and sprints to the football while rolling his wrists over each other. He lifts his mask into place and leans forward to the lead official, who faces the press box, rolls his hands over each other and points to the Cat side. He places the ball five yards back from the previous line of scrimmage.

"False start against the Cats. That brings up second and thirteen."

"Matthew jumped early, but I'm okay with it. I want him to show some aggressiveness."

'Noculars are raised. Football is hiked. Play is run.

"Hand off to Goose into the middle. Six yards."

"Kyle 'Goose' Frye with a tough six-yard run."

The active row ends, the future row starts.

While the officials spot the football, J-Dawg hustles to the sideline to get instructions from The Coach. He sprints back to the huddle. The teams reset along the line of scrimmage.

On the next play, J-Dawg rolls around right end behind Big G and Lights Out. Gain of 5 yards.

"Fourth down coming up. Let our boys hear you, Cats fans!"

'Noculars are raised. Football is hiked. Play is run.

"Handoff to the fullback. He's gang tackled."

"We got it."

The lead official sprints to the pile of players. He sights the ball relative to the sideline yardage marker and points over the Tiger Sharks players.

"Gain of three yards on the play. 'Beast Mode' Bannon. And that is enough for another Cats...First Dooown!"

Need for Speed and Blue Thunder each collect 4 yards on a pair of runs.

On third down, Bullet hikes the ball to J-Dawg.

J-Dawg slides the ball into Goose's "breadbasket."

"Quarterback hands off to Goose around left end."

Goose shifts the ball to his left arm as he sweeps around the left side.

Hit Man and Dirty Thirty tie up the Tiger Shark linemen at the point of attack.

Crackers, the wide receiver, occupies the cornerback.

Goose slides between the Hit Man and Crackers.

Run!

"He's free down the sideline!"

Goose soars untouched down the sideline.

"He's at the 30...the 20...the 10...Touchdooown! Touchdown, Goose! Goose on the loose!"

"Wow. The whole left side of the line blocked well," I say. "He wasn't even touched."

"Great blocking to spring Goose. Thirty-seven yards on the touchdown run. The score is Cats 26, Tiger Sharks 0."

In my mental "amazing coincidence" category: For the next music selection, the Music Man sets my head bobbing as the speakers flood the stadium with the pounding drums and blazing guitars to introduce lonely "Rock-n-Roll."

"Matthew is being subbed for now," Dan says. "He jogs straight for the bench under the tent to sit in the shade. I can see five minutes to take a break. Then I expect to see him on the sideline with his teammates, encouraging those still playing the field."

As the special team units set up for the extra point, the active log sheet line is closed out while nine Cats players crouch in a three-point stance along the line of scrimmage. One player, J-Dawg, drops to a knee ten yards behind the center, Nate Dog. A kicker, Skittles, stands a yard away and waits for the ball to be spotted upright. Eleven Tiger Shark players hop up and down along the line of scrimmage in an uncoordinated jumping jacks routine.

"We're going to try a kick."

"Surprising. After the Sophomore kicker's family moved back to Norway, I expected us to stick to runs or passes for extra point tries this season," Dan says.

Nate Dog hikes the ball on one hop to the kneeling J-Dawg, who tilts the ball lengthwise against the turf. Skittles steps into the ball and sends an arching drive several yards outside the right vertical goalpost.

"The kick is wide right. The score remains Cats 26, Tiger Sharks 0."

"Are you warm?" I ask while I update the game log sheet.

"A little."

I twist out of the announcer's booth and check the thermostat mounted on the back wall of the observation room. The thermostat indicates a 78°F room temperature even though the air conditioner thermostat controller rests at maximum allowable cooling (68°F). "The AC is having trouble keeping up," I shout.

The game progresses with the Cats exercising ball control while limiting the football touches their playmakers get on offense. Less than seven minutes remain in the game. A basic play unfolds like many others: The quarterback J-Dawg receives the snap, whirls to his left, and hands off the football to running back Need for Speed. He angles between the left guard Dirty Thirty and left tackle Hit Man. Both offensive linemen hold their blocks long enough for the back to gain four yards before the linebackers bring him down. During the play, a Tiger Sharks defensive lineman forces Dirty Thirty backwards, and he tumbles over the extended right leg of the Cat left tackle.

I follow the running back's progress and record the play on the game log sheet. Dan, binoculars focused on the field, rises from his chair. Players on both squads drop to one knee. Two coaches from the Cats sideline jog onto the field.

"Maroon jersey on the field," I say.

"It's Matthew. Down from friendly fire."

We watch in silence as one coach drops to his knee to talk to Matthew. After twenty or thirty seconds, each coach hefts Hit Man upward by his shoulder pads. Matthew does not put any weight on his right leg while both coaches support his hop-step to the Cat's bench under the sideline tarp.

"Was he ever helped off the field—in any game or any practice?"

"Never." Dan displays a scrunched forehead as he stares onto the field. "It feels a lot different when it's your boy who limps off the field. Football is a tough sport. It should breed tougher boys. I believe I'm making the right call by letting him play. At least, I pray I'm right."

A substitute Cats offensive lineman sprints onto the field into the huddle.

Dan stoops down to the mic and says, **"Let's give that young man a hand."** He holds down the mic button for a few extra beats so my hand claps echo from the announcer's booth through the stadium speakers. Dan stands, chiseled in place. His binoculars fixate on the far sideline.

The Cats conduct a running play I document in the game log sheet. Refocus on the Cat tent. Sean exchanges places with a junior high kid who was doing water boy duty and drops to one knee next to the seated Matthew, one hand on his son's lap. Matthew faces Sean: helmet off, face reddened, hair mussed, forehead sweaty, no tears. Sean hands him a water bottle and speaks to Matthew, who nods several times.

The Cats conduct another running play, and I update the game log sheet. Refocus on the Cat tent. Sean still kneels next to Matthew when a coach approaches him. Whatever the coach says triggers Sean to whip his head around and scream something at him. The coach raises both arms, palms outward in surrender, and backs up three paces before twisting back to the sideline. Not a good time to get between Sean and his son.

Matthew rises from the bench, unassisted, while his dad stands beside him. Matthew takes a cautious half step, then puts his full weight on his legs and flexes his right knee. He takes a few steps, nods to his dad, and sits back on the bench. Sean pats him on the shoulder pads and heads back to the sideline.

Dan issues a "whooo" sigh as he plops down in his chair. "Where are we?"

When the football changes possession, the Tiger Sharks attempt several passes but fail to threaten the end zone. The final score: Wildcatters 33, Tiger Sharks 0.

As the four officials, masks off, stride off the field to take their break, the players from each team uncoil from their sidelines along the midfield stripe in the traditional demonstration of sportsmanship. Matthew joins the Cats line—no apparent limp. The black and maroon helmets bob their heads as they pass one another. No hand touches. At the end of the procession, the winning Cats sprint back to the far sideline except for Matthew, who returns at a steady pace. The losing Tiger Sharks jog back to the near sideline. The fans in the stands, regardless of which team they support, stand and applaud the boys' efforts.

Dan's phone vibrates against the counter to notify him regarding receipt of a text message. "A text from Cheryl. Sean told her Matthew is fine. Only shaken up a bit. More scared than hurt."

"That's good news. Are you going to have a doctor check him out?"

"We'll see how he feels tonight. If he doesn't have any pain, and no pain or swelling tomorrow, we'll press on as normal. For the Monday practice, I'll ask The Coach to limit Matthew to non-contact drills, see how he does, see how he feels afterwards. We can't hold him out for no reason. If you don't practice, you don't play. It's a league rule."

"Sounds like a plan."

Final Junior game duty: auction the game football. The Wildcatters organization manager holds the game ball skyward as he paces back-and-forth ten yards inside the near sideline at midfield. Dan must be extra pumped—he starts the bidding at $100 instead of the usual $50. The Ball Bearer drifts his gaze from one side of the stands to the other and points and shouts when he sees a bidder wave to him.

"We have $250 now! Looking for $300. A lifetime memory. You may never, ever have this chance again. The chance of a lifetime! Put it on your fireplace mantle. Put it on a bookshelf, in a trophy case. I have a game football myself and glad to have one. We are at two fifty...Going once...Going twice...Last chance!"

The Ball Bearer raises both arms skyward and walks to the sideline.

"Sold! Thank you, sir. Please collect the football at the Cats table under the stands."

Does Dan generate extra income for the Cats organization through his enthusiastic auctioneering? Only the organization treasurer has the information. Do they ever compare football receipts with and without Dan as auctioneer? We'll never know.

"Good game for the good guys."

"Yeah. So far, our Cats organization is three wins, one loss for the day," Dan says. "The Senior games are often my favorites. They have the most experienced kids and more sophisticated play calls."

"Well, let's see how it goes for the first, and I hope the last, Senior home opener during a COVID global pandemic."

Chapter Eleven

When the Hurley Burley's Done

"Well, it's been a long day, but we've gotten through it. One more game to go."

"Yeah, but the booth is so steaming hot," Dan says. "This last game will be an ordeal."

"I'll check the air conditioner again." The thermostat indicates room temperature sits at 83°F. I slide in front of the overhead grill that should spew cool air into the press box and spread my arms wide apart. Nothing. No air flow. "The AC isn't working," I shout.

"Great," he replies as he texts the organization manager. "I'm texting the manager about the AC. I bet he jumps right on it as though he's sitting here with us."

Dan slides the cell phone onto the countertop. Less than a minute later, the phone rattles against the vinyl. "Too quick." He summarizes the text: "The league manager is checking on it. The school district gave him an emergency contact number for maintenance issues, so we'll see what they say."

"Limelight," a classic rocker about the stresses of performing before a mass audience, rushes from the stadium speakers.

The mob in maroon jerseys sprints from the south end zone to their tent on the far sideline. The black jerseys meander along the near sideline from the north end zone to their gray tent. Four officials stride toward midfield. One official points to each sideline before they have even reached the middle of the field.

The phone vibration draws our attention back into the booth. "Oh, no," Dan says as he reads the text.

"That sounds ominous."

"The press box temperature is computer controlled. Beyond a certain time of day, the air conditioner is regulated to a higher setpoint to conserve electricity. He doesn't know the setpoint. The AC is out of his control." He looks at me. "All these lightning delays kept us here longer than expected." He hollers to the rest of the press box: "Bad news, guys. The press box is getting toasty."

"Mid-nineties outside. Sunlight pouring through gaps in the clouds. It'll get boiling hot where we sit, right next to these windows."

"There's a heat index limit in place to protect the kids playing outside. Now we need one for the press box too," Dan quips.

"Well, it is what it is. The great travails of the press box don't affect the action on the field. We'll get through it."

From the big voice in the sky: **"I hope you are ready for some footbaaall! Cats football! Thanks for hanging in there with us today. We expect a great game between the visiting Pasadena Tiger Sharks and our Deer Park Wildcatters Senior squads."**

Three players from each sideline stride to the officials at midfield. Each official has tugged their mask to their chin. I record the player jersey numbers in the margin of the game log sheet.

"Here is your Senior Cat roster."

I recognize most of the nicknames from the Darts Junior team last season: Snake, Ghost, The Boom, Beast, Assassin, Mad Dog, Pac-Man, Krusher, Clutch and my favorite: Vicious—a natural fit with the first name, Sid. And I'm not a Sex Pistols fan.

The lead official aligns the two sets of captains to face each other to start the on-field ritual. The captains bob their heads at each other. No handshakes. The official displays both faces of the ceremonial coin to each captain. One of the visitor Tiger Sharks captains calls heads or tails, at least I presume so since I can't make out what they say to each other. No lip-reading skills. The official tosses the coin to head level and lets it fall to the turf. He picks up the coin and shows it to each captain.

Other names, likely incorporated from the Cats Junior squad, I don't recognize.

"Number 9. Paul 'Gunner' Forster, Wide receiver.
Number 17. Glen 'The Headhunter' Prejean, *Line*-man!"

I wince at the pronunciation of that name.

"Number 20. Manny 'Top Gun' Lorian, Wide receiver.
Number 55. John 'Hambone' Sherridan, Running back."

The official repositions the players face-to-face. The three Cat captains line up at the south 49-yard line and face north as the three Tiger Shark captains return their gaze from two yards away. The official taps the nearest Tiger Shark player on the shoulder, extends both arms in front of him, and draws them back to his chest. He claps his hands to send both sets of team captains jogging back to their respective sidelines.

"Ready?"

"Shoot."

Dan scribbles on scratch paper as I recite: "Cat captains are 1, 15, 88. Shark captains are 7, 22, 50. Sharks won the toss and will receive."

"Got it."

"Team captains for the Cats are Dan 'Ghost' Scully, Jake 'The Snake' Ramos and Alvin 'Krusher' Kricek. Captains for the Tiger Sharks are Ryan 'Patriot' Nicholson, Oscar 'Cobra' Dunham and Mark 'Hit Maker' Docken. Tiger Sharks won the toss and will receive the opening kickoff."

The two special team units jog onto the field under speakers that thunder the ominous opening beat from "Iron Man," a classic hard rocker re-popularized in a successful series of blockbuster movies.

The Cats align along the south 40-yard line with five players on each side of the kicker. The Tiger Sharks disperse players along their side of the midfield stripe, along the 40-yard line, and at the 25-yard line.

"By the way," I tell Dan, "If we were in Louisiana, your 'Pree-Jeen' name would be pronounced 'Pray-Zhahn'."

"Mm. My mistake. Every Thursday practice, I go from one squad to the next to collect the team rosters for the Saturday games and go over each boy's name pronunciation with a coach. Hah, I even read through the team roster names with our company receptionist on Fridays to make sure I get it right. In this case, I missed one."

"Sid 'Vicious' Anderson kicking off for the Cats."

The lead official points to the kicker, and the music stops. Vicious takes a dozen rapid staccato mini-steps to the football and drives it off the tee. A maroon-and-gold wave percolates downfield through the black-and-gray wall.

The football flies in a low arch, perhaps only ten yards high, and bounces once into the hands of a Tiger Shark deep return man, Cobra. He clutches the football and dashes up the far sideline.

Top Gun and Pac-Man shove the Cobra out of bounds at the 47-yard line.

"Ball advanced to their 47-yard line. First and ten Tiger Sharks."

The offensive and defensive units jog onto the field while I document the kickoff results in the game log. The Tiger Sharks array six linemen in a three-point stance along the line of scrimmage as a quarterback sets up in the "shotgun" position six yards behind the center. He raises both hands, perhaps one foot apart, toward the line of scrimmage. A lone running back bends over, hands-to-knees, to the left of the quarterback while the two wide receivers each split fifteen yards wide from their offensive line. One Tiger Shark player hunches hands-to-knees behind the right guard next to the center.

To counter, the Cats mount their defense with five linemen in a three-point stance opposite the crouched Tiger Sharks. Three linebackers stand several yards behind the defensive line to reinforce at the point of attack. Two cornerbacks match up against the wide receivers. A lone deep safety stands guard fifteen yards downfield from the football.

Meanwhile, the chain gang aligns their first down distance poles and ball marker pole per referee directions.

"Are you seeing this?" I ask.

"Seeing what?"

"The Tiger Sharks. They positioned a player behind the right guard."

He trains his binoculars toward the Tiger Shark formation. "Never seen that done before."

"It's an interesting bit of deception. He can slide along the line, set up before the snap, and act as an extra blocker at the point of attack before the defense can realign—a Neanderthal sledgehammer approach. Or he can step behind the center and act as a conventional quarterback. Or the snap might go to the shotgun quarterback for a handoff or pass from a position that does not require the QB to drop back. Lots of pre-snap options."

"Deception. I can use that," Dan says. "I wonder how our eleven- and twelve-year-old kids will handle the unfamiliar option offense."

'Noculars are raised. Football is hiked. Play is run.

"Handoff to the tailback. Plunge into the meat grinder over right guard. Short gain on the play. Sid 'Vicious' Anderson on the stop for the Cats."

The active row ends, the future row starts.

"I call your attention to the deceptive formation the Tiger Sharks employ. One of their players lines up right behind an offensive lineman near the center."

'Noculars are raised. Football is hiked. Play is run.

"Quarterback sweep to the right. Ryan 'Patriot' Nicholson with the carry. That brings up third and six."

The active row ends, the future row starts.

The press box door scrapes open. A diminutive gladiator in rubber cleats clomps through the observation room to the announcer's booth doorway. "Hey, Poppa," Cat Jersey 32 says.

I nod and send him a masked smile. "You gave us a little scare earlier."

Without diverting his gaze from the field, Dan says, "Matthew, what happened out there?"

"Somebody rolled onto the back of my leg. My knee hurt at first, but I'm okay now."

"Good!"

"I wanted to go back in, but the coach wouldn't let me."

"He probably wanted to get all the guys playing time," I say.

"Prob'ly."

"Is Cheryl still here?" Dan asks.

"Yeah. She stayed to watch the Senior game with her friends. Dad went back home to shower and sleep before he heads back to work tonight." Matthew waits several seconds and, not getting Dan's focused attention, asks, "Can you help take off my shoulder pads?"

"Sure," he says. To me, "Watch the game?"

"You got it."

Dan spins out of the chair. Matthew drops his helmet with a "thud" and raises both arms skyward for Dan to tug off his jersey and shoulder pads. I focus on the action on the field while a few "ouches" spew from behind me.

"You need to keep quiet in the large observation room. We're busy in here."

Matthew slips his jersey back on and asks: "Can I have some money for the concession stand?"

"Okay. Here's ten dollars. Earl, do you want anything?"

Eyes to the field, I shake my head no.

"Thank you," says Matthew as he dashes from the press box with no apparent limp.

"Of course, he leaves his helmet and pads here." Dan sits back down in his chair and asks, "What do we got?"

"Handoff to the tailback. Gain of two yards," I tell him. "Fourth down coming up."

"That brings up fourth down. Okay, Cats fans. Let...our...dee...fense...hear...you!"

"Somebody on their side jumped."

The far sideline official drops his yellow flag and sprints to the football while he waves his arms overhead. His mask dangles from one ear as he relays the penalty to the lead official. The masked lead official, who faces the press box, rolls his hands over one another in front of his chest and points to the Tiger Shark side.

"False start on the Tiger Sharks. That backs the ball five yards. Still fourth down. Cat fans, get cranked up again! Let our defensive players hear you!"

The press box door scrapes open. A maskless young man in a sweatshirt and orange baseball cap steps into the observation room. No sign of strained breathing.

"Hey, Dan."

"Hey, Jeremy," Dan yells back. To me, "Have you met Jeremy? The grandson of one of Cheryl's closest friends."

"I remember."

Jeremy rolls a chair to the counter and hunches over his cell phone.

"Hey, Dan," he hollers. "It's sure hot in here."

"Tell me about it," Dan yells back.

'Noculars are raised. Football is hiked. Play is run.

"Pitch to the tailback...around left side. He has the sideline! Forced out of bounds in Cats territory."

"How many yards?"

"Where did they spot it?"

"At the thirty-five."

"Sixteen."

"Sixteen yards on the run by Jack 'Dominator' Lewis. First and ten Tiger Sharks from the Cats 35-yard line."

"That missed tackle hurt."

The active row is finished, the future row is started.

Jeremy pushes the chair away from the counter and spins the rolling chair to face the rear wall. I bet he stands at the thermostat and tries to jab the set point tab lower. "Hey, Dan," he yells. "The air conditioner isn't working."

"Really?" I reply in a sarcastic tone.

The next play: **"Handoff into the middle of the line. Oscar 'Cobra' Dunham. Gain of five on the play."**

"Did you see that? The center hiked the football sideways, not between his legs, to the back spotted behind the guard. Our guys in the trenches were caught off guard," I say. "I'm glad our linebackers were all over the football."

Jeremy rolls his chair back to the counter and focuses on his cell phone.

"Hey, Dan," Jeremy shouts. "Did you see the SEC is going to play conference football games starting next month? Teams are checked for COVID three days before each game. All COVID positive players and coaches have to sit out the game."

"Yeah," Dan shouts back. "Big competitive advantage for the teams that manage COVID best."

The Tiger Sharks line up with quarterback Patriot in shotgun formation. The upback, Cobra, locates behind his right tackle.

Center Hit Maker snaps the football to Patriot.

Patriot takes one step to his right. He cuts inside.

Draw!

Headhunter, the Cat linebacker, whiffs as Patriot streaks past him.

Where's our deep safety?

"Quarterback rolls to...draw! Keeper through the middle! To the 20...the 10...Touchdown! Ryan 'Patriot' Nichols with 35 yards on the touchdown gallop."

"My God. It was like the parting of the Red Sea. The kid ran through the middle untouched to the end zone."

"Somebody was out of position. Maybe multiple somebodies," Dan says.

I close out the active row to document the touchdown while a classic rocker, a song that urges you to stay positive, fight through tough times, go ahead and "Jump," resounds throughout the stadium.

The special team squads line up for the extra point under the cascading music. The Tiger Sharks put nine players in the crouched, three-point stance. One player, ten yards behind the ball, drops to one knee. The other player stands a few yards further back. All eleven Cats jump up and down along the line of scrimmage while they thrash their arms overhead. Get Your Mind Right takes three long strides to the football and hooks the ball high to his left.

The Big Voice declares: **"The kick is no good. Wide left. The score remains Tiger Sharks 6, Cats 0. The Cats first opportunity on offense is coming up."**

"Hey, Dan," Jeremy shouts. "Did you see professional sports stadiums can open to fans now as long as they stay below 25 percent of total capacity?"

"Sure did," Dan hollers back. "The governor established some kind of standard for crowd size to avoid a superspreader event just in time for the professional football season. Hope it works."

"Recap?"

"Shoot."

"Six plays, 53 yards, 35-yard TD run."

"Scoring drive recap. The Tiger Sharks needed six plays to drive 53 yards, capped by a touchdown run of 35 yards."

The Cat return team jogs toward the south side of midfield while the Tiger Shark kickoff unit sets along the north 40-yard line.

The Cats form up with five players along their 49-yard line, four players across the 40-yard line and two at the 25-yard line.

"Walt 'Get Your Mind Right' Bishop kicking off for the Tiger Sharks."

A dynamic female vocalist blares from the stadium speakers with the defiant, self-confident message, no matter the challenge, you can't keep her down, so go ahead and "Hit Me With Your Best Shot."

The music stops as the lead official points to the kicker, who runs at the football and drives it in an arch to the Cat's 30-yard line. A Cat back, Clutch, catches the ball, cradles it in his arms, and sprints straight up the field. Three black jerseys smother the ball carrier at the Tiger Shark 47-yard line.

"Fine return by Owen 'Clutch' Pena sets the Cats up in Tiger Shark territory."

"Hey, Dan," comes yet another shout from the observation room. "No cash transactions allowed in college and professional stadiums. Credit cards only. They're trying to minimize direct person-to-person contact."

"That's all I use anyway," Dan hollers.

The Cats set their attack in a split backs formation with a wide receiver to each side of the offensive line. The Tiger Sharks oppose them with four crouched defensive linemen, four linebackers, two cornerbacks, and one deep safety.

"Even the Shark defensive alignment is unusual. Four linebackers offset behind four defensive linemen," I say.

"Handoff to the tailback into the left side. Nice run by Clive 'Tank' Bruckman! Gain of four yards on the play."

After The Snake ekes out one yard and Hambone generates another four yards, **"Toss sweep to the halfback around the right end. Forced out of bounds near the 35-yard line. John 'Hambone' Sherridan with the carry. And that is enough for Cats...First Dooown!"**

"Hey, Dan," comes a shout from the observation room. "It's getting too hot in here. I'll go sit with family for a while. See you later." Jeremy's chair rolls to the back wall and door scrapes open to announce his departure from the press box.

"He'd rather be outside in 95-degree heat under a tarp than in here with us," I say.

"I understand how Jeremy feels. A pleasant breeze from the Gulf with the storm front blowing through. No air circulation at all in here."

Clutch and Tank each conduct a run for a short gain. The next play comes out of nowhere.

"Hand...No. Quarterback keeper around the left end. He's free down the sideline! To the 20...the 10...Touchdooown!"

"How many yards?"

"Twenty-seven."

"Jake 'The Snake' Ramos with 27 yards for the touchdown. The score is tied at six apiece. Extra point try is coming up."

"Great fake to the halfback," I say.

"Had me fooled."

From the stadium speakers, "Sharp Dressed Man," a straight-forward classic rock song from a Houston hometown band about their efforts to dress to impress, fills the stadium.

In the booth, I close out the active row in the game log sheet to account for the score.

On the field, the Cats align in a three wide receiver shotgun formation. Quarterback Snake stands six yards behind the center with open hands extended forward. One running back stands, hands-to-knees, to his left. The Tiger Sharks oppose with six defensive linemen, two linebackers and three cornerbacks. The music stops when the referee signals for the play to start.

Snake hunches low to catch the ankle-high snap and throws the pass to his right a half-second before onrushing black jerseys reach him. The lone wide receiver to that side, Top Gun, angles toward the rear middle of the end zone. The cornerback hangs with the receiver and knocks the football to the turf.

"Incomplete pass. Intended for Manny 'Top Gun' Lorian. The score remains tied at six all. The Cats kickoff is coming up."

"This is a fun game to call. Two well-matched teams," Dan comments. "Enough experience so few penalties."

"It would be more fun if it weren't so hot in here. We can't prop the door open. It's hotter outside, no guarantee we get a breeze inside, plus we let in noise and insects. I'm bringing a fan next time in case we lose our AC again."

Both antagonists exchange blows into the second quarter. The scoreboard displays Visitors 13 and Home 12 with 6:44 left on the clock in the second quarter when the lead official waves his arms overhead and picks up the game football. The Cats jog to their dressing room at the SW corner of the stadium while the Tiger Shark players jog to theirs at the NE corner. The four officials trail after the black jerseys to get to the break room.

"No....No." I leave my binoculars and phone on the counter and scramble to scrape open the press box door. A long, continuous blare washes over me from beyond the north end of the stadium. "The lightning alarm horn is going off again," I holler.

"I know," Dan yells back. "Just got the text. A thirty-minute lightning delay has been triggered."

***

I push the press box door close. I'll stand outside a while and catch some of the breeze from the southeast. Tug my brand-new Cats cap tighter down on my head. Lower the mask to my chin. My maskless mouth sucks in moisture from the atmosphere—it's humid out here. After one minute, the horn goes silent to await an all-clear signal.

"I regret to pass on that a lightning strike has been detected in the vicinity of the stadium. The strike detection protocol requires a minimum thirty-minute delay. If lightning is detected again, then the thirty-minute delay restarts. During the delay, we *strongly recommend* that fans vacate the stands. We will announce when conditions are met that allow us to resume. Thank you for your understanding."

What does a bored engineer, without a smartphone, do at the top of an idle stadium? Well, I'm not studying cracks in the concrete. Look to the sky. No birds fly in this wind, but the majestic clouds impress. The aerial tidal wave from the gulf sweeps over the area that surrounds the stadium: an onslaught of dark streamers pour from bruise-colored clouds to hammer LaPorte to the east; a blanket of bulbous deep gray clouds roll past the stadium to the west and threaten to release a torrent at any moment; jagged flashes of lightning ripple against the swirling black clouds north of the ship channel, too far away to detect the associated thunderclaps; a merciful sliver of partly-cloudy sky from the southeast permits intermittent rays of sunlight to strike from above the stadium—all of which dwarf this man-made monolith to football.

The fans in the stands take the threat of the inclement conditions that hang over their heads in a stoic manner. I count six blue, four maroon, two gray, one white, and one red tarp. Half the tents remain occupied. Many fans sit on exposed metal seats with their umbrellas by their sides. The lone figure who sat by himself in the middle of the stands during the prior lightning delay has vanished.

Uh-oh. The spots between my right foot and toes contract in pain. Toe cramps. Lean forward, mesh fingers through chain-link fence, rock up and down on balls of both feet several times. Okay now.

The press box door scrapes open, and Dan emerges. He joins me by the fence, both our untucked shirts flap in the wind, our grotesque elongated shadows intertwine with the parked cars outside the east side of the stadium. After tugging his cap down, Dan says, "Hot with some breeze out here versus less hot with no breeze inside." He looks at me. "According to league rules, we're not supposed to be out here during a lightning delay."

I point through the chain-link fence at the police station roof on the opposite side of the main street through town. "Tough. They can dispatch their SWAT team. The police station is so close to the stadium, they could arrive in under a minute."

"Hah," Dan says as he swings his head around the stadium. "You do get a broad view of the area from here. High school buildings to the immediate north and east, homes to the west, and the church and elder care facility along the south road. Remember that old folks home? Dad stayed there a few years ago for a 30-day rehab period."

"I remember. That place sucked—old, understaffed, occasional whiff of urine. Wheelchairs that cross the entrance threshold emit frequent 'beeps' as octogenarians try to escape. Attendants chase after them to wheel them back inside. Rooms designed for one person retrofitted for double occupancy. No privacy. Personal items disappear from the room." I shake my head. "You put a bullet in my brain before you leave me in a pit like that."

"You can afford a much better nursing home. Tell whoever holds your medical power of attorney what you want."

"I still need a formal medical POA."

"Well, your relatives are around to help. If we are also in your will, our choice will be to keep you comfortable or to save your money for our inheritance. Hmm, I wonder what we'll choose."

Okay. Cross arms. Put scowl on my face. Stare into Dan's eyes. He gets my "just bite me" stare instead of my "you're full of it" stare.

"Just funning with you,"—Dan slaps my shoulder—"just funning. But you need to put your wishes in writing. I won't remember your long-term care desires."

"Won't remember. Your four years in youth tackle football didn't cause the degenerative brain disease that concerns professional players, and you're no...whatever comes after octogenarian. But I hear you. I don't want to overstress those who love me about my health care. I need to get my will and POA in order." Next year, for sure.

"I promise you're not ending up in an elder care facility as bad as that one. Dad sure hated it there. He wanted to get out of that place, get back home to mom, so he worked hard during his 30-day rehab period to build his strength enough so he could lift himself after a fall."

"Dad was plenty motivated. He realized he can't rely on Mom to cater to every single home care desire," I say. "I call Mom every Sunday evening, but she never tells me if anything is wrong. I assume things are all right at their house."

"Cheryl stops by there a couple times each week to make sure they're okay. I stop by...maybe twice a month. And James and Anne live a few miles away, so they see them every week. Make sure they are healthy, keep up with their meds. Make sure they have plenty to eat."

"Does Dad still wheel himself to the food pantry to see if the shelves are stocked? He always worries about the amount of food in the house."

"Dad and food are not my favorite subjects. In junior high, I asked him if I could go with him on a take-your-child-to-work day. He said 'No. Who would pay for lunch?'" Dan does not smile at the recollection. "I won't leave Matthew with a memory like that. Whether we eat at an expensive steak restaurant or a fast-food drive through, I get Matthew whatever he wants. Cheryl thinks I'm obsessive regarding food. 'Jordan'—she always calls me by last name when she gets aggravated at me—'stop spoiling our boy.' I do it anyway."

"I went on a parent-child workday once with Dad," I recount. "The trip was a bore. Since he inspected telephone poles for the phone company, we took a two-hour drive to a contract manufacturer in the middle of nowhere to look at creosote. No radio. No conversation. For lunch, he bought me a tuna sandwich from some mobile van that stopped by the plant site. He continued working while I ate in an empty lunchroom. After Dad finished work, a long, boring drive back home."

"Hmm." Dan looks inward to the stadium, crosses his arms and leans against the chain-link fence.

"Don't be too hard on the old man. Sometime later, decades after I left home, I asked Dad why we moved from the nice, two-story home in Pasadena to the oddball flat-roof house in LaPorte and then to the smaller house in Deer Park. He told me when we lived in Pasadena, he came home from work one day, saw the empty kitchen pantry, and didn't have enough money to buy groceries. After that, Dad resolved to move us to a house with lower monthly mortgage payments to make sure he could provide food for the family."

"I never heard that before," Dan says. He recalls, with a smile, "I remember Mom sure worked miracles with family meals. We never went hungry. She stretched meals enough to feed four boys. I remember a lot of oatmeal for breakfast. Spaghetti dinners on many evenings. And so much Hamburger Helper that I thought it was a basic food group."

"Yeah, parents are crucial for their children. Mom was the cornerstone for our family. I remember growing up, she helped me with my homework when she could. Not math, except in elementary school. When I grew from baths to showers, she sat on the toilet yelling out multiplication cards for me to shout out the answers from the other side of the shower curtain. 'Four times seven,' she yells. 'Twenty-eight,' I yell back. Hah. That's how I memorized my multiplication tables—across shower curtains. She drills and drills me on the math tables until the answer becomes automatic. It's funny the quirky little things you remember."

"So, she drills and drills you on a subject until the result becomes reflexive. Sounds a little like football practice in some regards."

"A little."

"Our mom is special," Dan agrees. "When her boys grew into junior high and high school, she wanted to find something more to fulfill her life. Learned to drive. Did volunteer work at St. Vincent De Paul. Got a secretary job for a small paint company with a one-room shack for an office. Were you off to college then?"

I shake my head "yes."

"After a couple years, she got a much better paying job for a stevedoring company near the ship channel. The owner, an old Dutchman, loved her work ethic, dedication to the job. They treated her well enough to make sure she stayed with them for the next couple decades."

"Our folks never had much money. They gave me an AM/FM radio—the nicest present they ever gave me—when I graduated from high school before I left for college. I was elated. I get to listen to FM music without annoying AM radio static. I needed five co-op semesters employed in a chemical plant to pay for college. My last year at A&M, Mom provided me with a zero-interest loan to help me get through the last semester. We all need help to get through life," I comment. "Parents, relatives, friends, schools and teachers, religion, sports...all parts of our help package."

"Mom helped me out too," Dan recounts. "She got me an interview with her company at the port. Started in the warehouse: grimy, sweaty clean-up jobs at a lower salary than I wanted, but decent pay for someone right out of high school."

"I didn't know you started in a warehouse."

"Yeah, the lowest paid position in the company. They later moved me to the container refurbishment area. Pretty soon, I trained others and became area supervisor. They transferred me to a coordinator function for the longshoremen jobs with the shipping lines we contracted with. After a decade, I moved on to a start-up stevedoring company. Met Cheryl when she dispatched trucks out of a portable building at the Barbours Cut container terminal. Worked my ass off. Rose to an executive position. We are where we are in part because of that simple start Mom gave me."

Dan twists back around, fingers poke into the chain-link fence, his face defies the incoming southeast wind. "My job put me in a favorable position to help Sean. I got him into the container yards, and it turned out better than I hoped. His supervisors tell me Sean is very conscientious, works hard, always willing to stay late or come in on short notice, gets along well with the other union employees. One told me Sean, for a smaller guy, performs the work of much larger men in his crew. Sean told me, on more than one occasion, 'The ILA saved my life...It saved my life.'"

Dan turns his face to mine. "It has been one long journey from Victorville. After Cheryl and I visited Sean there, God, we were so low...Cheryl in tears. We spent many nights questioning what we could have done differently, what we might have done wrong. Her son, Sean, and my son, Bryan, were both in elementary school only one year apart when we married. The two boys got along great, but turned out different, like...I don't know...caviar to a deep-fried taco. Bryan, an 'A' student, loved sports, played quarterback from youth football into high school, graduated with honors from North Texas in three years with a computer science degree, now an officer in the army. Sean did okay in school, but not the best student. We enrolled Sean in different team sports—football, baseball, basketball, soccer—but he never wanted to enroll for a second season.

"For a while, I hoped Sean would take up swimming." Dan smiles at the thought. "He enjoyed going to the community pool or Surfside Beach. When we went to the beach, he took it as a personal challenge to see how far he could swim from the shore. I see him now: Sean, fearless, strides straight into the sea. Then he vanishes into dark, muddy surf. He sometimes swims out so far I have trouble picking him out through the waves. About a half hour later he emerges from the surf, exhausted, and collapses next to us. I tell Sean he's swimming out too far from shore. If he keeps doing it, something bad is bound to happen. Sean shrugs me off. He tells me he is aware of his limits and can handle whatever happens out there." Dan stares at me. "He was an exceptional swimmer, a lot of stamina, but no interest in an organized swim team.

"He somehow got involved with the wrong crowd in junior high. We tried a change of scenery when we sent him to live with his biological father in Seattle, but he couldn't help Sean shake the drugs. So, in and out of prison until the last judge threatened him with an extended habitual repeater sentence."

My God. I've known Dan his entire life. Even though we're just an hour apart, our lives run in separate lanes. I had no idea of the angst, the pain, the efforts with their son. "Well, you and Cheryl turned things around with Sean. You should both be proud of the path he's on now."

"So far, so good," he says. "We're doing everything we can to make sure Matthew doesn't follow the same path as Sean. Cheryl is retired now, so she meets Matthew as soon as he gets home from school and helps him with homework until he finishes. Then Cheryl allows Matthew to immerse himself in video games. And now another threat for boys is social isolation and depression from all this online business." Dan shakes his head. "Matthew cannot end up on drugs. Not him. Youth sports are part of his help package. Matthew is going to play a competitive team sport, a sport that challenges him physically, mentally, emotionally. He'll have coaches, teammates, friends and parents to help him overcome the challenges, to help ensure he's ready to face today's world."

"He couldn't ask for more determined parents to guide him into adulthood," I tell Dan. My knees tell me it's time to sit for a bit. "Let's get off our feet," as I nod toward the press box and adjust my mask to cover my mouth and nose.

I hold the press box door open and follow Dan up the steps into the observation room. The Music Man and Dr. LePrince sit at two corners and bury themselves in their cell phones. "Gentlemen," Dan says as we roll our chairs to the counter. He dives into his phone and joins them in their collective isolated activity. I stretch the mask from my face to below my chin, towel off the sweat, and guzzle a room-temperature sports drink. The rubber band snaps the mask back into place. "Cheryl's still here," Dan tells me. "She's visiting with friends under a tarp below us, near the north 25-yard line."

"She must be fond of them to stay out in this heat."

"Matthew can't be happy about it unless Cheryl bribes him with money for the concession stand." Dan reads one particular text message and beams a smile. "Good news, guys. We'll be back in business soon." He hops out of his chair and long-strides to the announcer's booth.

From the voice in the sky: **"Update from the Cats organization manager. Play will resume in ten minutes. Repeat, play resumes in ten minutes. The first half will be completed from the point where the officials suspended play. The Golden Hearts drill team elected to forgo their halftime perfor-**

mance. There will be a five-minute break for halftime, and the second half will start."

***

The Music Man cranks up a classic rocker, a song with Cuban-Puerto Rican roots featuring conga drums, keyboards and brilliant guitars with all-Spanish language lyrics: "Oye, Como Va," or, translated to English, "Hey, How's It Going."

Meanwhile, the players for each team go through their pre-game exercise ritual: stretch, jump, run in place. The four officials, without masks, stride to the field. It's too hot to expect anyone to wear a cloth mask outside all day. The lead official resets the football while the far sideline judge directs the chain gang markers to the appropriate spots. The Cat offense and the Tiger Shark defense jog onto the field. The scoreboard froze in place when play suspended, so it's ready to go. Surprise—the game log sheet matches the circumstances at resumption of play.

"Thank you for hanging in there with us today. Fingers crossed, no more delays."

Play resumes and progresses to halftime with each team getting another possession. Neither team scores. For halftime, the scoreboard counts down from five minutes. The two squads retreat to their staging areas under their respective sideline tents to take a break before the second half starts.

Three Tiger Shark players sprint to the northeast area under the stands. A few minutes later, the same trio races back to their tent area. I empathize with their urgency.

As the special team players jog onto the field for the kickoff, the stadium speakers belt out a classic adrenalin pumper with lyrics that exhort the listeners to rev up their motors, get on the highway, fire their guns at once and explode into the title refrain of "Born to be Wild."

The Cat return team organizes to the south of the midfield stripe. The Tiger Shark kickoff squad prepares to charge them from the north 40-yard line.

"Walt 'Get Your Mind Right' Bishop kicking off for the Tiger Sharks."

The music stops when the lead official points to the kicker. Get Your Mind Right uses a five-yard running start at the football to drive it end-over-end to the Cat 35-yard line.

A deep back, Hambone, catches the ball and sprints up the near sideline.

The line of gray-and-black jerseys collapses toward Hambone while the maroon jerseys fend them off. A pair of Tiger Sharks shove Hambone out of bounds at the Cat 48-yard line.

"Nice return by John 'Hambone' Sherridan. First and ten Cats from their 48-yard line."

I update the game log sheet while the opposing offensive and defensive units jog onto the field. The Cats configure their attack offense as they did in the first half with a split backfield alignment. The Tiger Sharks oppose them with an adjusted defensive alignment. While four crouched defensive linemen set up against their offensive counterparts, one linebacker moves to one end of the defensive line. Three other linebackers stand at the more traditional five yards distance behind the line. Two cornerbacks match the Cat wide receivers, and one deep safety stands fifteen yards from the football.

Before the first play, the far sideline referee waves his arms overhead as he runs toward the ball and shouts to the lead official. The lead official points both arms to the Cat's side of the line of scrimmage.

"Timeout, Cats."

"What's going on?" I ask.

The sideline official escorts a maroon wide receiver off the field. The maskless Cats coach nearest the sideline approaches the official and flails his arms like he's in the throes of some spasmodic episode. That sideline official dons his mask to cover his face. Another Cats coach screams right into the helmet of the diminutive wide receiver. If a coach screamed point-blank into my kid's face, I'd be pissed off.

The momentary phone rattle against the vinyl countertop tells Dan he has a text message. "Hah. Cheryl texted me," he says. "She heard the coach screaming from across the field, 'For the rest of your life, never, ever step onto a football field without your mouthpiece in place.'"

"Oh, so an equipment violation triggered the issue."

"All kids in the field of play must wear a mouthpiece to protect their teeth and gum areas," Dan says. "Safety first."

"I didn't know the rule existed."

"A violation triggers an automatic timeout."

"What if no timeouts are available?"

"They get a delay of game penalty."

"I bet the kid never forgets to wear his mouthpiece again," I say. "In fact, after that spectacle, I bet the entire team never forgets to wear their mouthpieces."

"Okay. First and ten Cats."

'Noculars are raised. Football is hiked. Play is run.

"Quarterback...fake into the line...pitch to the tailback around left end. Clive 'Tank' Bruckman. Forced out of bounds after a 10-yard gain. And that is enough for another Cats...First Dooown!"

After the first down, the Cats run the football twice into the middle of the offensive line, once by Clutch, once by Tank.

On third down: **"Quarterback...fakes into the middle, rolls around the left end. Free down the sideline! The 20...the 10...Touchdooown! Jake 'The Snake' Ramos!"**

"Flag down."

"We have a penalty flag on the play."

"What happened?" asks Dan. "The football is coming back."

"Beats me. A referee is talking to one of our boys near the 30-yard line."

The lead official faces the press box, grabs his wrist, and then points to the Cat side. He paces seven yards back from the original line of scrimmage and resets the football. He holds his right index finger to the chain gang to inform them it's still first down.

"Holding against the Cats. First and long coming up."

"There's no such thing as a seven-yard penalty," I say. "Must be a spot foul, ten yards from the point where the holding occurred."

"The real penalty is it takes six points off the board."

On the next play, Snake dives between Headhunter and Beast.

"Quarterback keeper up the middle."

"Tough run. Snake broke a couple of tackles."

"He must be angry he lost the touchdown and showed it with an extra intense effort," I comment.

"*Determined* run by 'Snake' for a gain of nine on the play. Second and eight coming up."

The fullback, Hambone, carries the football for no gain on second down. Then, on third down: **"Quarterback...drops back to pass...to the sideline. Complete! 'Clutch' Pena with the reception. Gain of five yards on the play. That brings up a big fourth down for the Cats. Come on, Cats fans! Let our boys hear you!"**

The Cats reposition both wide receivers to the left of their offensive line. Both Tiger Shark cornerbacks relocate to their right side to match against the Cat wide receivers. The free safety drifts a few side-steps toward his right to reinforce against the Cat threat.

'Noculars are raised. Football is hiked. Play is run.

Ghost hikes the football to Snake.

Snake whirls right. He jabs the ball into Tank.

Tank follows Hambone into the line.

Hambone leads the way between Marine and Mad Dog. The trio creates a crease in the Tiger Shark D-line.

"Handoff over right tackle."

Tank slides through the line. Accelerate!

Free up the middle. Go, go, go!

"He breaks through the line! To the 20...to the 10...Touchdooown! Touchdown 'Tank' in for the score!"

"Way to hit that hole, young man!" I say.

"The score is Cats 18, Tiger Sharks 13 with the extra point attempt coming up."

The active row ends, the future row starts.

The special teams for each side set astride the three-yard line under the stuttered refrain of "You Ain't Seen Nothin' Yet" from the stadium speakers.

The Cats line up for the kick attempt. All eleven Tiger Sharks leap up and down and flail their arms overhead. Ghost hikes the ball in a smooth arc to Snake, who sets the ball in a vertical position and rotates the ball seams away from the kicker. Vicious takes two long strides and sends his right foot into the lower-middle part of the ball. Both officials beneath the goalpost raise their arms skyward.

"The kick is good! Right down the center of the uprights! Sid 'Vicious' Anderson. Two more points for the Cats and that makes the score Cats 20, Tiger Sharks 13."

I close out the active row in the game log to highlight the additional two points. "Nice drive," I comment. "Our boys overcame some big penalties to get it done."

"Recap?"

"Oh...seven plays, 52 yards, 27 yards on the TD."

"Scoring drive recap. Fifty-two yards on seven plays, capped by a 27-yard sprint to the goal line from 'Tank' Bruckman."

"Blitzkrieg Bop," a fast-paced punk rocker exhorting the crowd to go crazy at an arena rock concert, blasts from the stadium speakers.

For the kickoff, both teams establish the same configuration they used throughout the first half.

"Sid 'Vicious' Anderson kicking off for the Cats."

The official drops his arm to signal the start of play. Vicious sails a high, arching projectile to the Tiger Shark's 35-yard line. The kick height provides enough time for the maroon jerseys to blow through the initial line of black jerseys.

Dominator gathers the football in both arms, dashes toward the sideline, and cuts back toward midfield.

Headhunter, Ghost, and Mad Dog swarm over the Dominator.

"Jack 'Dominator' Lewis with the return. First and ten Tiger Sharks from their 39-yard line."

The Tiger Sharks use the same oddball shotgun offensive configuration as in the first half. To defend, the Cats counter with their standard alignment of five linemen, three linebackers, two cornerbacks, and one deep safety.

While the players establish their formations, the far sideline judge aligns the chain gang for the first down distance poles and ball marker pole.

In the booth, I update the game log sheet to document the kickoff and to prepare for the upcoming play.

"Handoff into the middle. Stopped cold! Frank 'The Boom' Mulder on the tackle. Second and ten coming up."

The next play fails to generate more than a couple of yards of forward progress.

On third down: **"Quarterback drops back...keeper into the middle. No gain! Barry 'Beast' Ellis blows up the play."**

"I couldn't tell if the quarterback intended a pass play or a quarterback draw."

"Either way, the middle linebacker blitz destroyed the play," Dan says.

"Okay, Cats fans. That brings up a big fourth down play. Make some noise! Let our defense hear you!

"Deep snap to the quarterback...under pressure...throws downfield to the right...Incomplete! Pass is incomplete! Isiah 'Captain' Contrera defended on the play. The Cats take possession at the Tiger Shark 40-yard line."

"He threw the pass up for grabs."

"No choice on a fourth down, do-or-die play," Dan says. "An attaboy to the safety who sprinted over to help."

"I'm glad the officials didn't call pass interference. Our kids look a bit 'handsy' to me."

"Now, if we can grind the ball down the field, if we keep the game clock running, and if score one more touchdown, then the game should be ours."

"That's a pretty healthy string of ifs."

The Cats capitalize on the favorable starting position to score another touchdown. The Tiger Sharks push across a touchdown late in the fourth quarter to make the final score: Wildcatters 27, Tiger Sharks 19.

The players conduct the post-game sportsmanship ritual by marching along the midfield stripe, nodding their heads as they pass one another. No hand touches.

"Please give a hand to our officials for today's game. They spent this long day with us to help our boys learn the right way to play the game."

The four officials, masks to chin, give a quick wave to the press box as they stride off the field.

"This one is in the books," Dan says. "That makes the Cats organization four wins and one loss for the day. Time to auction off the game ball."

"What better way to top off a memorable game than with the game football. Our organization manager is holding the football at the midfield sideline. Please wave to the person holding the football if you want to bid. Bidding is open to everyone from either team. We will start at $50."

The organization manager on the field, along with Dan and I from the booth, scan the stands for bidders. The Ball Bearer shouts and points toward the stands for each high bidder. The bids top off at $200. The Ball Bearer raises both arms skyward and jogs to the near sideline.

"Sold! Thank you, sir. Please collect the football at the Cats organization table under the stands."

"Not as much this time."

"Everyone is ready to get home," Dan says. "Besides, as the final game of the day, attendees for other games don't overlap, so the Senior game draws the smallest crowd. And no Golden Hearts halftime show today to hold those parents."

"Thank you for attending today's game. Please have a safe drive home," concludes the big voice in the sky.

Just for grins, I check the thermostat one last time: 86°F.

The Music Man triggers one final tune as the crowd drifts out of the stadium. A punk rock classic streams from the stadium speakers: "Should I Stay or Should I Go."

Chapter Twelve

Is Full Accomplished

"Successful day. A bit long. And not the most comfortable without air conditioning," Dan says. "I'm ready to roll."

"I hear that."

Dan returns the squeegee to the closet in the back observation room. Along the way, he offers his byes, good lucks and see you next games to the Music Man and Dr. LePrince.

I roll two chairs to the observation room counter, sink into one and lift my legs onto the other. I'm glad our boys won, of course, and I envy their simple post-game sportsmanship display. At the time I played, such a ritual meant nothing to me—just something to be done. I look back at those times and wish I could have gone down the procession line at least once as a winner. We lose every game.

It's strange how much of my youth football days I remember, perhaps because the football experience represents such a unique aspect of my life. I still remember the last two plays of my lone youth tackle football season. Less than a minute remains in the game. No timeouts left. No drama—we are down by three touchdowns. My coach on the field calls a pass play from the shotgun formation, three wide receivers out. My assignment requires me to block from the tailback position.

Clean shotgun snap to our quarterback. An untouched defensive lineman tears through our porous offensive line. I move to block his progress to our quarterback. He bounces off my chest, rolls to the quarterback and drives him into the turf. Sack. From one knee, the coach looks up at me and says, "Thanks a lot." After over 50 years, I still recall those exact three trivial words.

Enough time for one more play. The coach calls the same play again. Clean shotgun snap to the quarterback. The same defensive lineman, plus a linebacker, charge into our backfield. I crouch lower and launch my shoulder pads into the hips of the onrushing lineman, drive him into his attacking teammate, forcing the pair to my right. The two rushers tangle in each other's legs and collapse to the ground. Our quarterback steps to his left, cocks his arm and hurls a tight spiral twenty yards downfield to an open receiver streaking across the middle of the field. The football digs up turf five yards in front of the receiver's feet. Incomplete pass—the final play of my youth tackle football career.

Time to police the area. Chuck the empty bottles, scratch paper, roster notes into the trash can. Arrange the chairs in a single file along the back wall. Load my cleaning supplies into the cloth grocery bag, except for the spray alcohol solution. Dan returns and slides the game log sheets and organization binder into his leather case. I pump three alcohol bursts onto my left palm and rub my hands together. "Alcohol?" I ask.

"Hit me," Dan says as he extends both palms. Two quick pumps from the spray bottle and I move on to the next room.

I stick my head in the adjacent booth, where the Music Man rolls up enough cords for any and every occasion. "Marty," I say. "Last call for alcohol."

"Hah. I've heard that phrase more than once in my life. Sure, spray it on."

"Loved the tunes, man," I tell him. A few quick alcohol bursts into his cupped palms elicits a "thank you" nod. On to the video room.

Dr. LePrince moves in slow motion while he disassembles and packs his video equipment into the case, as though he's an actor in a film that advances frames at half speed. "Harold, care for some alcohol?" I ask.

Harold interrupts his packing, glances at his hands, and tells me, "Thank you. Sure. I can take some." I pump four alcohol bursts onto his open hands. He rubs his palms together, intertwines fingers, moves each hand across the back of the other before clasping each thumb and finishes with a fingernail rub into each palm—all before the alcohol evaporates. Someone knows the CDC guidelines for hand washing during COVID-19.

"You can handle getting this equipment down okay?" I ask.

"The case is not as heavy as it looks. The equipment is delicate, but the lightweight case has a hard cover and ample padding to protect against collision. I can manage."

"See you next home game," as I head into the bathroom. Back in the observation room, I meet Dan, leather case in one hand with helmet and shoulder pads in the other. "Is that yours?" as I point to the binoculars on the counter.

"Oh, thanks. I don't want to lose my three-hundred-dollar binoculars," Dan says as he slides them into his case.

Three hundred dollars for a pair of binoculars. Mine cost forty dollars.

I grab my jacket and cloth bag in one hand and hold the press box door open with the other hand. Dan wedges by me while he shouts, right next to my ear, "Great job, guys. See you next home game." "Later" and "goodbye" respond from the press box as the door slides closed.

***

No masks are seen on the descent.

The adults who brought canopies collapse the metal supports and the associated tarps. One toddler demonstrates her boredom by banging on a nearby metal seat. Long day for the preschoolers, too.

A few steps down, a baby cries as her mother cradles her, rocks the baby in her arms and issues a continuous "shhh." Not a gentle "shhh." An audible, frustrated "shhh," the kind of "shhh" that spews saliva toward any face in front of the "shhh."

The adult cleanup crew volunteers, and the children they draft to help them, double-time it along each 90-yard-long row to collect the stray trash. They dive to the ground and rise with an empty plastic bottle or candy wrapper, and repeat like hungry falcons focused on their prey.

I trail Dan as he wobbles down the concrete stairway. Both his arms sway at each downward step as he either swings the arm with his briefcase or the arm with the football equipment to maintain balance, reminiscent of an acrobat on a high wire who uses a pole for balance. I accommodate my barking knees with "granny" steps, two feet on each downward stair step. The lack of handrails warrants extra caution.

Dan, Cheryl and Matthew huddle together under the stands near the gate. Matthew holds his helmet and his shoulder pads in separate hands. "Hello, Earl," Cheryl says with a broad smile.

"Hello, Cheryl." I smile back from under my mask. No hugs or handshakes—or attempted elbow rubs.

"Dan tells me you lost air conditioning. That must be a miserable way to spend your Saturday."

"Not something we could control. In the end, we came, we saw, we survived—mission accomplished."

"All the home team parents love the broadcast. Some of the visiting parents around me got upset a few times about the broadcast slant toward the Cats."

"Tough. We're the home team broadcasters. Dan throws some visiting players name mentions to honor their efforts, but we are definitely homers. No apologies." To Dan, "By the way, I bet your tribute after the anthem hit home for a lot of people in the stands."

Dan gives me a nod while Cheryl, with a wrinkled brow, cocks her head toward him. He tells her: "After the anthem, I added a 'thank you' to the people in the stands for respecting the flag, honoring the veterans."

"Did you see the woman who walked in front of the press box during the anthem?" I ask him.

Dan shakes his head "no."

Cheryl points to my cloth grocery bag. "Going shopping?"

"Oh. The grocery store doesn't take cloth bags from customers during COVID, so I use this one to tote my cleaning supplies, Lysol spray or Clorox wipes, and alcohol hand spray."

Cheryl hunches over the sack. "That's a valuable collection. It's hard to get cleaning supplies now."

"Tell me about it. My grocer opens an hour early, at 6 a.m., for its over-sixty customers. I've waited in line for as long as thirty minutes to get inside. They let us in single file to avoid a group from bunching inside the store. The store aisles are marked with one-way arrows to help minimize contact with other shoppers, but the floor arrows are ignored, and everyone makes a beeline to the household cleaner section. I keep an eye out for disinfecting spray and wipes. I haven't seen bleach for months. And liquid soap ran low a few times, so much that I resorted to solid bars of soap for the first time in decades."

Dan chuckles. "Sounds like a scrum of retirees swinging elbows at each other to get that last can of Lysol."

"Hah, it's not *The Hunger Games*. Most people are courteous, aware of each other's situation. The grocery store does a decent job of getting off-brand replacements for the once-common sprays and wipes. The store places a two-item limit for most cleaners, so nobody scarfs up a dozen cans of anything," I say. "But I admit seeing a few shopping carts nudged out of the way to get to a disinfectant." I keep quiet about the time I give one of my two canisters of disinfectant wipes to a mother who's in tears about missing her opportunity to get a cleanser to help keep her family safe.

"I've gone to grocery deliveries. I place the order online, and groceries arrive at the front door within a few hours," Cheryl tells me. "It works out fine for our needs."

"Yeah, deliveries may be okay for boxed or canned goods, but I trust myself over a stranger to pick my fresh fruits, vegetables and meats. Since I cook more of my food now, I buy more fresh food than I used to. I've had an encyclopedia-cookbook by Chef Folse—you've heard of him—with Cajun recipes on my bookshelf for a decade. I read the history of evolving food influences from the different Native American, African, French, Spanish, and other immigrant groups into Louisiana. But I never tried making any of the dishes listed in the book until this year. Since I have plenty of time available during COVID isolation, I've taken a shot at about a dozen recipes. I haven't poisoned myself yet."

That last comment draws a smile from Cheryl.

"Sometimes the food is good. Sometimes not so much. Every batch of spicy black-eyed peas, an African-influenced recipe full of smoked sausage and ham, has tasted fine to me. Nothing else I make ever comes out the same way twice. I don't get it. The same recipe and different results. If plant operators reproduce their operating procedures as well as I duplicate recipes, their butts would be out the gate."

"Hah. You need to be careful with your starting ingredients. As many ingredients as possible should be fresh. Plant-based spices can't sit on your shelf forever and be expected to taste the same. Cook times and temperatures are crucial. And even the quantity you make at one time affects the taste. I hope you follow the exact recipe weights and volumes."

"Of course." You got me on that one. I have volumetric cups but no weight scale. Anyway, sounds like an engineering problem. Date the bottles for organic spices when opened. Rotate stock first in-first out. Stay with consistent batch sizes. Set the timer so stirring times are consistent. Freeze the excess. And stop cheating on secondary ingredients when you lack what you need. I learned the hard way you shouldn't substitute the spice you have for one you need because both spices are a similar color.

A metal pole bangs the back of my right leg. "Sorry," from the man wrestling with the poles on his way out the gate. Get a bag for that stuff, dude.

Cheryl nods to me. "I see you're wearing a mask."

"I must wear a mask. I fall into multiple 'endangered species' categories for COVID," I tell her. "I'm a little surprised I didn't see more masks around the stadium."

"I see masks at *indoor* public spaces," Cheryl says. "It's a county regulation for businesses to only admit customers who wear masks. All employees must also wear masks whenever they work with each other or with customers. I don't see many masks outside."

"I saw on the news that one of the local school districts, Clear something, Lake, Creek, whatever, requires their football players to wear masks when they play. It's okay to tackle and wrestle each other on the football field, but you've got to wear that mask," Dan says with a smile.

"Maybe a mask isn't needed in that specific case, but our brother's experience made me paranoid about COVID. James told me about his fever that peaked at 104 degrees and held steady at 102 degrees for three days. The doctor told him to stay out of the hospital while he could breathe. He alternated between bed and a cold-water bath for a week. The doctor also prescribed some super cough suppressant so James could get some sleep. Lucky his wife contracted a milder case, so Anne could help nurse him through it." I tell them, "I try to do everything I can to minimize my chances of contracting COVID."

I nod toward Matthew. "What about school? Do you still homeschool during COVID?"

"Thank God, no," Cheryl says. "The Deer Park district is optional attendance this semester, and Matthew goes to school. Masks are mandatory on school property unless you are eating or drinking."

"I'm glad to go back. I hated Nana teaching me," Matthew interjects.

"It was no fun for me either, kiddo." Cheryl turns from Matthew to face me. "The district provided a personal computer and teaching instructions for six subjects: history, science, math, PE, art, and one more...Oh, English. Five days a week for three months, we slogged through every lesson. I stayed by his side much of the time and worked with him one-on-one when needed. Sometimes we were up to midnight to finish the assignments. Hard for me to see how working parents coped."

"Some days my cousins got to swim in our pool, but Nana made me study until the lessons were done. Not fair."

"I'm such a hard taskmaster. You lead such a tough life, don't you?"

Matthew shakes his head up and down a few times as Cheryl continues: "We submitted completed lessons at the end of the semester, but the district brushed aside our work. They threw it away. The kids' grades stood where they were when classroom teaching was suspended in early March."

"We live in Pasadena but are lucky to be zoned into the Deer Park school district," Dan says. "Pasadena didn't have enough computers for all their students, and many of the parents didn't have home internet access. It was a mess."

"Yeah, nobody from the federal level to the state and local governments to individual households were ready for the ramifications of a global pandemic," I say.

"Well, thanks for taking a risk by venturing out among the crowd to help me out," Dan says. "The announcer's booth functions much more effectively when two partners work in sync to keep track of game action."

"I don't have many chances to do things with my younger brother," I tell him through my masked smile, "so I'm glad to help."

A screaming laugh provides an early warning to dodge the child who flashes by us.

"Do you have any preference for supper?" Dan asks. "Our favorite Tex-Mex place is open now. We need to wear masks to get seated. I hope we won't have to wait. Seating is limited since they must ensure all customer groups are at least six feet apart. Or we can get some carry-out and eat at our house."

"Thanks, but it's getting pretty late, so I'll head for home. The Astros are playing at Minute Maid in front of their cardboard cut-out fans tonight. It's still fun to watch them play, especially since they now add artificial background crowd noises to the broadcast. Sinking into an oversized chair, propping my feet up, watching baseball, nursing a cold one sounds like a nice way to end the day," I tell him. "Besides, I need to get home to my little girl."

"How old is she now?" Cheryl asks.

"Sandy is nine years old. I bet she's so hungry she's gnawed her cowhide doggie bone to the size of a stick of jerky. It's nice to have someone happy to see me when I get home. That big, yellow lab wags her tail so hard that every tail wag bounces her butt off the ground."

"All right. Thanks again. See you in two weeks for the next home game."

"You bet," I say.

"You have a long drive home," Dan says. "Be safe."

"Always safe, man. Always safe."

I toss them a wave—no handshakes—and trudge to my truck through a thinned-out parking lot. Tug my mask down to my chin. Man, it has been one long day. I learned, with a visceral passion, weather delays suck big time, especially when they trigger the loss of our air conditioning. Bring a fan next time as well as my antique Apple iPod with its over 300 classic rock albums. It's my only possession I consider irreplaceable—other than Sandy.

The public response to the pandemic was an eye-opener. I didn't expect to see so many people without masks. While some people show concern for strangers, most do not. If everyone doesn't wear a mask, the entire effort becomes futile. Not a popular opinion in Texas. The younger population—anyone under 50 years old in my book—may not need masks, but I wish more were considerate of the most vulnerable. Whatever. Ultimately you do what is best for your own health. My body will tell me in three or four days if I need to test for COVID-19.

Halfway to the truck, I stop and shake each leg to make sure my legs aren't cramping. Okay for the drive home.

The standout event of the day was Matthew's injury. Am I facilitating kids getting injured by helping Dan in the announcer's booth? I hope not. I would be quite the hypocrite to whine about the lack of concern the general population displays toward the more vulnerable in their midst during the pandemic, only to display the same attitude toward children who play youth tackle football. Does that make me a hypocrite?

No way. There's no way that's true. No way...I think. Enough COVID-19 data exists to warrant extra precautions for older adults, especially when obesity and Type II diabetes, and sleep apnea are involved. The data for youth tackle football related to long-term brain trauma are limited. A handful of young men who commit suicide show brain trauma effects that correlate to tackle football. The correlation was determined through post-mortem brain examinations. I believe the association is real. However, I'm not convinced serious brain trauma is common, especially when participation ends with youth tackle football or pre-college football. If medical science develops technology to quantify markers that show brain deterioration, now only available through autopsies, and if those markers show dangerous increases with tackle football participation, then I must end my involvement with youth tackle football. But now, a hypocrite? No way.

Another takeaway from today's games relates to the national anthem. Dan gets emotional whenever he hears the anthem. I'm glad he didn't notice the young Black couple who appeared indifferent to it. Was their behavior a silent protest to the George Floyd murder—caught on video only four months ago—or a self-absorbed activity for some immediate personal issue? I'll never know.

I toss the grocery bag with cleaning supplies on the passenger side floor of my pickup. From the driver's seat, one last look at the stadium in twilight. The passion for the game still amazes me. A global pandemic shocks every aspect of society, from a noble endeavor like an overseas church mission to more self-indulgent activities in nightclubs, but youth tackle football keeps rolling on. There's not much logic to it—many concerns in life are more important—but many consider youth football a valued aspect of our culture.

I should write a book. The oddball stuff that happens on gameday could yield an amusing story. Between retirement and pandemic isolation, God knows I have the time. I hear the critics now: Unconventional plot structure. Inadequate character arc. Insufficient depravity to entice the modern audience. A story told by an amateur, full of sound and fury, signifying...a slice of our lives. More than nothing.

Anyway, the game day ends. The kids had fun. The parents had fun, I hope. Dan had fun. I had fun, although it would have been more fun with a functioning air conditioner. I'm already eager to return to Abshier Stadium for the next home game announcing mission—COVID be damned!

Extended Epilogue: Family Fatality

Chapter Thirteen

Against a Sea of Troubles

Outside of important holidays, the last time I was with Dan, Cheryl, Matthew, and Sean was at the last playoff game of Matthew's final season in youth tackle football. That was a year ago. Another season, another youth tackle league super bowl victory for Matthew's team. After the season, Matthew started junior high, intending to play football at the next level. None of us ever imagined we would gather under these circumstances.

Still, I expect a nice service—at least as much as any funeral service can be nice. Dan wouldn't have it any other way.

The funeral home rests in a convenient, treed location off a major east-west artery through Deer Park. It's close to many relatives and near enough to the ship channel for coworkers to attend. The ceremonial chapel unfolds like a church: a foyer with double doors leads into a central aisle with perhaps two dozen pews line each side of the aisle; floor-to-ceiling dark-wood columns rise between the pews and an outer wall. An open casket rests on a raised platform at the terminus of the center aisle.

A frozen "fire-burst" of flowers explodes from the immediate base of the coffin area. I recognize pink and white carnations. And the roses, with their vibrant red, white, and yellow blooms. A separate vase of small blue flowers clustered off the top of green stalks stand beside the casket. Not bluebonnets—I know what bluebonnets look like—but I forgot what you call these flowers.

I recognize a handful of the attendees. My brother Dan, dressed in what I refer to as "business casual" attire, talks to guests in the front row. His wife, Cheryl, sits nearby the dais at the front of the chapel and visits with women unfamiliar to me.

Dan's two grandsons, Kade and Matthew, each one in a coat and tie, each one with a gloomy face that displays their discomfort with the present circumstances, stand beside an older gentleman also in suit and tie.

Bryan, Dan's son, stands near his father. Bryan epitomizes a warrior: a major, an Army Ranger, formal uniform with medals across his chest, 6-foot tall with no sign of excess body fat. He's close to forty years old. Man, I never looked so fit any time in my life. Dedication to the service demands staying in shape to parachute from planes and lead soldiers half his age. Dan told me Bryan runs five miles every morning regardless of the weather. When Bryan visits, he runs on the junior college track and then runs bleachers afterwards. I struggle to walk up stadium steps; I can't imagine running them.

Since neither of my uncooperative suits let me squeeze into them, I opt for a less formal attire of a sport coat with tie.

My brother James and his wife Anne wear their typical, impeccable Sunday church best. Their son and daughter with their spouses are also here in formal attire.

My youngest brother John, who wears a suit without a tie,—not able to get the top button on his shirt to fasten for a tie on his 6-foot-6-inch, three-hundred-pound frame—attends with his wife, Maria.

Mom wants to attend the service, but the cascade of ailments associated with a fall and hip injury keeps her inside her home. Dad, wheelchair bound with diminished mental capacity, never leaves his house.

The funeral home chapel fills over the half-hour that precedes the scheduled start time; standing room is required along the rear wall. We get to the funeral home early enough to select where we want to sit, so I squat on the back pew as far as possible from the open casket. My niece offers me some tissues, but I shake her off.

The classical music that cascades throughout the chapel sounds familiar. A prominent violin with supporting strings starts a sweeping melody of slow paced beats, matching the pace of a heartbeat; a second set of violins layers over the first, out of sync in a manner that both compliments and contrasts with the original; the cello strings—at least I think they are cellos, but my ear is not the most discerning—step into the mix; a bass accompanies with a discernible "plunk" in the background; the combinations unite to build in intensity; then the volume lowers and pace slows as a prominent violin steps forward to lead all the strings in a coordinated peak before a fade to silence. *Rollerball*, a classic science fiction movie about athletes in helmets and pads who skate around a rink and try to maim each other, includes the music during a scene of frivolous destruction of the local environment. To me, the string combination evokes feelings of tragic loss.

The music in the funeral parlor triggers a junior high remembrance. Mom decides to broaden my knowledge of the arts, of classical music, and acquires a pair of tickets to a performance at the local junior college. She feels ill the evening of the concert, so Dad takes me to the performance—three-piece chamber music. The recital is a mind-numbing, melatonin-producing, coma-inducing bore. We leave at halftime. The experience sours me against all classical music for much of my life. Gradual exposure to the genre leads me to respect and later regret not listening to a broader variety of the classics. I've never seen a live symphony. Not too late yet.

The music stops to signal the start of the eulogy. Dan speaks from a raised dais equipped with a mic that feeds the chapel speakers. "Why all the sad faces? Don't look so glum. We are here to celebrate Sean's life." The forced cheer doesn't last long. From several handwritten pages, the Big Voice recounts some hard times in his son's past, the drugs, prison, and how Sean, Cheryl, and Dan combatted those ordeals, how proud Sean was to be a longshoreman.

I can't focus on what he says. His reaction jabs at me, the frequent reach to the podium for tissues as he gives the lead eulogy. His tears are contagious. "Don't rub your eyes," I say to myself. "Let the teardrops dry in your eye sockets. My vision can blur. The tears for my brother's pain will dry."

Bryan, Sean's stepbrother, follows Dan. Bryan's reach for tissues interrupts the tribute to his brother. His eyes start out moist and red and do not get drier during his speech. Bryan recounts some childhood memories with his brother at my parents' house. My folks, after their four sons leave home and Mom has worked for more than a decade, save enough money to install a backyard swimming pool. Mom sits on the patio and surrounds herself with noise and mayhem as her grandkids and great grandkids swim in their pool. Dad floats in the pool, chews an unlit cigar to the nub, and revels in total idleness. "When Sean and I are in the pool with Granddad," Bryan recounts, "he develops an ever-expanding set of pool rules: no running around the edge of the pool, no horseplay, no diving, no hard football tosses and one extra rule made especially for us—never get grandpa's cigar wet. Of course, we break all his pool rules."

A female deacon from a megachurch north of Houston, one with televised services, speaks next. She recounts a garden. For the increasing number of funerals I attend these days, I can bet someone will speak about gardens. No one will talk of gardens at my funeral since my HOA forbids gardens. I'm not counting the jalapenos and habaneros I grow in pots on my back porch as my garden. "Sean's grandparents were regular attendees at our Sunday services. He often attended church with them during his visits. I remember him often telling me how he enjoyed working in his grandparent's extensive garden, all the tomatoes, squash,"—ugh—"peas, carrots, potatoes." I didn't know you could grow vegetables below ground level in this hot, insect-ridden clay soil. "He told me he planned to start his own tomato patch come spring. I was looking forward to his fresh vegetables." I never knew Sean was a gardener. I never knew Sean was a churchgoer.

The head of the local International Longshoremen's Union speaks last. He calls on the union members and their spouses to rise, upon which half the room stands. Without prepared notes, impeccably dressed in coat and tie, he recounts—as he swings his gaze between the crowd scattered throughout the room—"At first, I was concerned we would get an employee who shows up and coasts by on his father's name. But Sean proved my concerns unwarranted." He compliments Sean for his determination, his work ethic, his camaraderie with the other union members. He presents Cheryl with a Bible in commemoration of Sean's life.

For the last act of the ceremony, the attendees trudge down the central aisle past the open casket to the sons and parents. After the line dissolves at the casket, I let out a deep sigh and join the end of the line. The wave of perfume scents from the flowers hits me as I reach the casket. The super Claritin I took this morning suppresses sneezes. Even so, the allergy pill is ineffective in preventing my eyes from reddening—caused by the many flower scents, I'm sure.

I glance into the casket. The serene figure wears a pressed white shirt with deep burgundy tie, navy blue coat and corresponding slacks.. Two white envelopes rest atop the dark blue jacket.

I approach the fathers and sons who stand in a row to the left of the casket: I greet Matthew, mumble his name and shake his hand as I nod, step over to Kade and repeat the gestures, slide to Sean's biological father from Seattle and shake his hand. On to Dan.

"Fine job, man," I tell Dan while I shake his hand. "You had me tearing up with you."

"Thanks," he tells me through reddened eyes, "although I wonder if the ceremony did justice to Sean's life."

"You did well, very well."

Cheryl sits next to Dan. I reach down and grasp her hand, but what can you say to a mother who lost her son seven days earlier? I nod, express sorrow for her loss, and flee along the pews down the outer aisle.

As the attendees disperse, most of the family members mingle in the foyer and take turns visiting the bathroom. Dan approaches me in the hallway. "Do you have a map to the cemetery? Your GPS system may not get you to the exact spot where you need to go."

"I'm riding there with James and Anne."

"Good. Cheryl and I will head that way, follow the hearse in a few minutes. It should take less than two hours to get to Cheryl's family cemetery plot." Instead of the adjacent graveyard with a manicured St. Augustine lawn interspersed with oak trees, Sean will be buried in Cheryl's family plot beside his older brother. I never knew Sean had a biological brother.

"Nice job again with the service. I learned a lot about Sean's life I never knew." Dan nods his head while I continue, "When I passed by Sean, I saw a couple of envelopes with him."

"Yeah, the spiritual counselor, she suggested each son leave a handwritten note to Sean or to God or both. Since Sean's...departure was so abrupt, so unexpected, she thought it might help the boys to achieve some closure to leave a sentiment for him, a prayer to God for him. And to end the ordeal on a hopeful note." Cheryl catches Dan's attention with her wave. He shakes my hand and heads her way.

Dan told me he hoped the extended football experience would improve Matthew's mental and physical toughness, but I doubt any experience could prepare Matthew for the abrupt death of his father. Sean goes to sleep one night and never wakes up. At least Matthew's home life remains stable, unchanged since Dan and Cheryl obtained legal custody of the boy when he was four years old. The grandparents are old enough to have experienced personal loss in their lives, but I suspect loss of a child cannot be experienced without inherent pain regardless of any prior familiarity with death.

Once outside, I strip off my sport coat and tie, tug on the camo baseball cap and soak up the sun's rays. The twin smoke signals wafting to the sky from several cars away tell me where John and Maria stand. No caravan to the grave site. Here come James and Anne.

The immediate family makes their way in their individual vehicles, and I travel with my brother James and sister-in-law in their SUV to the gravesite at Cheryl's family plot, a ninety-minute drive to the northeast up the East-Tex freeway to the graveyard.

I have no idea what to expect.

Chapter Fourteen

Fear No More

This northeast artery from Houston often indicates blood red on the weekday morning drive maps, but traffic flows with no issues this December Saturday afternoon, so we reach the rural area outside Houston within ninety minutes. On the drive, we discuss the funeral service, the things we knew about Sean, the things we wish we had known while he lived.

Kade, who graduates from high school soon, has a settled home life with his mom, stepdad, and stepsisters. Matthew, younger than Kade, enters junior high with a stable home situation. He's been with Dan and Cheryl for a decade. As far as I know, Matthew isn't involved with his mother on the west coast. She didn't come to Sean's funeral.

One image lingers in my mind: two white envelopes resting atop a black suit inside the open casket. What would one say in a written message to God? To his departed father? If a boy were given one final chance to speak to Sean, what would he say? Perhaps Matthew would offer a "thank you" for coming back from drugs, from prison, to be a part of his life. To wish Sean peace he could not find in life. Would he ask God to look after Sean, to forgive Sean's faults? I hope both boys realize opportunities for the living to pray to God regarding the souls of their loved ones exist every day.

To pass some time, I also note the businesses along the highway that re-opened after the pandemic, the ones that closed forever, the American flags that dot the businesses along the highway—as well as numerous flags associated with the Houston Texans professional football team: red, white and blue colors incorporated into an image of a horned bull, with a lone white star for an eye whose five tips represent pride, courage, strength, tradition and independence.

The SUV guidance system doesn't lead us right to the gravesite, but Dan guides us by phone to a single yellow-flashing light at a stop sign on a Farm-to-Market road, the gravel lane where we turn at a specific Methodist church and where the graveyard rests in relation to the church. The cemetery encompasses five or six acres surrounded by a chain-link fence with live oaks along the border on two sides to provide a bit of shade. Birds, jays or grackles, provide an intermittent racket that disrupts the silence of the field.

The cemetery lies at the mercy of the sun. The stiff, cracked soil—with fissures wide enough to swallow a cell phone—betrays the drought that has inflicted the area for several months. The barren ground displays little grass but also few weeds. Vases with flowers dot the landscape. Patchworks of plots display red or yellow roses beside a half-dozen markers. A couple of white magnolias, the size of my hand and fingers, lie in front of one tombstone. Dense globular clusters of gold-yellow petals, maybe marigolds, rest by a few other markers. Another marker featured a flower—I can't identify it—with white petals not yet unfurled around the yellow core. All the flowers exhibit varying states of vigor, from brilliant bloom to faded beauty. Intermittent streams of fire ants rule the ground cover, so we don't dare stand in one spot too long.

A canopy—a blue tarp with white trim along the edges—covers an area near an open gravesite at the northwest corner of the cemetery. Six brown metal folding chairs are set up under the tarp. At least this dry, hard ground prevents anyone's chair from sinking into the earth. I hope someone sprayed for ants around the gravesite.

Anne makes a beeline to Cheryl and Dan while James and I pass through a gateless gap in the fence and meander among the markers, our dark shadows hugging the ground a few feet to our east sides. In my youth, I never reflected on my mortality. Turning 30 years old bothered me more than turning 40 years old, or 50 years old, or 60 years old, or—not there yet. Now that I'm certain that I'm nearer my life's end than beginning and my contemporaries have started to pass away, I have more of a what-the-heck attitude with my own mortality—not that I'm in a hurry to reach the inevitable. Nobody wrestles with death and comes out on top. But everybody fights. And so should it be.

We stroll among the graves. The markers vary in shape from flat against the ground to three feet tall with tops that range from flat to pillowed. Most stones are dull granite, but some are shiny marble. The gravestone rows are more jagged than straight, and denser patches of markers intersperse among the rows. Clusters of tombstones exhibit the same last names with dates to indicate the family members who lived from a single month to those who lived for one hundred years. Some grave markers date back to the 1870s. One thick stone vase rests cocked against a marble headstone: Geneva Blessinger, beloved wife and mother, born August 12, 1945, and died February 12, 2021. I stand up the vase and recenter it in front of the headstone. A few red rose petals drift downward from the bloom. Tiny "rust spots" dot the leaves on the stem. No water in the vase.

"I like the gravestones that incorporate a photo of the deceased," James says. "What kind of headstone do you want?"

"I don't want one. Stick me in the ground the cheapest way possible."

"No, you're getting a grave marker."

"I don't care now if I get a marker, and I bet I care less after I'm gone."

"You're getting one and you can't do anything about it. I'll put 'World's Greatest Brother' on it."

"Spare me. Name and dates are plenty good."

"But the most interesting markers have personal information, like the two-year-old girl who died of influenza in 1922 or the one with the photo of the Korean War veteran in uniform who passed in 1989."

"Well, I don't have any noteworthy associations. I worked for a chemical company for forty years—and if you put a company logo on my gravestone, I'll come back to haunt you, your kids, and your kid's kids. You can slap my college logo in one corner as long as you make sure it doesn't look like an ATM money machine sign."

"Deal," James says.

We drift in a circuitous route to the northwest corner of the cemetery, where John and Maria join us near the gravesite. Locomotive puffs of smoke emanate from John's lips to signal his approach. Without a breeze, the smoke lingers around his face for an extra beat. Big John has shed his coat and wears a short-sleeve dress shirt so his arms display his "don't you dare tread on me" tattoos: a semi-coiled, hooded-head cobra on his left arm rises to a strike position; a screaming bat, wings at its side, pounces from his elbow toward his right wrist; from his knuckles to past his left wrist, a helmet-topped rifle projects from a burial mound with "some gave all" arched over it and "all gave some" below it, the image superimposed over a red, white and blue flag.

"Hey, guys," John says in a husky voice that makes each word sound like an independent statement.

"John. Maria." James and I nod to them while I tell John, "We're talking about grave markers. What kind do you want?"

"No worries. The VA buries me."

Maria cocks her head, wrinkles her brow and looks at us as though wondering, I imagine, "What kind of macabre stuff are you guys talking about?"

The immediate relatives who attended the funeral home service join a different set of relatives from Cheryl's side of the family, perhaps forty people in total. Cheryl, Dan, Kade, and Matthew sit under the canopy near Sean. Bryan sits behind Dan and Cheryl, while the older gentleman, Sean's biological father, sits behind Kade and Matthew. Meanwhile, the other attendees cluster around the tarp perimeter. The crowd includes men, women, and children of approximate ages five to seventy. Footwear encompasses polished boots, dress shoes, tennis shoes, and slip-ons. Clothes range from formal suits and dresses to blue jeans. Some have bare heads, baseball caps, and a few with immaculate, pressed cowboy hats. Several people wear sunglasses. Of course, I forgot mine.

A smaller grave for a child, where the date of birth matches the date of death in 1980, rests next to the open pit beside the blue tarp. The sentiment etched on the marker: "Born in Heaven." The first name etched onto the tombstone: "Matthew."

"Your attention please," the funeral director addresses us. The gravesite grows quiet except for the groaning metal chairs under the blue canopy and the chirping green leaf canopy overhead. "Thank you for attending this ceremony at Sean's final resting place. Once we have concluded, I ask everyone to depart from the gravesite so we can complete the burial. And now, the family tells me that Sean's uncle will read from the Bible."

All hats are removed. All heads are bowed. James steps forward and reads passages from the Bible, starting with a New Testament passage: "Let not your heart be troubled; believe in God, believe also in Me" (John 14:1 NASB).

After several Bible passages, Dan says a few words thanking the attendees to close the service, and the crowd disperses so the funeral parlor employees can complete their business at the gravesite. James, Anne and I meet Dan and Cheryl before they leave for the luncheon for the attendees.

"Here are directions to where we're going." Dan hands the note to James.

"It's my brother's farm," Cheryl says. "My great grandparents on my father's side of the family bought several hundred acres in the area after the turn of the century—the previous turn of the century. They raised some cattle and owned a small dairy farm. Along with the watermelon and corn, they did okay. They survived the Great Depression and the many ups and downs that accompany farming. Over the decades, the property has been divided among their heirs. My brother who owns a farm near here has over one hundred acres."

"Cheryl owns forty acres," Dan interjects.

"It's not working acreage. I just want to hang onto the land for a while longer."

"Okay," Dan says. "We're heading that way. See y'all there in a bit."

While James sets the SUV navigator to the new target location, I watch Dan hustle to the end of the row of vehicles outside the cemetery fence line. Bryan has stripped off his uniform inside the mid-size silver rent car he drove here and now looks like your average physically-fit super stud. After a brief conversation, Dan embraces his surviving son. Not a casual hug, but a tight, sustained hug from a father who fears losing his oldest son.

***

We drive to the farm owned by Cheryl's brother: pass through the flashing yellow light and drive straight for four miles, turn right on the county road with a Civil War year number (FM 186-something), drive for six miles—the road isn't wide enough for two vehicles to pass each other at the same time, so prepare to pull over for oncoming vehicles—then turn left on the half mile drive to the ranch-style farmhouse with a steep, shiny metal roof.

The family serves us a comfortable meal of lasagna and salad with a home-made cherry cobbler that contains tart cherries and tons of sugar. I go back for dessert seconds, just to be polite, of course. Is this proper funeral etiquette? We eat outdoors in a covered pavilion area set a hundred feet from the house: several hundred square feet of broom-finished pavement with surface cracks and shaded by welded, corrugated metal sheets supported by metal pipe posts. Rust spots are present at the base of the posts. Where's the inch of grout between the bottom of the posts and the pavement?

The sheltered area accommodates several wooden tables with attached benches. In general, people who know each other cluster together. We four brothers who provide a tip-of-the-iceberg persona of the current family generational image—an army combat veteran who now works as an operator in a chemical plant, a no-nonsense business executive in the port shipping trade, a county civil servant and church deacon, and a retired engineer from the petrochemicals industry—sit at one table.

John attacks his meal with enthusiasm, a forkful of lasagna at the ready for mouth insertion as soon as he swallows the previous portion.

"Hungry?"

"Very." John sees me watching him gobble the food. "I always eat fast when I eat outside. A habit I picked up from ten months in the sandbox—or 'dung heap' to me. I liked the MREs when they're hot, except for the always nasty vegan meals. But I ate the meals as soon as possible, before tons of fine desert sands 'spice' my food or another god-awful cloud of flies swarms the space between the open MRE and my mouth. No more wads of fly guts with my food."

"Let's say grace," James says. John freezes mid-chew. Dan and I set down our silverware. We all bow our heads, and James continues, "Lord, please bless this food that nourishes us. And thanks to You for allowing us to gather on this important occasion. Please watch over the living and extend Your mercy to the recent departed. All glory to God. Amen."

In chorus: "Amen."

"Thanks for coming," Dan tells us. "This week has been hell, and I appreciate my brothers being around to support us."

"Bryan not here?" I ask.

"No, he drove straight to Bush to catch a plane back east."

I see Matthew tossing the football around with a couple of his cousins in the expansive grass field beside the pavilion. "How's Matthew doing?"

Dan twists around to watch Matthew for several seconds. He turns back to us and says, "About as well as to be expected. Kade is several years older than his brother, so he helps us console Matthew, to help him get through his father's death."

Dan tries the lasagna. "Um, that's good." He swallows and continues: "Matthew has Sean's Air Jordan shoes now. All eighteen pairs. The boxes overflow from under his bed and spill out into his room. Cheryl gets a bit aggravated with him since he can't even wear the larger shoe sizes, but Matthew doesn't want to give them up.

"And Matthew has adopted Lori. He dotes over Sean's dog as though she's a baby sister. We set Lori's doggie bed in the living room so she can be around us when we're there in the evenings, but she's still adjusting to our house. She mopes around; the tracks of her tears crust up around her eyes." Dan swings his eyes between us. "For Matthew's sake, everyone needs to remember to bring a gift for Lori when we celebrate Christmas later this month."

That statement raises a smile. I guess I can spring for a doggie bone. I'll have to get one for Sandy too—wouldn't want her to get jealous.

"Sean...he complained of body aches, swelling, and blisters in his mouth on-and-off for weeks, and his regular doctor couldn't figure out what was going on. Cheryl scheduled him to see a specialist at the Texas Medical Center. Sean passed away in his sleep only three days short of that appointment,"—Dan looks down and shakes his head—"only three days."

We finish our meals in silence. I'm glad to be here for my brother, but I'm also glad when this day ends.

Sean died in his sleep. I wish I knew why. I want to ask Dan about the cause of death, but I can't bring myself to do so. Maybe I'll find out later.

Chapter Fifteen

Is Determined, Not Concluded

Four months after the funeral, I connect with my brother on the phone to discuss our parents' health expenses.

"We visited Dad in the nursing home today," Dan says. "He recognized me but didn't know Cheryl. She reminded him she's the person who brings him strawberry shakes from Whataburger. He smiled at us and said, 'Yes, the strawberry shake girl.'"

"Hah. He's having a good day if he recognizes his sons. James told me he recognizes Anne as 'the cherry pie girl.' She brings the boxes of cherry fruit pies he keeps in his room."

As for most phone conversations, I listen via speakerphone so I can multi-task. Tonight, I'm ordering items online, a personal habit that accelerated since the start of the COVID-19 global pandemic. The list includes all kinds of "essential" items: six pairs of white socks, ink cartridges for my printer, music CDs for obscure rock groups from the 1960s and 70s—still more CDs than downloads for my music tastes. The TV, with sound muted, tunes into whatever sport most interests me at the time. This evening, it's a replay of the final Astros spring training game. Sandy lies on her rug and watches me while she pants in her typical open-mouthed manner.

After reviewing our parent's financial wherewithal to pay health care expenses, I ask Dan about his family's health. "All doing pretty well. No major health issues but Cheryl and I still worry about Matthew. Junior high school was where Sean mixed with the wrong crowd, who exposed him to drugs. We are determined to make sure Matthew avoids that trap. We keep a close eye on his associations and encourage interactions with the kids we like, the ones with parents we know, ones with good grades, ones involved in sports, ones who have their act together."

Dan describes the preparations for the Deer Park school district football programs. "Matthew's heart is not into football right now. The Deer Park program is very competitive, very popular. Each junior high has an A and B squad, and the high school has three freshman football teams this season. The district keeps its supervised weight room open four days a week during the summer off-season, and you can bet some boys are in there every day. Matthew doesn't want to take part, but I told him he has to lift weights at least two days a week if he might play again."

"Kids change interests, especially in their teens. We survived without playing high school sports."

"True. But since he was six years old, Matthew has been so enthusiastic about football. I have a pair of season tickets to the Texans, and we go to most of their home games. Matthew isn't as interested as he once was."

"I hope he appreciates what you do for him," I say. "I only remember going to one Oiler game with Dad in the late '60s when he got a couple of free tickets to a game in the Astrodome. If we didn't get a free ticket to a pro sports event, then we weren't going." The Oilers lost. The field goal kicker needed to make a fifty yard field goal for the win. He wasn't close.

"That's one more Oiler game than I ever saw with Dad. Even if Matthew doesn't appreciate it now, I want him to one day look back with fond memories of the times we spent together. No matter what, I want Matthew to have positive outside interests. Organized religion is not a big part of our lives, so I hope sports help provide positive direction. He is not going the way of his parents—no drugs in Matthew's life."

After several seconds of silence, Dan says: "It took four months, but I have Sean's autopsy report now."

Cease multitasking.

Fix gaze to phone.

Sandy sees my change in demeanor and lifts her head off her paws to more intensely stare at me. She almost rises.

I remember that early Sunday morning in late November when I learn of Sean's death. The default ringtone activates while I'm asleep. Roll over and check the alarm clock. My blurry eyes see five-something AM. Who's calling at this hour? Throw off the sheets and stumble to the charging phone. Of course, the tone stops singing before I answer it. "Missed call" indicates Dan tried to reach me. Before I hit redial, the phone vibrates in my hand with a text message: "Seans deceased were waiting for medical examiner."

What! Redial missed call.

"Sean's gone, man, he's gone." Dan's voice cracks between sobs as he stutters.

"What happened?"

"Sean's father, who's been staying with Sean for several months now, found Sean this morning—unresponsive, cold, pale skin. Sean just went to bed ...like any night. We don't know...don't know. The EMTs and police are here...someone else just drove up. I gotta go. Gotta go."

Holy crap.

I don't recall my specific reaction, but I can guess. I'm rocking back and forth a few times, my off-hand flailing about while I hold the phone, mouth agape, as many gasps as breaths. Sandy sees my awkward face and body language, hears my voice. She senses my distress, my feeling of helplessness as I react to Dan's tearful account of the death of his son only an hour earlier. I hear the patter of paws across the living room tile floor as she comes toward me. Sandy lays her head on my lap, places one paw next to her head and whimpers. She looks up to me, each eye with its dark pupil in a caramel-colored pool, a white crescent sliver along the base of that pool. Sandy shows me she's here for me. Just her presence is a comfort.

I've been curious about Sean's cause of death since that morning. But ask my brother about the autopsy results for his dead son—no way. Now, Dan is about to tell me.

"Overdose. Pain pills—laced with fentanyl."

"Oh, man, I thought he was clean. His life was moving in such a positive direction."

"His death, the autopsy results...we never saw it coming. If a drinking issue was the problem, then we would have noticed it for sure. When Sean lived with us for a year after a stint in the halfway house, he got into my liquor cabinet one evening and started doing shots of Cuervo Gold. You would not believe the personality change. Sean demanded my car keys. He had been drinking. He was on probation. I was not letting him get behind the wheel of my truck and set him free on the open road. Sean butted his chest into mine, tried to push me against a wall—at least as much as anyone 100 pounds lighter than me can push me anywhere—and screamed at me: 'I have the right to live my life as I choose now.' By the next day, he forgot all about the incident. He was never like this growing up. Sean never talked about his prison experience, but I wonder if prison planted this aggression inside him.

"Anyway, I emptied our home bar, gave away all our liquor bottles to the neighbors. Moved my margarita machine from the outside patio kitchen to the attic. When Sean got his own place, I checked there for hard liquor. Never found any, just an occasional beer in the fridge. We could uncover a drinking problem. But fentanyl...we wouldn't know how to even recognize the issue."

"Do you have any idea what might have happened?"

"His last girlfriend...I may have told you, Sean was a felon in possession of a stolen firearm the last time he was arrested."

"No. Never heard that before."

"That firearm offense, with illegal drugs, meant hard time at Victorville. After he got out of prison, he was a changed man—determined to go straight. But he never shook his low self-esteem. He didn't see how a former addict, an ex-con, could ever attract a decent woman. I tried to build him up, to get him to look on the positive side, to look at the challenges he overcame. He had a good job, the best pension plan in organized labor, the respect of men he respected, a house, a car, a settled, productive life. Not enough. He never shook his second-class citizen self-image."

Dan sighs.

"Well..."—I have to say something—"ex-convicts are not throwaway lives. You and Cheryl did everything you could."

"I wish something we tried worked. Two stints in drug treatment centers didn't take. A change of scenery to live with his biological father in Seattle didn't help. When he was there, he got into harder drugs—meth."

"Damn." Dan can't see me shake my head. "I didn't know Sean well, but I bet if he could tell you, he would say the years he experienced with you and Cheryl and his sons after Victorville were the best period in his life since childhood."

"Only 42 years old." Dan lets out an audible sigh through the phone. "I checked online. Fentanyl overdoses took over 68,000 lives in 2020—over 1400 deaths every week! It was like...like..."—Dan stutters over the phone as he gropes for what to say—"Sean spent most of his life swimming out from the beach. We helped as much as we could, taught him how to swim, more than enough for him to stay afloat, but in the end, he swam so far out that he could not get back to shore, could not escape his past. He went under.

"We failed Sean. But not Matthew. Drugs will not happen to Matthew. Not again. We intend to do everything we can to support his mental and physical ability to withstand any challenge life throws at him."

"Life exists on a field of conflict—full of threats, of challenges we need to overcome to obtain and appreciate the simple pleasures, the simple joys, the loves we collect during life," I say. "Sports can help build positive traits: instill discipline, improve health through exercise, build teamwork, encourage training habits, teach one how to deal with failure or success, build greater resilience."

"Toughness."

"Or toughness, if you prefer. As Matthew progresses in his journey through life, he'll exercise more independence. A team of caring parents and relatives, reliable friends, teammates and coaches, perhaps Faith, a spouse, will provide support—but nobody can predetermine an outcome. In the end, regardless of where the currents or tides of life steer us, each of us selects our own path."

"You know," Dan says, "the emotions never end. The concern. The love. I'll worry about my son and grandchildren until the day I die, as they will about their children. It's just the way life is."

And so it is. An eternal truth to the endless cycle of the human condition and the associated parental love for one's children: There is never a "The End."

Chapter Sixteen

The Future Comes Apace

Dan and I announce for the youth tackle football organization's home games until Matthew graduates from the youth tackle football program. Then we "retire" from the youth football stadium announcing job. Dan still works fifty-plus hours per work for his stevedoring company. Actual retirement is not on his radar screen.

As the hub of broad family activity, Cheryl does whatever it takes to sustain the family, so we all thrive at work, at school and at home. A variety of activities to support a wide circle of family, elderly in-laws and friends exemplify Cheryl's compassion: transporter for doctor visits, educator for medical instructions, food shopper and chef, morale officer to boost spirits, wedding shower coordinator and all kinds of other things I can't think of now. She never asks for anything in return.

After youth tackle football, Matthew plays football as the junior high offensive line center in a shotgun offense. Freshman high school football may come next. We'll see. Since his father's death, his heart isn't into football. Matthew still spends too much time online playing video games. (Cheryl wishes he would read a book once in a while.)

The pursuit of a writing career provides more personal fulfillment in retirement than swilling Shiner Bock and watching sports on TV. Sandy doesn't mind since she gets to lie on her rug next to me.

The year after Dan and I surrender our game announcing duties, my niece enrolls her first-grade son, Kyle, to play youth tackle football. The six-year-old is a great kid: a skinny, forty-seven-pound dynamo who likes traditional superheroes—his favorite is Spiderman—and who spends too much time playing video games and whose favorite food is cheese pizza, the kind with white Alfredo sauce instead of traditional red tomato sauce. Even though he's the smallest kid on the team, he throws himself with enthusiasm into any role the coach assigns him.

During his first year, he comes off the bench to play defensive line or cornerback. Kyle thinks he's the best player on the team. His parents see he loves the athletic and social aspects of the team sport of youth tackle football. "Nightmare" wants to sign up for a second season.

A few years removed from the stadium announcing gig, Dan and I find we miss the action. Dan still has his brown leather case somewhere around his house—in case some relative wants their youth football games announced.

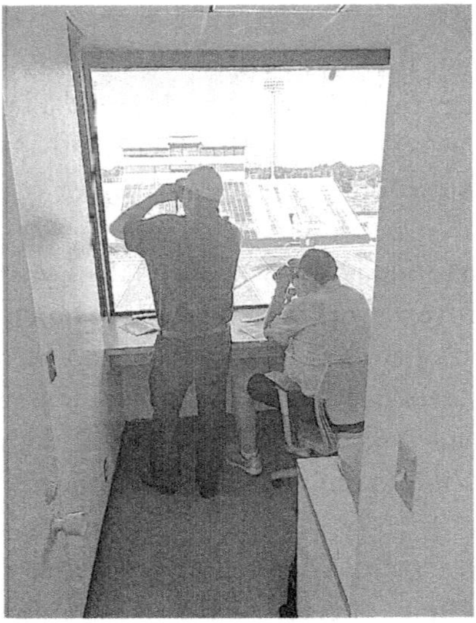

Two brothers in the announcer's booth.
Photo courtesy of Katrina Highfill.
The picture, taken from behind the announcers as they scan the field, captures their best sides.

Made in the USA
Coppell, TX
22 May 2026

77712849R00128